NO
TRIUMPHANT
PROCESSION

NO TRIUMPHANT PROCESSION

The Forgotten Battles of April 1945

JOHN RUSSELL

WITH R. DE NORMANN

ARMS AND
ARMOUR

*This book is dedicated
to those who fought and died
in sight of peace*

Arms and Armour Press
A Cassell Imprint
Villiers House, 41-47 Strand, London WC2N 5JE.

Distributed in the USA by Sterling Publishing Co. Inc.,
387 Park Avenue South, New York, NY 10016-8810.

Distributed in Australia by Capricorn Link (Australia)
Pty. Ltd, 2/13 Carrington Road, Castle Hill,
NSW 2154.

British Library Cataloguing-in-Publication Data:
a catalogue record for this book is available from the
British Library

ISBN 1-85409-234-0

Cartography by the author.

Designed and edited by DAG Publications Ltd.
Designed by David Gibbons; edited by Jonathan
Falconer; printed and bound in Great Britain.
Hartnolls Limited, Bodmin, Cornwall.

CONTENTS

LIST OF MAPS

INTRODUCTION

This book tells the story of battles fought during a campaign uncelebrated by history. It encompasses a series of actions fought between the British and the Germans in northern Germany during the closing days of the European campaign when the war's result was no longer in doubt and, for the Allies, the race nearly won. The battles were not momentous, they had no impact on the inevitable outcome of the war and the casualties compared to other battles were relatively few. Yet they were fought with a ferocity that was the equal of anything the British had experienced in the North West European campaign thus far, checking them in their advance to the Elbe.

Why has this campaign and its battles remained unknown? To historians, the final weeks of the European campaign fought after the Rhine crossing have been of little interest. Most British narratives that cover the war's closing days, hurry from the Rhine crossing to the surrender on Lüneburg Heath and at best make only very brief passing reference to the bitter actions fought en route. The contemporary newspapers glossed over the tough fighting and the proximity of such indelible events as the relief of Belsen, Hitler's suicide and then VE Day also combined to blot them out. This lack of coverage of the fighting in the closing weeks has given rise to a perception that there was virtually no fighting and that the advance through Germany was little more than a formality – nothing could be further from the truth. Montgomery's 21st Army Group was to suffer some 30,000 casualties between the crossings of the Rhine and the Elbe, nearly a quarter of the total for the campaign as a whole.

The book focuses on the actions fought between the German 2.Marine Infanterie Division and divisions of the British VIII and XII Corps during a two-week period in April 1945. The German division's stand represents the last formal resistance by a coherent German formation against the British Army during the Second World War. My research for the book had its beginning in the early 1980s when I was stationed in Fallingbostel, a British Army garrison situated on the North German Plain mid-way between the cities of Hannover and

Hamburg. The catalyst for my research was the presence in the nearby woods of the foundations of a large wartime prisoner-of-war camp, Stalag XIB. From investigations into the history of this camp, my interest expanded to encompass the events that preceded its relief and it was then that I discovered that intense fighting had taken place on the rivers Weser and Aller not far to the west. Although regimental and formation histories and war diaries clearly revealed the toughness of the fighting, each naturally tended to describe it from a unique viewpoint, and with published records of these little-known events so scarce and the fighting left largely unrecorded, I determined to write the story, using as many personal accounts as possible before memories faded. My first formal expression of thanks is therefore to the veterans of the battles who willingly cast their minds back to the traumatic events of 1945.

It has been my intention to record the battles from the German as well as the British viewpoint. Despite the ruin and utter confusion that prevailed in Germany in April 1945, it was surprising to find that some German units were still keeping war diaries; and even more surprising to find that some had survived. I wish to thank Kurt Mehner of Rinteln, Germany, for his most generous assistance with this material and for providing me with his most comprehensive work on Wehrmacht formations. Without his help my book would have been a one-sided account and I am indebted to him. I also wish to thank Günther Milkau, Oberst Ulrich Saft, August Jahns and Heinz Oelkers, the latter living next-door to the site of the Elfriede strongpoint.

On the British side, I would like to record my gratitude to Roderick de Normann who devoted substantial amounts of time and resources to research and acquire personal accounts; I am extremely grateful to him. I am also indebted to Philip Buss MA for allowing me to tap his encyclopaedic knowledge of the Wehrmacht. His assistance helped unravel the complexities of organisations which would otherwise have remained beyond me.

I would also like to thank the many regimental headquarters, museums and individuals who have helped me with material, both written and photographic. Excellent assistance has also come from the staff of the Photographic Department of the Imperial War Museum, the Public Record Office at Kew and the Central Library of the Ministry of Defence; all have been unfailingly helpful. Last, and by no means least, I wish to thank my wife Virginia and my children, Alice, William and Tom for their forbearance over the years that it has taken me to complete this story.

To help keep track of affiliations, I have listed at Annexes A and B respectively the orders of battle for the British and German formations as they were composed in mid-April 1945. All details of weapons, vehicles and aircraft have been relegated to Annexe C where those wishing to know more can read brief summaries. I have left the titles of all German formations and units in the original German; this has not been done to confuse the reader who does not understand German but rather to maintain historical accuracy and avoid the ambiguity that can creep in trying to afford them equivalent British Army descriptions. The reader may however find this short glossary useful:

Abteilung (Abt.)	Detachment of no fixed size
Ausbildung (Aus.)	Training
Ersatz (Ers)	Replacement
Fallschirm	Parachute
Pionier (Pi.)	Engineer
Panzer (Pz.)	Armoured
Panzerjäger (Pz.Jg.)	Anti-tank
Kraftfahrzeug (Kfzg.)	Transport

Ranks used for both sides will be those held in April 1945; readers might find it useful to be able to compare the British Army equivalents to the German naval ranks that will be encountered:

Matrose	Private
Matrosen-Gefreiter	Corporal
Matrosen-Obergefreiter	Sergeant
Maat	Staff Sergeant
Ober-Maat	Warrant Officer
Fähnrich zur See	Officer Cadet
Oberfähnrich zur See	2nd Lieutenant
Leutnant zur See	Lieutenant
Oberleutnant zur See	Captain
Kapitänleutant	Major
Korvettenkapitän	Lieutenant Colonel
Fregattenkapitän	Lieutenant Colonel
Kapitän zur See	Colonel

At the risk of sowing some linguistic confusion, German nouns are used in the singular throughout, even where they should be in the plural. All titles, British and German, and other terms requiring abbreviation are given first in full, followed in brackets by the abbreviation which will be used thereafter. All maps are by the author, and copyright is indicated on all original photographs where known.

John Russell,
Omagh, January 1994

PROLOGUE

The morning of Tuesday 10 April 1945 broke quietly on the North German Plain. As the night grudgingly gave way to day, an obscuring mist rose from the meandering river to cover the sodden beet fields and pastures. The sound made by the British soldiers as they trudged wearily across the heaths and through gloomy pine forests was deadened by the moisture-laden air and all that could be heard was the occasional cough and clink of metal on metal. Although the men were tired as they had been on the move all night, morale was high with the enemy nowhere to be seen and the advance had been without incident. There was no reason why the capture of a crossing point over the next river should not be as easy as it had been for the last and the imminent end of the war brought even closer.

As the first infantrymen emerged from the forest, they saw through the mist ahead of them featureless pastures stretching away into the murk. The advance halted and the men lay down wearily where they stopped. The company commander moved up to be with the leading platoon to confirm their whereabouts. Despite the mist, he knew that his objective, a prominent road junction, was not far away and he determined to secure it as soon as possible to comply with his commanding officer's wish that they press on, a requirement that had been the theme of the orders held the previous evening. He ordered the company to shake out into open formation to cross the fields and the soldiers got to their feet once more and began to advance. The move began with no incidents more serious than soldiers catching their battledress on the low, barbed wire fences and slipping in drainage ditches, to the accompaniment of curses from their NCOs and the ill-suppressed comments of their comrades. As they advanced, they heard the distant rumble of artillery, followed a few moments later by the crump of exploding shells on an unseen target a mile or so to their front. This sudden reminder that the war was not over brought a rush of adrenalin and the fatigue of the long night march was quickly forgotten. The noise of the artillery fire was soon joined by the sharper crack of rifle bullets as unseen enemy hiding in the copses and scattered farm buildings took pot shots at them. The advance pressed on.

When the leading platoons crossed a cobbled lane that lay at right angles to their advance, the rifle fire from some nearby houses increased and the first soldiers fell wounded. The advance checked momentarily whilst the soldiers fought some short and bloody skirmishes to clear the enemy from the houses and gardens. The enemy wore the thick, navy blue shirts of marines, and the soldiers noticed that those who had surrendered did not display the usual looks of exhausted resignation or cheerful relief that were the hallmarks of the majority of the German prisoners which they had captured over the last two weeks. With the houses cleared, the advance began again. Ahead, the leading soldiers began to make out the outline of a large brick and timber barn as it emerged through the mist.

At a distance of 300 yards from the barn, the still of the morning was shattered by the violent, terrifying and unforgettable noise of MG42 machine-guns. The effect of the guns firing at their awesome cyclical rate of 20 rounds per second was devastating and the advance stopped in its tracks. The machine-guns were joined by a withering torrent of bullets from rifles fired through holes cut in the barn's walls. Some of the soldiers were cut down where they were, whilst the luckier ones grabbed the meagre cover available in the open fields and started to fire back. Moments later their exposed position became even more dangerous when the machine-gun fire was joined by a deluge of shell-fire which fell amongst them.

For these men of C Company 1st/5th Battalion The Welch Regiment, and for those from many other battalions and regiments of British VIII and XII Corps, the war was still far from over and their battles to cross the rivers Weser and Aller, and then subsequently hold bridgeheads, involved them in fighting of a ferocity the equal of anything that they had experienced so far.

1
'FROM PILLAR TO POST'
23 MARCH – 8 APRIL

The spectacular advance by the Allies following the successful conclusion of the battle for Normandy, had by early September 1944 carried them across France and Belgium. The Wehrmacht appeared to be incapable of stopping the flood of armour and men from rolling on across the Rhine and on to Berlin and many thought that the war would be over by December. Despite the appearance of imminent victory, the war was however far from won and the Allies had still to face months of bitter fighting. Logistically they were near breaking point, for every gallon of petrol and every shell and bullet had still to be trucked from the Mulberry harbours in Normandy as the port facilities on the French and Belgian coasts had either been demolished or were resolutely defended by the Germans. Although Antwerp was in British hands, the port could not be used until the Germans were cleared from the island of Walcheren, which dominated the sea lanes in the Scheldt Estuary, and the advance now slowed to a near standstill whilst the British and Canadians swung north to take on this strategically vital task. The battle for the Scheldt Estuary was to last for two months and it was not until late November that the first merchant ship reached Antwerp. Whilst the battle to clear southern Holland and the Scheldt began to get underway, an abortive attempt was made to seize crossings over the Maas and the Rhine with airborne landings at Nijmegen and Arnhem. The failure of Operation 'Market Garden' lost further momentum for the Allies and the eastward advance by Field Marshal Montgomery's 21st Army Group was blocked by the German 15.Armee, which had been allowed to escape from Belgium, and by the recently formed 1.Fallschirm Armee. The situation to the south was no better, for the Americans had become embroiled in slogging battles against the concrete bunkers of the Westwall (better known to the Allies as the Siegfried Line) in the forests on Germany's western border, and their advance too had slowed.

The restrictions placed on the Allies by their logistic problems forced them to make headway only when sufficient materiel was available, with the result that the advance had dwindled to a series of alternating jabs across the front against which the Germans had been able to use 'fire-brigade' tactics with their meagre reserves, preventing anything more than limited localised successes. During the closing weeks of 1944, under the expert leadership of Feldmarschall von Rundstedt, the German armies in the west made timely use of the Allies' difficulties by raising Volksgrenadier divisions[1], plugging gaps, particularly in the fortifications of the Westwall, and forcing the Allies to fight a gruelling winter campaign as they attempted to close up to the Rhine. Whilst these events were taking place, far more ambitious preparations under Hitler's direct supervision were in hand to mount a counterblow against the Allies. Two newly reconstituted armies – 6.SS and 5.Panzer – had been formed for an offensive which would strike the weak American forces in the Ardennes before swinging north-west towards Antwerp to cut-off the 21st Army Group. On 16 December the German offensive codenamed 'Wacht am Rhein' ('Watch on the Rhine') was launched. Despite achieving surprise, the offensive was to last only two weeks before the Allies recovered from the shock and mounted counter-offensives. By 16 January the so-called Battle of the Bulge was over and the Germans were back in their original positions having lost some 50,000 men and many hundreds of armoured vehicles. With the German offensive spent, the Allies could look once again to crossing the Rhine.

For this crossing to be successful however, the remaining German armies west of the Rhine had first to be defeated. In early February 1945, Montgomery launched his offensive into the Rhineland, Operation 'Veritable', and for the next five weeks a battle raged of an intensity that had not been known since the worst of the bocage battles in Normandy the year before, only this time the fighting took place during the worst winter for years and produced conditions that would have been familiar to the fathers of the soldiers of both sides. Although the Germans fought courageously and ferociously in defence of their homeland, they could not hold back the Allied armies. The battles between the Maas and the Rhine delayed Montgomery's armies a further month and cost some 20,000 casualties, but they had succeeded in essentially destroying the last German army in the west – 1.Fallschirm Armee – and in defeating it west of the Rhine, had destroyed the forces which could have been used to oppose the river crossing. Although defeat was inevitable, the totality of the defeat suffered by the Germans was wholly due to Hitler's refusal to allow any withdrawal to the right bank of the Rhine.

Eisenhower's plan was to cross the Rhine in two areas - the British 21st Army Group in the north between Emmerich and Wesel, and the

United States 12th Army Group in the south between Mainz and Karlsruhe. The character of the two operations could not have been more contrasting. Whilst the Americans looked to bouncing a crossing over the Rhine, Montgomery planned a complex assault only rivalled in scale by the Normandy landings. In broad outline, Montgomery's plan involved the Canadian 1st Army providing security on the left flank whilst the British 2nd Army crossed between Rees and Wesel and the US 9th Army, which was under British command at this time, crossed on its XVI Corps' front in the Rheinberg area. Under his command were 27 divisions: 17 infantry, eight armoured and two airborne. In addition Montgomery had five independent armoured brigades, a British commando brigade and an independent Canadian infantry brigade. The crossings, which would take place at night, would be supported by massive bombing and artillery programmes and would be supplemented the next day by the two airborne divisions landing in depth on the Rhine's right bank. Once the German defences had been overcome, Montgomery promised that his forces would, 'crack about in the plains of Northern Germany, chasing the enemy from pillar to post'.[2] His plan for these subsequent operations involved the Canadian 1st Army driving north to cut off the German forces in the Netherlands, 2nd Army striking out across the North German Plain towards Berlin, whilst the US 9th Army moved in a south-easterly direction as the northern hook of the manoeuvre to seal the Ruhr.

However, on 7 March troops of the US 27th Armoured Infantry Battalion captured intact the railway bridge across the Rhine at Remagen and at once the balance of Allied strategy swung to the south. Eisenhower naturally decided to exploit this unexpected piece of good fortune. Bradley's US 12th Army Group and the southern thrust to envelop the Ruhr now took on a greater urgency and degree of importance than activity in the north where 21st Army Group was still only at the planning stage for its crossing operation. Although the initiative had swung to Bradley, Montgomery benefited directly by this early American crossing as the Germans hurriedly switched most of their available reserves to south of the Ruhr to try to seal off the American penetrations.

The German Army headquarters responsible for the West Front was Oberbefehlshaber (OB) West. Three days after the debacle at Remagen, Feldmarschall von Rundstedt, commander of OB West, was sacked for the third and final time by Hitler who replaced him with Feldmarschall Albert Kesselring, whose last command had been Heeresgruppe C in Italy. Kesselring was expected to repeat the successful delaying battles he had fought in Italy which had cost the Allies so heavily in time and men, but the conditions that existed on the Western Front bore scant resemblance to Italy and he would not be allowed by either Hitler or the Allies to fight another delay battle on his terms. He described his situation as being akin to 'a concert pianist who is asked to play a Beethoven sonata on an ancient, rickety and out-of-tune instrument'. To achieve his mission he had a nominal 65 divisions with a real strength of less than half that number. By this stage of the war most of the German Army's formations and units were shattered remnants, and the use of impressive titles such as 'Armee', 'Korps' and 'Division' usually had little bearing on the size and quality of formations generally comprising handfuls of troops with little or no experience, very few heavy weapons and virtually no armour. Indeed the continued use of these titles added to the German's delusion that their army was akin to the formidable fighting organisation of former years. The infantry divisions were severely understrength and were made up of the sweepings from broken formations reinforced by raw recruits combed from industry and the Volkssturm[3], whilst armoured formations had fighting strengths of tanks and assault guns numbered in tens. The parachute formations held their title in name only and were based on a few veterans bumped up with the remains of Luftwaffe field divisions, redundant ground crews and any other members of the Luftwaffe without a proper role. They bore no resemblance to the highly trained, élite units that had fought at Eben Emael or Crete. Kesselring's problems were further compounded by chronic fuel shortages, which either prevented or severely limited deployments; by a Luftwaffe which had virtually lost control of the Reich's air-space; and by Hitler's interference in even the lowliest of tactical decisions. Although Hitler had for some years been playing an increasingly interfering role, with his Directive of 21 January 1945 the Army field commanders finally lost the last vestiges of scope for independent action, and this extract from an extraordinary document represents the final triumph of the Corporal over the General Staff.

'I order as follows:
1. Commanders-in-Chief, Commanding Generals and Divisional Commanders are personally responsible to me for reporting in good time:
(a) Every decision to carry out an operational movement.
(b) Every attack planned in divisional strength and upwards which does not conform with the general directives laid down by the High Command.

(c) Every offensive action in quiet sectors of the front, over and above normal shock-troop activities, which is calculated to draw the enemy's attention to the sector.

(d) Every plan for disengaging or withdrawing forces.

(e) Every plan for surrendering a position, a local strongpoint or fortress.

They must ensure that I have time to intervene in this decision if I think fit, and that my counter-orders can reach the front-line in time...'[4]

Amazingly, despite the desperate situation, the will to resist still remained and Hitler's grip on his commanders and troops, mainly imposed by fear, remained absolute. Death became the standard punishment for the most trivial offence and an order of 5 March typifies the increasing savagery of the edicts served on a German soldiery who had already borne an immense burden of death and misery for their Führer.

'As from midday 10 March, all soldiers in all branches of the Wehrmacht who may be encountered away from their units on roads or in villages, in supply columns or among groups of civilian refugees, or in dressing-stations when not wounded, and who announce that they are stragglers looking for their units, will be summarily tried and shot.'[5]

Signed: Blaskowitz. Obst.Gen

In mid-March 1945 the German forces of OB West remaining in Holland and opposing the Allies from the right bank of the Rhine in northern Germany came under the command of the author of that edict, General Johannes Blaskowitz. Blaskowitz had only recently taken over command of Heeresgruppe H from Generaloberst Kurt Student who had been sacked by Hitler for alleged poor performance in the Ardennes offensive. Heeresgruppe H comprised General Günther Blumentritt's 25.Armee in the Netherlands, and in northern Germany General Alfred Schlemm's 1.Fallschirm Armee. Schlemm's army had suffered very severe casualties in men and equipment during the battle for the Rhineland and despite the resolve of its soldiers to defend the Fatherland, the prospect for them to be able to repel the impending crossing of the Rhine was distinctly bleak. 1.Fallschirm Armee faced the greater part of 21st Army Group's strength and its three formations were deployed on the Rhine's right bank from north to south as follows: on the right flank and facing the British XII and XXX Corps was General Meindl's II.Fallschirmkorps containing the three parachute divisions 6, 7 and 8; in the centre facing US XVI Corps was Straube's LXXXVI.Armeekorps, which was made up of the infantry divisions 84, 180 and the various units comprising Kampfkommandant Wesel; whilst on the left flank facing US XIII Corps was General Abraham's LXIII.Armeekorps with two divisions - Infanterie Division Hamburg and the 2.Fallschirmjäger. Schlemm had a very small armoured reserve in General Lüttwitz's XLVII.Panzerkorps, comprising two divisions - 116.Panzer and 15.Panzergrenadier - which were held some 15 miles north of Emmerich on the army's right flank. The two divisions mustered a total strength of only 35 tanks.

Following the demolition it had suffered in the Rhineland, 1.Fallschirm Armee was in a parlous condition and in no operational state to fight a major battle. Meindl's II.Fallschirmkorps was the only formation in the army capable of effective resistance and it had received reinforcement following its withdrawal across the Rhine. However, the men it received were very young, wholly inexperienced and with few weapons, and virtually no replacement had been made of the losses in armour or artillery. II.Fallschirmkorps only had 10-12,000 fighting troops and no more than 80 field and medium guns and 12 assault guns to cover its frontage of some 25 miles. Most significantly, it had no reserve to counter airborne landings. On 21 March the Germans suffered a severe setback before battle for the Rhine crossing was even joined when the redoubtable General Schlemm was seriously concussed in a RAF raid which caught his headquarters near Wesel. His concussion prevented him playing a leading role in the battle which was soon to follow.

At 1530 hours on 23 March, Montgomery gave the order to mount Operation 'Plunder', the crossing of the Rhine. At 2100 hours the same day, the soldiers of the 51st Highland Division and the 9th Canadian Infantry Brigade made the first assault crossing of the river, landing in their Buffaloes south of the town of Rees. One hour later, the commandos of 1st Commando Brigade crossed in Buffaloes and assault boats to land on the right bank downstream from the Highlanders. Their objective was the town of Wesel but the commandos stopped short of the town to allow 200 Lancaster bombers reduce it to rubble before they moved in to mop up what was left of its defenders. Although the Highlanders met extremely heavy resistance from members of 6. and 7.Fallschirmjäger Division, further to the south other crossings by the 15th Scottish Division and the US 30th and 79th Divisions from XVI

Corps were achieved against minimal opposition. The subsequent advance by the Americans was to cause particular problems for the Germans as it was made along the boundary of Straube's LXXXVI.Armeekorps and Abraham's LXIII.Armeekorps. In an attempt to throw back the first lodgement before the main assault began, Blaskowitz ordered General Lüttwitz to release 15.Panzergrenadier to counter-attack the Rees area. This conveniently conformed with Montgomery's design for the battle which aimed to draw German forces away from the area of the southern bridgehead.

On 24 March the land operation was followed by Operation 'Varsity', the airborne landings in depth by the British 6th and US 17th Airborne Divisions. Despite heavy losses from Flak during the fly-in, the landings were a success and virtually eliminated the artillery and service elements of 84.Division. Day one ended with Schlemm facing disaster at Rees, at Wesel and on his left flank where US XVI Corps was close to achieving a breakthrough south of the River Lippe; all that was available to counter these three threats was 116.Panzer Division. Meindl's II.Fallschirmkorps was in a particularly shaky situation as the collapse of 84.Division from the neighbouring LXXXVI.Armeekorps had exposed his left flank and the failure of 15.Panzergrenadier Division to eliminate the bridgehead south of Rees had forced him to pull back his paratroopers still remaining on the Rhine. Blaskowitz now ordered Lüttwitz to despatch 116.Panzer Division to counter the threat posed by US XVI Corps as he believed that this was the greatest danger. However, as it would take time to obtain the additional fuel needed to move the division from the right to the left flank and as daylight movement was suicidal, the earliest this move could be made would be on the night 25-26 March.

Although 116.Panzer Division eventually managed to reach the left flank it had insufficient strength to counter-attack and could only block the Americans. This it did, however, with some success. Due to the difficulties being experienced to their north by the British against II.Fallschirmkorps and 15.Panzergrenadier Division, the Americans were hampered by a lack of real estate in which to generate 9th Army's massive superiority in men and armour and the Germans were therefore able to hold the attackers to limited gains. They fought bitterly throughout the bridgehead for the next two days but the weight of numbers inevitably began to tell and the first major crack in the defence came on 28 March when paratroopers of the US 17th Airborne Division, mounted on the decks of Churchill tanks of the 6th Guards Armoured Brigade, broke through north of the River Lippe and raced on 17 miles to outflank 116.Panzer Division. At about this time the Allies completed their first bridges across the Rhine and 1.Fallschirm Armee was now no longer able to hold back the flood of men and armour that was unleashed. On the right flank II.Fallschirmkorps fell back to the north-east, Abraham's LXIII.Armeekorps had largely ceased to exist on the left flank, whilst in the centre Straube's LXXXVI.Armeekorps collapsed and was forced to retreat in a north-easterly direction, opening a rift in the front which was rapidly exploited by the US XVI Corps. The ensuing American advance drove the remnants of Lüttwitz's XLVII.Panzerkorps and Abraham's LXIII. Armeekorps south into the Ruhr to join Model's Heeresgruppe B, driving a gap between the two Heeresgruppe that was never to be closed.

Blaskowitz now thought it timely to warn Hitler of the situation on the Western Front, going over Kesselring's head to do so. As a result of Heeresgruppe B's problems in the Remagen area, Blaskowitz believed, correctly, that it was only a matter of time before the Americans would be east of the Ruhr and in a position to cut him off. He therefore sought authority to withdraw his entire force behind the river Weser some 125 miles east of the Rhine. The manoeuvre would be covered by 1.Fallschirm Armee from the first logical delaying position, the wooded ridge of the Teutoburger Wald. Both Hitler and Kesselring were infuriated by Blaskowitz's report, the former for his defeatism and the latter for his ignoring the chain of command. Not only as Blaskowitz's request refusewd, but it was also decided that Student should be sent to 'assist' him in his further prosecution of the war, a calculated rebuke to an officer of Blaskowitz's standing.

In addition to Student's move, Hitler made a series of other major changes in command on 28 March. Schlemm finally succumbed to his injuries caused a week earlier and the command of 1.Fallschirm Armee was transferred to Blumentritt, who was in turn replaced at 25.Armee by General Kleffel. Despite the crazy merry-go-round of changes, the state of the German forces was now far beyond anything that could be set right by the appearance of new commanders, however competent. Indeed, the changes not only damaged further what little cohesiveness still existed but also ceased to have any significance to the commanders concerned. For those in the highest command appointments, this was a time fraught with danger as increasingly the Gestapo and SS were disposing of those who did not exhibit blind obedience to the Führer's orders, however absurd.

Major changes were also forthcoming for the British, although for them it affected operations rather than command. With the Rhine crossed and the bridgehead established, Montgomery's intention had been for 2nd Army and the US 9th Army to mount a massed drive to the Elbe and thence on Berlin. The right of 9th Army would be directed on Magdeburg and the left of 2nd Army on Hamburg. By the end of the fourth week of March, the bridgehead had expanded to a width of 40 miles and a depth of 25 miles and concentrated within this perimeter Montgomery had amassed 20 divisions and 1,500 tanks. The capture of Berlin and final victory seemed within his grasp. But on 28 March, the very day on which the final great advance would begin, Eisenhower announced his historic bombshell which took not only Montgomery but also Churchill completely by surprise. After the conclusion of the operation to encircle Model's Heeresgruppe B in the Ruhr and 9th Army had reached the Paderborn/Kassel area, Eisenhower required the American formation to revert to Bradley's control. Furthermore US 12th Army, not 2nd Army, would now make the main Allied drive eastward to the Elbe, but not with Berlin as its objective but rather the industrial and political complex of Leipzig/Dresden; Berlin was to be left to the Soviet armies in whose future zone the city lay[6]. Eisenhower was further influenced by the threat posed by the forces thought to be massed in the Alpine National Redoubt and he did not wish to become embroiled in the fight for the ruined capital city when a greater danger was thought to exist to his south. Although this threat never materialised, the lives of thousands of Allied servicemen were saved by his decision not to go for Berlin. Montgomery's 21st Army Group from now onward was destined to play a secondary role. The Supreme Headquarters of the Allied Expeditionary Force issued a new directive to 21st Army Group designed to meet Eisenhower's revised operational objectives. The group was ordered to continue without pause its advance to the river Leine and Bremen, thereafter launching a thrust to the river Elbe in conjunction with, and protecting the northern flank of the Central Group of Armies. The group was to seize any opportunity to capture a bridgehead over the river Elbe and be prepared to conduct operations beyond the river. In his directive[7] issued that same day to reflect the change, Montgomery made the following statement.

'...there are no fresh and complete divisions in the German rear and all the enemy will be able to do is to block roads and approaches with personnel from schools, bath units, pigeon lofts and so on.'

He was soon, regarding one German formation in particular, to be proved somewhat precipitate in this prediction.

By the end of March the battle for the Rhine bridgehead was nearly over and Blaskowitz's forces in north-west Germany reduced to a desperate state. In the centre 1.Fallschirm Armee, now commanded by Blumentritt and containing only Straube's LXXXVI.Armeekorps, was receiving a severe mauling as it pulled back and was capable of offering only limited and localised resistance. An attempt was made to patch together Straube's Armeekorps following its near annihilation during the battle of the week before and he had been allocated three divisions which had formally been under Heeresgruppe H's direct command: Division Nr.471[8], Division Nr.490 and 325.(Schatten)[9] Division. All three were woefully weak infantry formations consisting of low-grade personnel, such as older men and convalescing wounded, who were able to make only an extremely limited contribution. These divisions would soon disappear as they were over-run and mopped-up by the rapidly advancing 2nd Army and the only reason LXXXVI.Armeekorps survived was because it had been allocated two armoured formations. Following the battle for the right bank, XLVII.Panzerkorps had withdrawn southwards into the Ruhr with what remained of 116.Panzer Division, leaving 15.Panzergrenadier Division, although now reduced to little more than Kampfgruppe strength, to join LXXXVI.Armeekorps. The other armoured formation was Panzer Ausbildung Verband 'Grossdeutschland' which joined 15.Panzergrenadier Division in the reconstituted LXXXVI. Armeekorps. The Verband was a brigade-sized formation which had formed in Schleswig-Holstein during March 1945 as the successor to the original replacement formation, Ersatzbrigade 'Grossdeutschland', which had been rushed to the Eastern Front. Although a training unit, it was well-led and relatively well-equipped. Blaskowitz's left flank was in thin air.

In marked contrast to the cadaverous German forces, the British 2nd Army was a potent, battle-hardened formation with overwhelming superiority in armour and artillery, and supported by 2nd Tactical Air Force which had near total mastery of the air. For the British, maintaining the speed of their advance was paramount; at the operational level it was essential to prevent the Germans regaining balance, whilst strategically it was vital to reach Schleswig-Holstein ahead of the Soviets to stop them investing Denmark. Despite their apparent strength, the British were exhausted not only from the recent months' bitter fighting but also from the cumulative effects of six years of war and they had become extremely casualty-conscious with the end so obviously close.

2nd Army broke out of the Rhine bridgehead and started the eastward advance on a three-corps front with XXX Corps on the left, XII

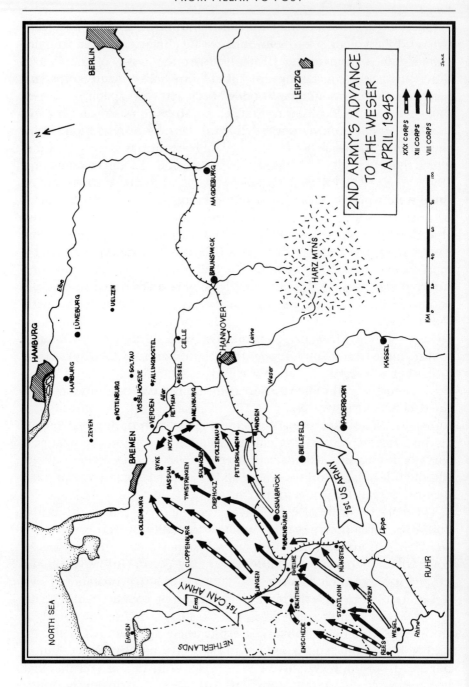

Corps in the centre and VIII Corps on the right. The corps were to experience advances of markedly contrasting character against Blumentritt's 1.Fallschirm Armee and Armeegruppe Student. On 2nd Army's left, Lieutenant General Horrocks' XXX Corps faced tough opposition from the outset from Armeegruppe Student. The Corps did not start its advance from the Rhine bridgehead until 30 March, and on the next day in an attempt to take the offensive, Hitler ordered that an attack be mounted by Heeresgruppe H using forces on its right flank to strike the advancing XXX Corps. Generaloberst Jodl, Chef der Wehrmachtführungsstab (Chief of the Wehrmacht Operations Staff), subordinated General Schwalbe's LXXXVIII.Armeekorps and General Meindl's II.Fallschirmkorps to Student for this operation, with the new formation being grandly entitled Armeegruppe Student. The counter-move was stillborn as Student had insufficient fuel, ammunition or manpower to undertake it and Kesselring ordered him instead to conduct mobile operations in defence of the northern Holland-Emden area. Despite the state of his forces, Student carried out this defence with tenacity and XXX Corps had to fight hard to capture the towns of Bentheim and Lingen, which were not cleared until 4 and 6 April respectively. Although the advance then continued across the North German Plain, it was continually slowed by the rearguards of Student's forces and 1.Fallschirm Armee as they made a fighting withdrawal back towards Bremen.

On the right VIII Corps, commanded by Lieutenant General Barker, was able to exploit the vacuum left by the collapse of LXXXVI. Armeekorps and accordingly made rapid progress as it advanced on its axis towards Osnabrück. By 31 March it had reached Emsdetten, some 50 miles east of the Rhine, and bridgeheads had been won over both the Dortmund-Ems canal and the river Ems. VIII Corps had been in reserve for some time prior to the Rhine crossing but had been reactivated for the final advance. The Corps was made up of formations of markedly different character: 11th Armoured Division, a conventional armoured division; 6th Airborne Division, consisting of out-of-role parachute and airlanded brigades; 15th Scottish Division, a standard lorried-infantry division; the four commandos of 1st Commando Brigade, providing the equivalent strength of two fully-manned infantry battalions; and the three Churchill tank battalions of 6th Guards Armoured Brigade. Fortunately the Corps was launched against Heeresgruppe H's weak left flank as its organisation was not as well suited as the other corps for maintaining high rates of advance against a properly conducted fighting withdrawal. Despite the lack of transport in the airborne division and the commando brigade, their ability to take advantage of opportunities for rapid advance was unimpaired due to a phenomenal capacity for improvisation and every method of transport from limousine to wheelbarrow was pressed into service.

In the centre XII Corps, commanded by Lieutenant General Sir Neil Ritchie, was initially to face stiff opposition from the remaining armour of LXXXVI.Armeekorps. XII Corps at this time consisted of 7th Armoured Division, the famous 'Desert Rats' of the North African campaign, and two infantry divisions: 52nd Lowland and 53rd Welsh. 7th Armoured and 52nd Lowland led the Corps' breakout from the bridgehead and although opposition from the parachute units in Borken and Stadtlohn and damage caused by bombing in the bridgehead area initially slowed their advance, these leading divisions made rapid progress and by the start of April had reached the Ems. The Corps was then confronted not only by this obstacle but also the town of Rheine, lying at the centre of a ring of well-defended airfields, and further to the east the Dortmund–Ems canal.

Whilst XII Corps began to clear the Rheine area, 11th Armoured Division of VIII Corps crossed the Dortmund-Ems canal, moved into the sector allocated for the future use of XII Corps and then became involved in very fierce fighting around the town of Ibbenbüren. This town dominated the main road where it crossed the Teutoburger Wald, one of a number of steeply-wooded ridges that rise sharply above the plain in this area of Germany. The town and the approaches to it, which lay in narrow gorges and then crossed a small river, were held by officer candidates of the Fahnenjunker Lehrgange der Infanterie[10] from Hannover. These men, offering fanatical resistance, were aided by the thick woods which made observation, and artillery and close air support difficult.

Owing to the lack of bridges in the Rheine area, 7th Armoured Division was unable to advance further. It was therefore decided that operations here would be concluded by 52nd Lowland Division, freeing the armoured division to cross via the same bridges as 11th Armoured Division and relieve VIII Corps from the Ibbenbüren battle; 11th Armoured could then press on eastwards. Once Ibbenbüren had been cleared, 7th Armoured would advance towards Nienburg, the next major town on its axis, which lay to the east on the Weser. On 3 April, the division began to move into VIII Corps' bridgehead on the right bank of the Dortmund-Ems canal and started to take on the battle for Ibbenbüren.

Whilst his Corps were battling their way forward, Montgomery on 5 April ordered the 2nd Army to secure the line of the river Weser, capture Bremen and then to advance on the right to the line of the rivers Aller and Leine. Bremen would be held whilst bridgeheads over the Weser, Aller and Leine were secured. Thereafter the army was to be prepared to advance to the line of the Elbe. But events were now moving very fast and VIII Corps, relieved from the Ibbenbüren battle, had already been continuing the eastwards advance against light opposition and had made good progress with two of the Corps' brigades having reached the Weser on the same day that Montgomery issued his order. These were the first 2nd Army formations to reach the river. By nightfall, 6th Airlanding Brigade, which belonged to the airborne division, had reached the river three miles north of Minden at Petershagen, whilst 29th Armoured Brigade and 159th Infantry Brigade, both from 11th Armoured Division, reached the river in the area of the town of Stolzenau and plans were immediately made for bouncing crossings over the river.

Although making good progress, XII Corps did not have such an easy advance against Blumentritt's 1.Fallschirm Armee. On relieving 11th Armoured Division in the battle for Ibbenbüren, 7th Armoured Division found that a quick victory was not forthcoming. Both 131st and 155th Brigades were committed in an attack on 3 April but made little progress against stubborn resistance. Attacks ground to a standstill against the fire of snipers, roving machine-gun teams and endless Panzerfausts which the Germans skilfully employed by allowing the attacking troops to pass them, before attacking from the rear. House after house was set on fire, but the Germans fought back from the blazing ruins. Whilst the infantry brigades continued to wear down the defenders of Ibbenbüren, it was decided to maintain the Corps' momentum by allowing 22nd Armoured Brigade to by-pass the town to the south on VIII Corps' axis. This move took two nights on appalling roads with very bad traffic congestion, and it took until the evening of 4 April before the brigade could push ahead over the high ground of the Teutoburger Wald to relieve 11th Armoured Division at a captured bridge over the Ems-Weser canal at Halen. The Ibbenbüren battle had delayed XII Corps for three days and it was not until 5 April that General Ritchie was able to direct Major General Lyne, Commander 7th Armoured Division, to secure as early as possible the area bounded by the towns of Verden, Nienburg, Sulingen and Bassum. Flanks and mopping up were to be disregarded and bridges were to be captured over the River Weser between Verden and Nienburg. 7th Armoured Division with 22nd Armoured Brigade in the van now raced ahead of the Corps' infantry and secured Diepholz that same day. For the infantry divisions the pace of operations was less rapid. 53rd Welsh Division took over the final stages of the Ibbenbüren battle and the town was finally cleared by 71st Infantry Brigade on 6 April. 52nd Lowland Division, on the Corps' left flank, was making slow progress against elements of Panzer Ausbildung Verband 'Grossdeutschland', and the divisional bridgehead across the Dortmund-Ems canal was not secured and the advance taken up again until 5 April. 52nd Lowland Division's task was now to secure the Corps' long, open left flank.

Against negligible opposition 22nd Armoured Brigade made rapid progress from Diepholz as it advanced toward its next objective, the road and rail bridges over the Weser at Hoya. Throughout the night of 6-7 April, 1st Battalion The Royal Tank Regiment (1 RTR) and 2nd Battalion the Devonshire Regiment (2 Devon) kept up the advance, travelling as fast as starlight permitted with the infantry clinging to the tank decks. When the column was only two miles from the river, a tremendous explosion was heard over the noise of the tank engines as the German demolition teams fired their charges and dropped the bridges into the river. The tanks and infantry, although disappointed at having come so close to their prize after a 60-mile night advance, spent the rest of the morning of 7 April reorganizing in the Hoya area, capturing 40 prisoners in the process.

The 8th King's Royal Irish Hussars (8th Hussars) meanwhile made for the bridge to the west of Verden, but any plan to rush to it had to be abandoned as it was strongly protected by infantry and guns. On the division's left, 131st Infantry Brigade had broadened the advance and had units on the outskirts of Bassum and Twistringen. As it was clear however that the Weser could not be crossed until much larger forces could be brought forward, no further move was made towards the bridges at Verden or to the north and so the division consolidated its gains. Early on 8 April it was ordered to advance northwards to cut 1.Fallschirm Armee's withdrawal routes to Bremen. However, 22nd Armoured Brigade had first to be relieved from its positions on the left bank of the Weser in the Hoya area before it could take part in the division's advance, and it was decided that 160th Infantry Brigade from 53rd Welsh Division should come under command of the armoured division and move up to Hoya to replace it.

Once relieved from Hoya, 22nd Armoured Brigade and 131st Infantry Brigade led the new advance and the towns of Riede and Syke were captured. However, opposition thereafter began to stiffen considerably and it became clear that the battle for Bremen would be long and hard and, moreover, one for which an armoured formation was ill-suited. Furthermore, the decisive direction was east not north, and the armoured division would be needed to spearhead XII Corps' advance eastwards to the Elbe. To pave the way for this advance by 7th Armoured Division once it had disengaged from Bremen's approaches, 3rd Infantry Division temporarily came under command of XII Corps and began to relieve 7th Armoured Division of its responsibilities on the left flank, releasing it to move south-east to a concentration area near Nienburg. General Ritchie's plan was now for 53rd Welsh Division to secure crossings over the Weser, then move rapidly to seize the important bridge over the river Aller at Rethem. Having secured a bridgehead on the Aller's right bank, the division would sidestep north-wards and advance on the axis Verden-Rotenburg-Tostedt opening up the axis for the armoured division's advance to Hamburg and the Elbe.

By the end of the first week of April, both VIII and XII Corps had made excellent progress in reaching the Weser. Notwithstanding their success, these had not been easy days and the advance into Germany had been no easy matter. The flavour of the advance has been evoca-tively captured by General Sir David Fraser.

'For their part the Allies advanced with caution. It was inevitable, with the outcome so certain and so imminent, that men did not wish to court death if risk could be avoided. Operations, in many cases, were understandably sluggish. The challenge of earlier days, the exaltation of liberation of occupied territories, was past. The advancing columns would run on to the defences of a village. A few tanks would be hit, a few casualties would be inflicted. The place would be masked while the following echelons deployed to find a way round. A well placed anti-tank gun on the edge of a wood, probably using its last rounds of ammunition, would take toll from this manoeuvre and withdraw. An artillery programme would be fired, time would be spent, another unit be pushed through to take the lead. A few prisoners would come in, a few of our own dead be hastily buried, a few more miles advanced. Then some route would be found where few defenders were in evi-dence and a larger leap forward achieved. Acts of heroism in such cir-cumstances – and there were many – are the more meritorious. Casualties – and they were not few – become a little more poignant. The final battles were seldom easy, but to fight them was to engage in a race where the result was already known. The necessity was clear but the stimulus flagged.'[11]

27

NOTES

1   Volksgrenadier (People's Grenadier) divisions were raised in the latter half of 1944 from the remnants of broken divisions, replacement units and depot staff. With a divisional strength of only 8,000 and their training standards set by Himmler's assertion that their close identity with the Waffen-SS, Party ideology and the people was of greater significance than military skills, they were not surprisingly of limited value.

2   Extract from Montgomery's Order of the Day for 23 March 1945 issued to his armies prior to the launch of Operation 'Plunder'. Montgomery's frequent use of hunting and cricketing metaphors irritated many British soldiers who did not see war in similar sporting light.

3   The Volkssturm was the people's militia. Formed in September 1944, its mission was to contain airborne landings, eliminate sabotage groups, guard key points, reinforce depleted Army units, plug gaps in the front, man quiet sectors and crush uprisings from slave labourers. Recruits were given a 48-hour training and were expected to master the main infantry weapons. Few received weapons and many militiamen went to war unarmed. The Volkssturm was commanded by Reichsleiter Bormann.

4   H. Trevor-Roper, *Hitler's War Directives 1939-1945*, Sidgwick & Jackson.

5   Milton Shulman, *Defeat in the West*, Secker and Warburg.

6   The row over this change still simmers on. Even if 2nd Army had managed to reach Berlin before the Soviets, it is highly doubtful that it would have had either the strength or the energy to capture the city, even with the US 9th Army retained. By 1945 the Russians alone had the stomach for this scale of battle.

7   21st Army Group Directive M563 dated 28 March 1945.

8   Division Nr. controlled replacement and training units within a Wehrkreis and were not therefore proper front-line divisions. With the Reich under direct threat, efforts were made to standardise them on a three infantry and one artillery regiment basis so that they could be deployed; command was usually vested in a recalled officer. Division Nr.471 came from Wehrkreis XI (Hannover) and Nr.490 from Wehrkreis X (Neumünster).

9   The term 'Schatten' means 'Shadow'. These divisions were formed from early 1944 onwards and contained fighting echelon troops only. As casualties fell mainly on the infantry, then next on the artillery and engineers, the Schatten Divisions contained two infantry regiments, an artillery Abteilung and an engineer company. It was not intended that they should fight as an entity but be used to bring damaged divisions back to strength.

10   Officer candidates had already experienced active service prior to selection to attend the four-month officer candidate course. This particular course was all that remained of an infantry officer candidate school - Schule VIII - which had moved to Wehrkreis IX.

11   General Sir David Fraser, *And We Shall Shock Them*, Hodder and Stoughton.

2

'ROCK OF RESISTANCE'
MARCH – APRIL

The river systems of the Weser and its tributary the Aller dominate the western area of the North German Plain. The Weser is a substantial river with a total length of some 400 miles. It rises in the hills of Hessen in central Germany and takes a generally northerly course as it flows to the North Sea. The major towns of Kassel, Hameln, Minden and Nienburg are all located on its banks and the great mercantile city of Bremen lies at the end of a long estuary some 40 miles from its mouth. Due to its depth and width, the river is navigable by barges for much of its length and ship-building has been possible far inland.

Some 25 miles east of Bremen at the town of Verden, the Weser is joined by the river Aller. This river rises in the Harz and flows northwest to its confluence with the Weser. The Aller is in turn fed by the Leine which joins the Aller just north of the village of Schwarmstedt. All three rivers provide barriers to west-east movement as they meander their way over the Plain to the sea. The Weser is some 300 feet wide, the Aller 230 feet and the Leine 150 feet and in April 1945 all were swollen with flood waters from snow-melt in their head-waters; although they had not burst their banks, they were flowing with a smooth, deceptive power. In 1945 the rivers had extensive meadows on either bank which were prone to flooding and were marshy.

The ground across which the rivers flow is typical of the North German Plain. Although much of the Plain is gently rolling, on the flattest areas are large expanses of gloomy peat moors and pine forests; the land between the Weser and the Aller being characteristic of this type of landscape. Where the ground is higher the soil turns sandy, and mixed oak and coniferous woods give the countryside a lighter feel. Despite the flatness of the terrain, this was not good armour country; areas of boggy heathland were commonplace and the land was heavily wooded, which further restricted manoeuvre. Beside the woods, the many streams and drainage ditches provided obstacles to armoured movement and despite British expectations, there was no chance of being able to launch the armour on a great sweep across the Plain and the advance was for the most part restricted to the roads and tracks.

The main roads were good but the secondary roads usually had narrow cobbled surfaces, sometimes with a wide sandy verge which soon broke up under heavy traffic, although remaining passable. Tracks too were generally passable by all types of vehicles where they crossed high ground but were liable to collapse under heavy traffic in low ground. Spring had come early in April 1945 and the days were pleasantly warm, the fruit trees were in blossom and the numerous forsythia bushes which are a feature of the area were in bright flower.

The area today is still heavily rural in character and dotted with villages and hamlets. Most of the farms and houses are concentrated into the villages and relatively few buildings are found away from the settlements. The farmhouses are typically large as they consist of the farmer's house at one end with a barn and cow byres at the other and despite post-war modernisations, the half-timbered farmhouses of red brick and tile roofs still predominate. The larger towns of the area, Nienburg and Verden, as well as the smaller, Hoya and Rethem, are located on the two rivers where they have developed from crossing points. Germany's very comprehensive railway network was connected to all these towns.

During the first week of April 1945 the situation for the German Army on the North German Plain became yet more difficult and to the hard-pressed and exhausted German soldier the weather and scenery were of secondary importance. On the right flank, II.Fallschirmkorps and LXXXVI.Armeekorps of Student's Armeegruppe were conducting a desperate but successful fighting withdrawal back towards Bremen against XXX Corps and had fought hard to delay the British at the towns of Bentheim and Lingen. Extensive use was made of mining and demolitions to exact delay and impose heavy burdens on engineering effort and logistics. The demand for bridging caused by demolitions had been immense during the campaign and 1,509 Bailey bridges would eventually be built between the Seine and the Elbe – a total length of some 30 miles of bridging.

The collapse of the German forces on Heeresgruppe H's southern flank left no forces available to block the advance of VIII Corps which was having a virtually clear run to the Weser. On 5 April Blaskowitz signalled OB West to say that Student was in danger of being outflanked, that 1.Fallschirm Armee was already by-passed by the Anglo-American threat to the Weser and that he could only defend the area south of Emden and prevent an Allied advance into the North German Plain if he received reinforcements. Despite the threat and the urgent need for a decision, there was little chance of Blaskowitz receiving a sensible reply, far less reinforcements, as the decision whether to defend the line of the Weser or to rest the flank on Holland, Emden and Wilhelmshaven was the subject of leisurely discussion between Hitler and his OKW staff. With decision-making atrophied, Kesselring could do no more in his reply than to tell Blaskowitz bluntly that it was his task to stop the advance to the ports of Emden, Wilhelmshaven and Bremen with what he had, even if this led to him losing contact with other German forces.

The general withdrawal of all forces within OB West had made it increasingly difficult for Kesselring to exercise command and control over these most northern elements. It therefore became necessary to form a new headquarters, entitled OB Nordwest, to command the defence in this area. The unfortunate Blaskowitz was now moved sideways to command the increasingly beleaguered 25.Armee in Holland and the headquarters for OB Nordwest was formed from his Heeresgruppe H's headquarters, with Generalfeldmarschall Ernst Busch, an officer well-known for his Nazi views, being appointed to its command. Shortly after he took command, Busch attempted to fire his troops with vehemence for the fight ahead with these none too uplifting words.

'Soldiers, Comrades!
The time for long speeches and words is now over!... The war gets ever more intense and we are now battling for the freedom of our land!... A calm, sure heart is needed for victory!... The Führer's will is clear: the very freedom of our German soil. The way ahead: fight to the end!

Your Commander-in-Chief, Busch, Generalfeldmarschall'

Not surprisingly these empty words had little or no effect and further changes of command now followed swiftly. On 5 April, Student relinquished command of his Armeegruppe on the Heeresgruppe's right flank and the formation was broken up with II.Fallschirmkorps returning to 1.Fallschirm Armee and LXXXVIII.Armeekorps to 25.Armee. Student was despatched by Busch to organise the defence of the riverlines of the Weser, Aller and Leine and was ordered to form a new Armeegruppe from the Ersatz Heer (Replacement Army) formations that were in the area. Although the rivers lay in the path of the British XII and VIII Corps and the US 9th Army, offering the last opportunity to conduct a defence based on obstacles before the Allies reached the Elbe, no plans had been made for their defence. To Student's south there was a vast gap with only the hastily raised 11.Armee available to block the Americans. There could be no prospect of a successful defence.

The primary formations which would be available for Student's Armeegruppe were XXXI.Armeekorps z.b.V.[1], 2.Marine Infanterie Division and Stellvertretendes XI.Armeekorps. Within XI and XXXI.Armeekorps the majority of the units came from the Ersatz Heer which had been under the command of Reichsführer-SS Himmler since the previous September. Attempts were made to create an armoured reserve for the Armeegruppe in the shape of Panzer Division 'Clausewitz' which had begun to form in the Soltau area from the last cadres of troops undergoing armoured training. The division was something of a forlorn hope and never developed beyond a strength of two or three battalions of infantry, eight guns and 20 tanks.

Although the declared mission for Student's Armeegruppe was to attempt to stabilise the front by defending the lines of the rivers Weser and Aller and thereby win time for the formation of Wenck's 12.Armee in the Harz, there was another reason, over and above the fear of summary execution, why some German forces were prepared to continue the fight when every indication was that all was lost. German sources have suggested that they fought to delay the British advance to the Elbe so that six million soldiers and refugees would be bought time to cross the river ahead of the Soviet armies. It is interesting to note that this motivation was diametrically opposed to the one driving their comrades on the Eastern Front, where many were resolved to continue the fight against the Soviet armies under the delusion that the Western Allies would inevitably join forces with the Germans against a common, communist foe. For these men the arrival of the Allies could not come soon enough and the delay being imposed on the Western Front would have been seen as disastrous.

Student's Armeegruppe was ordered to hold the lines of the rivers, concentrating on the main crossing-points. His right flank consisted of Bremen itself and the line of the Weser between the city and the town of Verden. The flank's defence was based on XXXI.Armeekorps z.b.V., otherwise known as Korps Ems. Korps Ems had been formed as an emergency measure to provide defence for Bremen with its headquarters found by taking staff officers from Generalkommando Stellvertretendes (Stellv.) X.Armeekorps from Wehrkreis X. The German Army has always been structured on a strong regional basis and the Wehrkreis headquarters as part of the Ersatz Heer were responsible not only for the territorial administration of their areas but also for raising the successive waves of recruits and for the subsequent reinforcement, manning, equipping and basic training of new formations and units for their affiliated field formations. The headquarters bore a different title depending on which of the functions they were carrying out: territorial command -Wehrkreiskommando, and training command – Generalkommando Stellv. Armeekorps. Stellvertretendes literally translated means 'substitute', and corps bearing this prefix therefore substituted back in the Reich for the Field Army fighting formations bearing the same number.

In late March 1945 the final wave of recruits was called up, codenamed 'Aktion Leuthen', and the Wehrkreis headquarters were themselves mobilised, dropping their Wehrkreis functions and taking under their command battlegroups formed from the Wehrkreis training establishments and replacement units. This was a last ditch measure as it obviously spelt the end of the Army's ability to provide trained replacements. Most of the units thus raised were infantry although three skeleton panzer divisions, of which 'Clausewitz' mentioned above was one, were also formed. The infantry groupings were then despatched to the fronts bearing the quaint titles of either 'Ostgoten' (East Goths), if they went to the Eastern Front or 'Westgoten' (West Goths), if they went to the Western. Capable of offering some resistance if the ground favoured them, these units could offer virtually no opposition to manoeuvring armoured formations.

Korps Ems was commanded by General der Infanterie Siegfried Rasp, an exhausted man who had until recently commanded 19.Armee during its long retreat from southern France. His corps consisted of Division z.b.V.172 and Division Nr.480[2] and the multifarious units that went to make up Kampfkommandant Bremen. Although the two divisions had been hastily thrown together and were based on training and reinforcement units, including 'stomach' battalions, police units and marines, they were at least not exhausted by battle. Korp Ems' infantry fighting potential was concentrated in the Grenadier training regiments 22 and 269 and the SS training and reinforcement battalion, SS-Panzer Grenadier Ausbildung und Ersatz Bataillon 18 'Horst Wessel'. As there were virtually no artillery units available for allocation to Korps Ems, the Korps was supported instead by the anti-aircraft guns of Generalmajor Schaller's 8.Flakdivision, the provider of Bremen's Flak defences.

The central sector of the Weser-Aller Line lay between the towns of Verden, Nienburg and Schwarmstedt, and was allocated by Student to the 2.Marine Infanterie Division. The division, which will from now onwards hold centre stage in this account, had formed in

Schleswig-Holstein in February 1945 at the marine barracks at Glück-stadt and Itzehoe and was one of six marine divisions manned by oper-ationally redundant naval personnel offered up for ground forces by Grossadmiral Dönitz. The marines came from many backgrounds and locations: U-Boat crews waiting for boats to be built, crews from the surface ships of the High Seas' Fleet who no longer had ships to man, and dockyard personnel and men from the Baltic bases overrun by the Soviet armies. In recognition of their suspicion of both the Grossadmi-ral's motives and their probable sacrificial role, they gave themselves the ironical nickname 'Die Dönitz-Spende'; the English translation – 'The Dönitz Donation' – having a rather apt alliteration. These divi-sions were not marine in the modern understanding of the term, but were more akin to the British naval battalions of the Great War.

By 1945 the German ground forces had become desperately short of manpower and the Luftwaffe, Navy and industry were continually

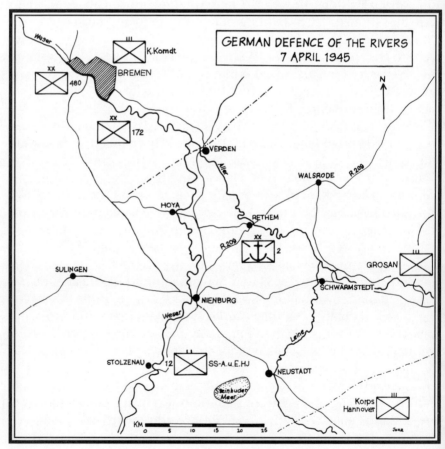

being combed for additional resources. Even industrial firms whose output was critical to the war effort were forced to surrender manpower and the topic was a frequent agenda item on the conferences held between Hitler and his various Wehrmacht commanders. Fortunately our knowledge of the naval aspects of these conferences is quite good as a collection of documents known as the 'Führer Conferences' was among the German naval archives captured by British and American intelligence officers at Tambach. During the conferences Dönitz or his deputy used to take rough notes and these were later written up as minutes. Those conferences Dönitz attended with Hitler in 1945 contain numerous agenda items discussing the raising of naval units to participate in the land battle. At the conference held on 20 January 1945 Dönitz placed 20,000 members of the Kriegsmarine at the disposal of the Army, and it was decided that these men would replace 22 Army replacement battalions located in Denmark, releasing these battalions for the Eastern Front. Nine days later Dönitz asked that he be allowed to retain a part of the 20,000 so that he could create a naval division.

The establishment of 'private' armies was very much de rigueur for the leaders of the Third Reich, with Himmler controlling the Waffen-SS – by 1945 an organisation of over one million men – and Göring sporting a total of 22 Luftwaffe infantry divisions and a tank division, in addition of course to the parachute divisions. With the intense rivalry that existed between these men, it was only to be expected that Dönitz would therefore seize the earliest opportunity to create his own land force. Both Keitel and Jodl agreed to Dönitz's request and Hitler directed that all naval personnel yet to be transferred to the Army would be held back to form the division, to be called 1.Marine Infanterie Division. With Hitler's permission granted, the division immediately began to form around two marine formations already in existence, 1.Marine Schützen Brigade and Marine Schützen Brigade Nord. Göring, who was always looking for ways of improving his reduced status, offered Flak guns mounted on trucks and trailers to provide the division with the necessary artillery. The calibre of these weapons could not have been impressive given their ad hoc method of carriage and they would have been no substitute for field artillery.

The first specific mention in the minutes of the Führer Conferences of a second marine division is made for the meeting held on the afternoon of 9 February 1945. At this meeting Dönitz asked Jodl to help supply the division with equipment and arms as the Navy could provide almost nothing except the personnel and had to depend on the

Army for everything else. The minute ends with Dönitz stating that the equipping of the division was in accordance with the Führer's decision, a well-worn trump card played at these conferences. Two days later Dönitz's representative at Hitler's headquarters, Admiral Wagner, was still demanding resolution of the supply problem. He stated that he could not consent to any arrangements made by subordinate naval representatives with corresponding Army headquarters for the supply of small-arms and motor vehicles to be furnished by the Navy. The Navy was apparently so short of small-arms that Dönitz had ordered all arms on naval vessels to be mobilised in order to equip one of the marine Flak Abteilung at Gotenhafen (now Gdynia) on the East Prussian Baltic coast, as it was about to be thrown into the land battle.

The air of unreality that now pervaded the deliberations of Hitler's conferences and the wholly unrealistic expectations placed on newly raised formations is clearly revealed by a report given by Dönitz to the conference of 14 February, following his inspection of 1.Marine Infanterie Division two days before. His report could have described either of the two naval divisions then being formed. He asserted that he had gained a very good impression of the troops and their readiness for action. Shortcomings in training were still apparent although he felt they could gradually be eliminated. Equipment, particularly heavy weapons, was still badly needed and he complained that Himmler had withdrawn the assault gun brigade that was supposed to support the division. He predicted that the division could adapt itself well to mobile warfare in time, but that he had doubts whether the middle-ranking officers from battalion commanders upwards could cope with the demands of modern warfare. Hitler asked the Reichs-führer-SS's deputy to urge him to return the assault gun brigade and remarked that he believed the naval division capable of great perseverance regardless of its lack of experience in land warfare. In this at least he was to be proved correct.

On 1 March Hitler stated that in line with a suggestion of Himmler's, he was in favour of transferring the second division's battalions, as they became operationally ready, to join the first division on the Oder Front in the area of the town of Angermünde, lying midway between Berlin and Stettin. However, with the equipping of the division still incomplete this could not be achieved, resulting on 3 March in Hitler demanding that it be equipped at once. These demands of Hitler's, made from the cloud-cuckoo-land of the Führerbunker in Berlin which he was now to occupy until his death, had become meaningless as the Reich's capacity to provide anything but the most basic weapons and munitions was near exhausted. He then declared that the division was to be assigned to the area south of Stettin in order to get further training behind the front on a battalion or regimental scale. Dönitz reported that it could deploy 10 days after it received its equipment and that, according to the divisional commander, it must be sent to a training area to practise artillery cooperation before being sent to the front. Hitler rejected this proposal stating that there was no time available, but that there was nothing to prevent them from carrying on this training in the area behind the front, without restriction as to the use of weapons.

The remainder of the month was spent feverishly trying to equip 2.Marine Infanterie Division. This delay in its deployment began to work in the division's favour. Attention for its deployment now began to swing to the Western Front - an infinitely more promising prospect for the marines' long term survival. During the conference of 30 March, Chief of the Oberkommando der Wehrmacht (OKW), Generalfeldmarschall Keitel, suggested that the division might be best deployed to the Emden area, as it was feared that there could be a paratroop or sea-landing in this area. With an indecisiveness which had by now become the hallmark of his leadership, Hitler stated that he would not make the decision whether the division went to the Eastern or Western Front until just before a deployment was necessary. The next day his dilemma was resolved. Dönitz suggested to Hitler that the division be sent to the Western Front due to the difficult situation developing there and that the units which were comparatively fully equipped be transferred immediately. Hitler agreed and on 2 April the signal went out from the Seekriegsleitung (Admiralty) to Marine Oberkommando Nordsee allocating the division to Heeresgruppe H. Admiral Wagner, Dönitz's deputy, was directed to arrange a speedy transfer with the proper authorities so that he could advise the Führer of the exact date of the operation. By 6 April the details were arranged and the decision taken to deploy it towards Osnabrück on the Western Front. Here it was to prevent a breakthrough by the British, for the speed with which the front was collapsing required the division, as OB Nordwest's last reserve of any quality, to be moved immediately to block the gaps that had been torn in the front. However, due to the time wasted by Hitler's prevarication, any hope of the division reaching Osnabrück in time had disappeared with VIII and XII Corps' rapid advance across the North German Plain, and it was decided instead that 2.Marine Infanterie Division would be allocated to Armeegruppe Student for the defence of the Weser-Aller Line.

The committal of the division would represent the appearance of the first fresh German formation of divisional strength since the Allied crossing of the Rhine, and it would be the strongest infantry formation facing 2nd Army's axis, although the consequence of the premature deployment was that the marines' training in basic infantry skills was never completed. On receiving notification that the division was to join his Armeegruppe, Student's intention was that it would defend in turn the lines of both the Weser and the Aller with responsibility for the defence of the area between Verden, Schwarmstedt and Nienburg, encompassing the central sector of his line. Lying in the direct path of a British main thrust, this area was virtually undefended and the bridges over the rivers Weser at Verden, Hoya and Nienburg, and over the Aller at Rethem and Essel, would clearly be objectives for the British.

The 2.Marine Infanterie Division was organised on the lines of the Infantry Division 45 establishment, and had a reported strength of some 10,000 men. The 45 establishment was flexible and could be anything from the full-strength division of over 11,000 men, down to a Type IV establishment of only 5,000 men. From 1943, the Germans revised the establishment of their divisions to reflect the requirement for manpower economies and the improvement in firepower from an increase in automatic weapons, resulting in a drop in strength from about 20 to 10,000. The Division 45 establishment was almost identical to the Volksgrenadier Division which had been created by Himmler in September 1944.

The divisional commander was Vizeadmiral Ernst Scheurlen who had been plucked from his appointment as Admiral Deutsche Bucht (the German Bight, well known from shipping weather forecasts) to its command. Two years before, Scheurlen had gained notability as a capable and energetic commander for his effective organisation of the successful evacuation by sea of 17.Armee, cut-off in the Caucasus. This emergency had been inflicted on the Germans when their lines of withdrawal from the Caucasus had been cut following the fall of Stalingrad and the Soviet's recapture of Rostov, and Scheurlen had hurriedly to gather together every transport and escort vessel available in the Black Sea to effect the escape. The evacuation centred on the Crimean port of Kerch and in a two-month period from the end of January 1943 he managed to save 105,000 men, together with large numbers of horses and vehicles, whilst being subjected to continuous Soviet air attack. Although a success, this evacuation must have borne an unpleasant parallel to the British experience of Dunkirk.

In its unreinforced state, the division comprised three infantry regiments, which were entitled Marine Grenadier Regiments (Mar.Gren.Rgt.) 5, 6 and 7[3], an independent infantry battalion, Marine Füsilier Bataillon 2 (Mar.Füs.Btl.2), and the normal supporting arms and services. The three infantry regiments each consisted of two battalions, each of four companies. Each battalion's fourth company should have been a heavy weapons company equipped with two 15cm IG33 infantry guns, MG42 machine-guns and 8cm GrW34 mortars, but due to the chronic shortages of armaments at this stage of the war they never received their full complements of weapons. Each regiment also had two regimental companies, numbered 13 and 14 – 13.Kompanie was a regimental heavy weapons company and was equipped with two 15cm IG33 guns and eight 8cm mortars, whilst 14.Kompanie was roled as tank hunter or Panzerjäger. In this role it should have been equipped with Pak 40 anti-tank guns, but as it never received its guns it was used as a three-platoon infantry company, equipped with the Panzerfaust and Panzerschreck anti-armour weapons. The marines in the infantry companies were equipped with a number of different types of small-arm reflecting the problems of availability. Whilst many were issued with the 7.92mm Stg.44 assault rifle, the mainstay continued to be the Mauser 7.92mm G98/40 rifle. Each platoon had three 7.92mm MG42 machine-guns capable of being employed in the light or medium role and Panzerfausts were liberally issued throughout the battalions. Mar.Füs.Btl.2 was a 700-strong battalion and was in theory the divisional reconnaissance unit. However, as recce was not high on the list of tactical requirements for the Germans by this stage of the war, it was employed as a seventh infantry battalion and was organised on exactly the same lines as a battalion of a grenadier regiment. Although the troops of 2.Marine Infanterie Division were very inexperienced and young - the average age was 20 - they were enthusiastic, many were still in their formed crews and, above-all, they were not battle-weary. They represented a rare commodity in Hitler's Germany of 1945 and there was no comparison between these fit, motivated troops and the usual scrapings of old men and young teenagers swept-up into the army's ranks. Despite their undoubted motivation, Dönitz issued a decree on 7 April to make certain there was no back-sliding.

'We soldiers of the Kriegsmarine know how we have to act. Our military duty, which we fulfil regardless of what may happen to right or left or around us, causes us to stand bold, hard and loyal as a rock of the resistance. A scoundrel who does not behave so must be hung and have a placard fastened to him, "Here hangs a traitor who by his low cowardice allows German women and children to die instead of protecting them like a man".'[4]

This was no idle threat and summary hanging for desertion by the Marine Küsten Polizei, the naval police, provided powerful inducements to loyalty.

The division was supported by a number of arms and services. The eight batteries of Marine Artillerie Regiment 2 (Mar.Art.Rgt.2) provided the division's integral artillery support and were equipped with a mix of horse-drawn 10.5cm le FH, the standard German Army field gun, and Russian artillery pieces of the same calibre. However, the regiment was unable to deploy at the same time as the grenadier regiments as there were insufficient horses to move the guns and it was forced to remain in the Schleswig-Holstein area whilst they were acquired. The dependence on horses was later to have dire consequences for the artillery regiment. Anti-tank and anti-aircraft firepower was held within the three-company Marine Panzerjäger Abteilung 2 (Mar.Pz.Jäg.Abt.2) which consisted of two anti-tank companies equipped with 7.5cm Pak 40 and a Flak company of three platoons each equipped with three 3.7cm Flak 43 mounted on Steyr trucks. Presumably these guns and trucks were part of the Göring bequest to the Kriegsmarine mentioned earlier. Battlefield reinforcements were supplied by the three companies of Marine Feldersatz Bataillon 2 (Mar.Felders.Btl.2), which deployed with the division, and a limited combat engineering capability was available from the divisional engineer unit, Marine Pionier Bataillon 2 (Mar.Pi.Btl.2). Similar to all German engineer units, the soldiers of the pioneer battalion would be expected to fight as infantrymen whenever needed. The division was supported by a signal Abteilung and a supply regiment. As the marines' knowledge of the tactical skills necessary for fighting a land battle was low, every company had attached to it two army instructors to assist and advise. In addition, Mar.Pz.Jäg.Abt.2, Mar.Felders.Btl.2 and the four Abteilung of Mar.Art.Rgt.2 were commanded by army officers and each regimental and battalion commander had an army Major or Leutnant as an infantry adviser.

Scheurlen's division was reinforced by two regimental-sized groups: Kampfgruppe Grosan and Regiment Totzeck. Kampfgruppe Grosan was formed of troops from the armour training school at Bergen and primarily consisted of six weak infantry battalions, two of which were Hungarian; an armoured group of three Mk VI Tigers, a Mk V Panther and seven 8.8cm Pak 43 anti-tank guns; and an anti-tank group of some 20 men equipped with Panzerfausts and bicycles! Regiment Totzeck was formed from personnel from the Nebelwerfer school at Celle and comprised three very weak infantry battalions and a Nebelwerfer battalion of two batteries.

Although Student could be confident that his centre held by 2.Marine Infanterie Divison would put up resistance, he could have had no such confidence for his left flank. The Armeegruppe left flank was the responsibility of Stellv.XI.Armee Korps. This grouping, also known as Korps Hannover, had a strength of little more than a regiment. The Korps was commanded by General der Infanterie Walther Lichel and was formed around the static headquarters of the military district Wehrkreis XI[5]. Its primary strength had been provided by two infantry training regiments from Division Nr.471, but these were no longer available to Lichel having been allocated as army troops in Heeresgruppe H and both had become swept up in 1.Fallschirm Armee's confused fighting withdrawal to Bremen. Another unit of Korps Hannover which had also been in action were the officer cadets from the Fahnenjunker Lehrgange Hannover, who had offered such stiff resistance to the British at Ibbenbüren. By early April, Korps Hannover had been broken up and bypassed by the rapid advance of the US XIII Corps and its ability to influence events had become minimal.

The northern elements of Armeegruppe Student began to deploy to their battle positions during the first week of April 1945. 2.Marine Infanterie Division was ordered to deploy on 4 April and the marines left their barracks the same day meeting troop trains at the three Schleswig-Holstein towns of Husum, Glückstadt and Eckernförde for the journey to the front. Despite the enormous damage that had been wreaked on the German railways, the extensive redundancy in the network allowed trains to be re-routed to avoid areas of destruction and the railways remained amazingly efficient right to the end. The deployment of the marines was spread over two nights to allow for re-routing and to avoid the now constant threat of Allied fighters which made day movement too dangerous. The marines' destinations were the stations at the towns of Verden and Rethem, from where they would deploy on foot or on limited road transport to their regimental sectors. Although Scheurlen was required by Student to defend the lines of both the Weser and the Aller and on his left flank the Leine, time was not on his side and it was quite apparent that the British would reach the Weser before he had time to prepare for a full defence. He therefore decided to deploy such forces forward to the Weser as were sufficient to provide only delay, leaving his main effort for the defence of the Aller.

The first regiment to arrive was Mar.Gren.Rgt.7. This regiment, commanded by Kapitän zur See Karl Neitzel, an ex-U boat skipper, reached Verden on Friday 6 April and immediately deployed its two battalions to defend the division's right flank. Neitzel's regiment was however held back in the general area of the town and did not deploy southwards to the Aller, a decision which was to have serious repercussions as the battle unfolded. Bataillon I./7 deployed on a southeasterly orientation between Verden and Neddenaverbergen, whilst Bataillon

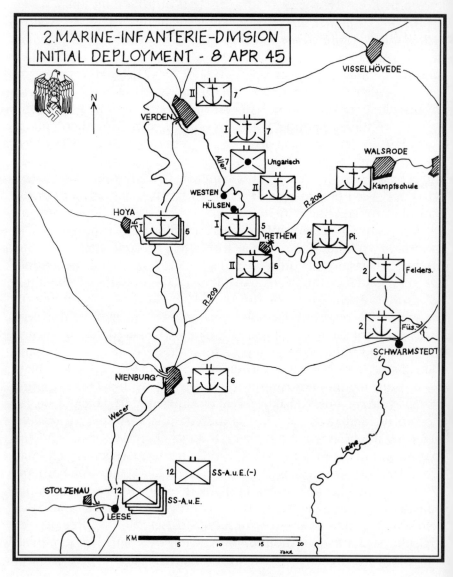

II./7 remained in close proximity to Verden. Some companies crossed the Aller and occupied positions in the villages situated in the triangle of land between the Weser and the Aller.

The rest of the division was moved by train to Rethem, which the regiments progressively reached without incident on 7 and 8 April. Mar.Gren.Rgt.5 commanded by Kapitän zur See Hermann Jordan, a former Luftwaffe officer who had been transferred to the Kriegsmarine, deployed on the Aller's left bank to hold the division's central sector. Jordan was ordered to deploy troops forward immediately to defend the Weser. Regimental Kompanie 14./5 occupied positions in buildings on the right bank facing the town of Hoya, whilst marines from the other regimental company, Kompanie 13./5, deployed in groups to cover the likely routes that the British would use once they had crossed the Weser. The marines from Kompanie 14./5 were joined by some middle-aged soldiers from Bataillon 65 of Gren.Ausb.u.Ers.Rgt.269, about 50 equally old transport drivers and the party of engineers who had blown the road and rail bridges at Hoya. The probability that either the Hoya or Nienburg forces would repel assault crossings of the Weser was remote but it was hoped that they would afford some delay to allow time for the further development of the main defensive positions to the east on the Aller.

Kapitän zur See Werner Hartmann, the commander of Mar.Gren.Rgt.6, was a well-known former U-Boat commander and holder of the Knight's Cross with Oak Leaves. Unlike the other two regimental commanders Hartmann had some experience of dealing with land forces, for between December 1944 and February 1945 he had been responsible for organising elements of the East Prussian Volkssturm[6]. On his regiment's arrival at Rethem, he immediately deployed his Bataillon I./6 forward the 15 miles to the Weser in the area of Nienburg, whilst Bataillon II./6 took up positions in depth opposite Rethem on the right bank of the Aller in the area between the villages of Hohenaverbergen and Otersen. This battalion was also the divisional reserve. Mar.Pi.Btl.2 deployed to the area of the village of Bierde, whilst Mar.Felders.Btl.2, commanded by Major Stoschke, marched to Hodenhagen. The Kampfschule from Mar.Felders.Btl.2 was held in depth covering Route 209 from the western edge of Walsrode; this road was assessed as the enemy's main axis of advance as it affected the division.

Mar.Füs.Btl.2, commanded by Korvettenkapitän Josef Gördes, also deploying on foot, moved to the area of the villages of Essel and Schwarmstedt to defend the road and rail crossings over the Leine and

Aller on the division's left flank. When the battalion arrived in its area of responsibility, it deployed forward battalion headquarters and the three rifle companies to the Leine; one company to cover the bridge at Bothmer, one to provide protection to the south in the area of the hamlet of Grindau, whilst the third deployed with battalion headquarters to the village of Schwarmstedt. The fourth, the heavy weapons company, with its mortars, infantry guns and medium machine-guns together with the other supporting arms remained on the right bank of the Aller to provide depth and fire support for the forthcoming battle. These forces concentrated on defending the road bridge which lay to the north-east of Essel, and positions were prepared on the slightly higher ground above the river from which the guns could fire in the direct role against targets on the left bank. Backing these positions was an extensive and thick coniferous forest which followed the course of the Aller and provided excellent cover for infantry movement. It would appear that Gördes expected the main enemy thrust to be directed at his battalion from the west and his widely spaced companies were deployed to cover the likely crossing points of the Leine.

As events turned out, his appreciation of the enemy's most likely approach was partly correct but the use by the British of an additional and unexpected approach was to render his defence of the Leine a short-lived affair. With Mar.Füs.Btl.2 isolated from the division's centre of mass in the Rethem-Verden area, the battalion received the only armour available to Scheurlen in the form of an element of the Fallingbostel-based Pz.Jäg.Abt.71 equipped with two Elefant heavy tank destroyers. The Abteilung also possessed two of the deadly 8.8cm Pak 43 anti-tank guns and was accompanied by 120 men from 11./101 Festungs Pak Abteilung (Fortress Anti-Tank Abteilung) who, despite their grandiose title, were only equipped with small-arms. Gördes was also given a platoon of four 7.5cm anti-tank guns from a platoon of the divisional Panzerjäger Abteilung. It is interesting to note that the supply of rations seems to have broken down completely and the marines of the Füsilier battalion were dependent on the generosity of the local population for their food. The two additional regimental groups which had been allocated to Scheurlen – Kampfgruppe Grosan and Regiment Totzeck – were also deployed to the division's left flank. Oberst Grosan's Kampfgruppe was positioned in the area of the village of Ostenholz, in depth of Mar.Füs.Btl.2, and was to play a significant part in the battles to follow, whilst Oberst Totzeck's regiment deployed on the right bank of the Aller to cover the river and the road leading east to the small town of Winsen.

As the division's own field artillery had yet to reach the front, Scheurlen would be dependent on the support which could be offered by Flak batteries. The division had been allocated support from a number of Flak batteries which had become redundant from the air battle and had come under the collective command of Flakregiment 122(E)[7] to support the Army. This Flakregiment originally consisted of a number of railway Flak Abteilung located throughout Luftgau XI - the Hannover-Hamburg air region. However, by March 1945 its 10 Abteilung were spread far and wide across northern Germany, and in April the regimental headquarters was itself deployed to command all Flak units supporting the army on the Weser line between Verden and Stolzenau. Concentration of effort was placed on the likely crossing sites at Stolzenau, Nienburg and Hoya and the Flakregiment headquarters came under command of 8.Flakdivision[8], which formerly had been responsible for the air defence of the Weser-Ems area and Bremen but had now become part of Armeegruppe Student. It is however something of a mystery how the guns received target information as the Flak batteries naturally had none of the command and control resources, such as forward observation officers, for fighting in a land battle[9]. Their effectiveness, other than in the direct fire role, would therefore be limited.

The batteries allocated to support Bataillon II./6 at Nienburg were grouped under Leichte Flakabteilung 859(E), commanded by Major Helmig, who was also the Kampfkommandant Nienburg. Despite its description as a light, railway Flak unit, this Flakabteilung had grouped under its control a number of powerful motorised batteries: 1./521 Reichs Arbeit Dienst (RAD)[10] with four 10.5cm Flak 39 heavy anti-aircraft guns; 2./137 with five 8.8cm Flak guns and three 2cm Flak 30 light Flak guns; 3./607 with four 8.8cm Flak guns; 4./132 with six 8.8cm Flak guns and Batterie z.b.V. 6969 with 11 3.7cm light Flak guns. The batteries allocated to support the forward deployed elements of Bataillon I./5 were 2./604 RAD with four 8.8cm Flak guns and three of the four-barrelled 2cm Vierlingsflak, a highly effective light anti-aircraft weapon; and the heavy Flak batteries 4./117 and 4./162 each equipped with four 10.5cm Flak 39 and three 2cm Flak 38. Batterie 4./117 occupied gun positions in the vicinity of the hamlet of Ahlhusen, just over a mile to the east of the Weser, whilst 4./162 deployed in Hassel. At Eystrup railway station were the five 10.5cm Flak mounted on railway flats of combined Batteries 1. and 4./125(E), and also in the area were elements of Flak Abt.z.V.294, one of two army Flak Abteilung formerly responsible for providing anti-aircraft cover for the V-2 launching sites.

The Weser Line to the south of Hartmann's Bataillon I./6, between the towns of Nienburg and Leese, was held by a number of units under the command of Kampfkommandant Leese. The mainstay of the defence of the Weser's right bank in this area was to be an SS training and reinforcement battalion, SS-Panzer Grenadier Ausbildung und Ersatz[11] Bataillon 12 'Hitlerjugend', (SS-Ausb.u.Ers.Btl.12 HJ). Although the battalion was not at this stage under Scheurlen's operational command, it was soon to become so and will later play a significant part in the forthcoming battles on both the Weser and the Aller. Four companies of the SS battalion were allocated to the defence of the town of Leese, located on the right bank opposite Stolzenau, and a heavily camouflaged factory producing V-2 rockets hidden in the woods to the north of the town. For their defensive task, the companies would be supported by a number of light and heavy Flak batteries and a reserve battalion of engineer officer cadets, Reserve Offizier Bewerber-Pionier Bataillon Nienburg (ROB-Pi.Btl.Nienburg).[12] The remaining four companies of the SS battalion were dispersed among the villages and woods in depth of Leese. To the south of the battalion and holding the area opposite Petershagen were troops from an engineer formation entitled Pi.Sperr-Brigade.1100.

Although SS-Ausb.u.Ers.Btl.12 HJ was first formed at Arnhem in the summer of 1943 as the training and reserve battalion for 12.SS Panzer Division 'Hitlerjugend', in early September 1944 this original battalion was renumbered '16' to serve 16.SS Panzergrenadier Division 'Reichsführer SS'. A new battalion was subsequently formed two months later at the SS training barracks at Kaiserslautern but moved to Nienburg in November 1944 and occupied the Hindenburg barracks at Langendamm on the outskirts of the town. Here during the same month, it was joined for five weeks by the remnants of 12.SS Panzer Division 'Hitlerjugend' which came to Nienburg to be brought up to strength for the Ardennes offensive following the disaster of the Falaise pocket and the withdrawal from France. In early 1945 the battalion received its last recruits, aged between 17 and 19, from seven Hitler Youth companies in the Nienburg area. These companies joined the battalion headquarters, the permanent staff company and the NCO training (Unterführer Lehr) company which were already at the barracks, and the Hitler Youth proceeded to receive a very short but hard training using limited and poor equipment. Although by the end of this training they were far from the hardened soldiers normally associated with the Waffen-SS and were little more than Hitler Youth in soldiers' uniform, they were fired with its fanaticism and were commanded by officers and NCOs

46

with considerable combat experience. The battalion gave itself the nickname 'Panzer-Teufel' – 'Tank Devils'. Found later on a captured member of the battalion was this brutish pamphlet, with its sham philosophy revealing the effort that was put into imbuing the youths with callousness for the task ahead.

'Panzer-Teufel – Always shoots first! The man who shoots first lives longer!

'I or you: this is the question that will soon every minute of the day affect you and your opponent. At the front there is no mercy at all. Men fight, shoot, strike, bite, scratch and trample in an orgy of physical destruction. You're ill-prepared for battle if you are not quite clear as to what battle means; it means that you must kill if you want to stay alive! Killing is the Englishman's natural inclination. He pictures war as a sport. An old English "wisecrack" says, "Hunting lions[13] is good, hunting man is better, hunting Germans is best of all".

'And so, as you can understand, it means nothing to him to maul and maim women and children with high explosive and phosphorous. This is why his fighter-bombers harass you with bomb and cannon. This is why it happens that you alone, a solitary gunner, are engaged by a whole battery of English guns. For your enemy in the west, KILLING IS A SPORT!

'We Germans take neither joy nor pleasure in killing.

'Perhaps, one day, you will catch yourself laughing and rejoicing when the enemy is being shot to pieces, when men are being mown down by the hundred in the fierce fire of your company. That's how it should be – you must overcome your reluctance to kill. Abandon the thought that you not only kill the man, but bereave his mother, wife or children. One second, Comrade, just one second of such thoughts can bring death to you or the soldier next to you. And if you die, the enemy's bullet brings the same sorrow to your family or your comrade's. And they are many thousand times more valuable than a bloody bolshevik's flock of brats!

'KILLING IS YOUR DUTY!

'Prepare for it. Practise with your weapon and learn to master it. And make your heart very hard! Then you will not shrink from the realities of war. Bleeding wounded, torn maimed men in frightful death-pangs, stiff corpses; these are the sights you must be accustomed to seeing. If you don't kill, you may soon be lying among these groaning victims. You must realise, that if you lack the courage to look all these horrors squarely in the face before you go into action, you will suffer all the more in the fury of battle.

'If ever weakness threatens to overcome your will to annihilate the enemy, then think of all the thousands of your comrades, the thousands of women and children that you, and you alone, must revenge. Our enemies have done them to death with cynical cruelty. War abolishes all laws that forbid you to kill. War brings God and the Earth into unison; it sanctifies the Earthly task of killing through the Heavenly power of your dedication to yourself.

'And so, in the hour of war, the law of the soldier is this: BE READY TO KILL!'

The commanding officer of this unsavoury battalion was Hauptsturm-führer[14] Peinemann, a former policeman. On 4 April the battalion, together with its Unterführer Lehr Kompanie departed from Neinburg to take up defensive positions at Leese to face the point at which VIII Corps was threatening to cross. The battalion's mobility was improved by Peinemann hijacking 10 Sd.Kfz.251 half-tracks which had been passing through Neinburg en route for the 'Grossdeutschland' formation fighting on the approaches to Bremen. The SS battalion was also allocated artillery support from redundant Flak units: Batterie 5./280 RAD equipped with three 8.8cm Flak 37 and Batterie 4./871 equipped with a number of 3.7cm and 2cm Vierling light Flak. Additional light Flak support was provided by Leichte Flakabteilung 859(E).

Student's situation on the eve of battle was beset with difficulty; he was compelled to defend a very wide frontage with forces woefully weak in training and heavy weapons; he had negligible armour; his reserve, the skeleton panzer division 'Clausewitz', was unlikely to be able to influence the battle; he was unable to create depth to his defence, other than at a strictly local level; and the enemy had air supremacy. Despite these overwhelming disadvantages, in the central sector he had troops who were capable of putting up a fight and the marines and young SS soldiers were fresh and determined to acquit themselves well in their first and probably last land battle. For both sides, the bridges over the Weser and Aller were of major tactical importance and many, soldier and civilian alike, were to die in the towns, villages and surrounding countryside between 5 and 17 April 1945.

NOTES

1   The initials z.b.V. stand for 'zu besondere Verwendung' – 'for special employment'. This was a commonly used suffix which was used for many different types of formation and unit and generally meant a non-standard or specially raised organisation. The description could thus be applied to anything from a penal battalion to a corps.

2   Division Nr.480 is a good example of the Ersatz Heer's ability to reconstitute itself. In September 1944 one of the original Wehrkreis X replacement divisions, Division Nr.180, was deployed as an emergency measure to counter the Allied airborne landings in the Netherlands. Elements left behind began to rebuild the replacement and training structure to form a new division, Division Nr.480. This capacity to rebuild replacement formations kept the army effective despite the horrendous losses suffered from 1942 onwards.

3   The German system of unit numbering using roman and arabic numerals will be used throughout this account. Regiments and companies received arabic numbers (eg Mar.Gren.Rgt.5 or 3.Kompanie) whilst battalions had roman numerals (eg II.Bataillon). By using a back slash, affiliations could easily be created, thus Bataillon I./5 would be the first battalion of the fifth regiment. As the first battalion's companies were always numbered 1-4, and the second's 5-8, the parent battalion can be omitted from the description, thus Kompanie 4./7 would be the fourth company (from the I.Bataillon) of the seventh regiment.

4   Peter Padfield, *Dönitz – The Last Führer*, Victor Gollanz Ltd.

5   There were thirteen Wehrkreis within Germany proper, with an additional two in Austria and a further four in other areas such as Danzig and Poland.

6   Hartmann's sea-going commands were U37 and U198. In addition to these commands, he served on Dönitz's staff in 1940 and commanded the training establishment, 2.U-Boots Lehr Division in Gotenhafen. In 1944 he was at HQ U-Boats Mediterranean. He was awarded the Knight's Cross on 9 April 1940 to which the Oak Leaves were added on 5 November 1944. Hartmann later became a prisoner-of-war and was held in a camp at Zedemgen in Belgium. After his release, he joined the Bundesmarine which he served with distinction. He died in 1963 and was buried in Glückstadt with full military honours.

7   '(E)' stands for 'Eisenbahn', i.e., railway.

8   Anti-aircraft defence was in the main the Luftwaffe's responsibility. A static division, such as 8.Flakdivision would normally control two or more Flakbrigades, each of between two or more Flakregiments. A regiment would control between four and six Abteilung, the basic Flak unit. There were four main types of Abteilung: Schwere (heavy), Leichte (light), Gemischte (mixed) and Scheinwerfer (searchlight).

9   The motorised Flak units which operated with the field armies were infinitely more capable of supporting a land battle and were frequently called upon to provide fire support against ground targets.

10   The RAD was the German labour service. From 1935 every German adolescent male had to perform 6 months' service in the RAD prior to Wehrmacht call-up. By 1945, since so many Flak crews had been sent to the fronts, whole units of RAD were converted into Flak batteries. Other members of the organisation were less fortunate and were swept up into four RAD divisions which fought as infantry on the East Front.

11   All field army divisions, Heer and Waffen SS alike, had an Ausbildung und Ersatz Bataillon as their home based training and replacement unit. Each division then deployed with its own training and battle casualty replacement battalion, the Feldersatz Bataillon.

12   An ROB was a reserve officer applicant. Qualified volunteers and suitable conscripts from the ranks were designated as reserve officer applicants. They attended a 10-month course, usually conducted by the headquarters of the relevant replacement and training unit, which would train them to be section, or equivalent level, commanders following which they would be transferred to a field unit to prove themselves. If successful they would be appointed officer candidates (Fahnenjunker) and sent on an officer candidate course. The men of ROB-Pi.Btl.Nienburg were therefore at the start of their military training.

13   This might have been marginally more credible had it said foxes!

14   The Waffen-SS used a system of rank titles which differed from those of the German Army. The equivalent British rank for Hauptsturmführer would be Captain.

3

THE BATTLE FOR THE LEESE
BRIDGEHEAD, 5–8 APRIL

The battle for the Weser-Aller Line was first joined on 5 April on VIII Corps' axis some 30 miles to the south of Hoya. On this day small bridgeheads were established across the Weser against initially weak opposition from Armeegruppe Student. On the Corps' northern axis 29th Armoured Brigade had captured Stolzenau on the Weser's left bank, but not before the road and rail bridges were blown. During the afternoon G and H companies of the 8th Battalion the Rifle Brigade (8 RB) crossed the river and formed a small bridgehead on the right bank, allowing bridging operations to start. At the same time 1st Battalion the Herefordshire Regiment (1 Hereford) from 159th Brigade[1] reached the river 2½ miles to the south of Stolzenau at Schlüsselburg where it captured a ferry intact and formed a bridgehead with two companies. Further upstream, on the southern axis, 6th Airlanding Brigade from the airborne division had reached the Weser in the Petershagen area and established a small bridgehead on the right bank. Meanwhile, 3rd Parachute Brigade, also from 6th Airborne, together with elements of the US 5th Armoured Division captured the town of Minden, which lay on the boundary of 2nd Army and US XIII Corps; unfortunately all the town's bridges over the Weser had been blown. The intention for VIII Corps for the next day was to enlarge its bridgeheads allowing 15th Scottish Division to pass through in the south and 11th Armoured Division in the north.

On 6 April, extension of the southern bridgehead on 6th Airborne's front took place as planned. 6th Airlanding was ferried across the river during the course of the night and by midday had pushed out the bridgehead to a depth of one mile. The 5th Parachute Brigade also crossed and established itself in position to protect the construction of two bridges at Petershagen. During the course of the afternoon the bridgehead was counter-attacked by a small force of Tiger and Panther tanks, but they were beaten-off successfully and the Class 9 bridge was completed. Unfortunately, further north in the Stolzenau area, 11th Armoured was faring less well and had received clear evidence that the Germans intended to hold this area. Although bridging operations had got underway under cover of the small bridgehead formed by the 8 RB companies, young SS Panzergrenadiers from Kompanie 3, 5, 7, and 10 of SS-Ausb.u.Ers.Btl.12 HJ, supported by light Flak and 8.8cm Flak from the RAD battery 5./280, were putting up a fierce resistance from positions strung along a railway embankment on the western edge of the village of Leese, effectively dominating any movement on the right bank and preventing any expansion of the bridgehead. An un-named Oberscharführer from the SS battalion describes his part in the battle.

'I was an instructor in the battalion. My own service had been with the Leibstandarte in Russia. Usual decorations, Iron Cross, Infantry Assault, Close Combat and Wound Badge in silver. I lined my platoon along the railway embankment which stands about 20 feet above the ground between the River Weser and the village of Leese. The first British probes were easily repulsed – our field of fire was excellent. We could see every movement that the Tommies made. I had my mortars behind the railway embankment with the reserve sections and three, tripod-mounted MG42 firing on fixed lines. The battalion had ammunition enough. We had been ordered to hold to the last. We did not know it then but there was a V-2 assembly plant about 2 kilometres (one mile) behind the railway line, just north of Leese, and it was our task to hold until the civilian scientists had got away.'[2]

During the course of the morning the weakly held bridgehead was subjected to a strong counter-attack by the SS which was only beaten off with great difficulty by the two 8 RB companies; the next attack would be likely to over-run them. Fortunately help was close at hand in the form of 45 Royal Marine (RM) Commando, the lead unit of 1st Commando Brigade, which had reached the Weser during the night before and was now ready to cross the river to support the companies and expand the bridgehead. The commando brigade, commanded by Brigadier Mills-Roberts, had spent the last 24 hours clearing Osnabrück but had been ordered to push on to the Weser as fast as possible to reinforce 11th Armoured Division, which had insufficient infantry resources to mount the river-crossing. 45 (RM) Commando was now placed under command of the armoured division and, in the highly vulnerable assault boats, immediately crossed the river about a mile south of Stolzenau, drawing very heavy fire from artillery, mortars and 2cm Flak. Once across, the commando fought a hard close-range battle to secure a shallow bridgehead and make contact with the beleaguered 8 RB companies to the north. The young men of the SS were reported as being excellent shots and any member of the commando who raised his head above the bank was shot, invariably through the eye, and it was readily apparent that the commando was not strong enough to do more than help the riflemen hold the bridgehead. With the arrival of 45 (RM) Commando on the right bank, the two 1 Hereford companies in the bridgehead to the south were evacuated to the left bank having spent an uncomfortable day under continual 2cm fire.

The Stolzenau bridgehead was not only attacked from the ground, for the Luftwaffe was also thrown into the fray to mount some of its last attacks. The aircraft came from Luftflotte Reich, the once-mighty organization that had been responsible for Germany's day and night defence against the Allied bomber offensives. The Luftflotte, commanded by Generaloberst Hans-Jurgen Stumpff, had been squeezed into an enclave around Schleswig-Holstein and committed to a desperate last struggle to defend the homeland against the enemy air and land attacks. Considering the losses it had sustained, it is surprising to note that the Luftwaffe had no shortage of aircraft at this stage of the war and there were huge numbers of replacement aircraft held in well-camouflaged and well-defended storage parks. However, there was a

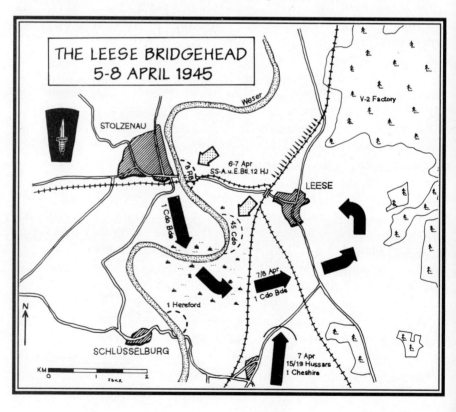

crippling shortage of fuel and pilots, particularly those with combat experience, and this prevented any deployment in strength.

Initially in early April the Luftwaffe had the upper-hand for not only was a spell of poor weather hampering 2nd Tactical Air Force's operations but the Allied aircraft were still operating from airfields well to the west, resulting in lengthy response times and short duration on task. The Luftwaffe had started to interfere with the bridging operation at Stolzenau as soon as work had started on 5 April, and to the astonishment of the British soldiers the first aircraft to appear overhead at 50 feet was a Stuka, an aircraft which had not been seen by day for some time. This aircraft, which was soon joined by others, came from one of the three Nachtschlachtgruppe which operated the Stuka in the night ground-attack role; night operations being the only way in which this obsolete, but once greatly-feared aircraft, could hope to survive. Soon the air was filled with noise as the explosion of the first bombs mingled with a cacophony of small-arms fire as the British fired every automatic weapon that could be brought to bear. Despite the wall of tracer, the attack from the air was pressed home successfully by a 20-strong assortment of Junkers Ju 88, Ju 188 and Ju 87 Stukas and the bombing caused damage and casualties throughout the bridging site. Worse was to come on the next day.

Eight Focke Wulf Fw 190s in the fighter-bomber role attacked the bridge during the mid-afternoon of 6 April and scored direct hits on the approaches and on the end of a floating bay. The attack killed and wounded 40 sappers, put out of action a large amount of pontoon equipment and badly cratered the approaches to the bridging site. In response to the previous day's urgent requests for help, Hawker Tempest Vs from No 83 Group had been fitted with long-range fuel tanks and were already flying east to protect the bridging site when the attack began. The first British aircraft to arrive were from No 56 Squadron which immediately attacked the enemy aircraft orbiting the area; two Fw 190s were promptly shot down by Squadron Leader Mac-Kichan and Flight Lieutenant Payton, although one of the British aircraft was also shot down by ground fire. At 1730 hours a further attack was mounted by five Fw 190s which were intercepted by Tempests from No 80 Squadron and a further two enemy aircraft were shot down. Although the Tempests thereafter mounted patrols up and down the line of the river, the Germans continued to mount sneak attacks hiding in the cloud and only appearing when the Tempests were at the extremities of their 'beat' to dive down and bomb the area. When the Tempest pilots realised what was happening, they doubled back and drove off the enemy attackers. During one of these attacks the head-quarters of the 23rd Hussars in Stolzenau was attacked, spreading confusion among a group of officers who had the good fortune to discover an enormous store of wine. The last attack on 6 April was mounted at 2000 hours by four Stukas. The lumbering aircraft were set on by Tempests from No 486 Squadron and Flying Officer Sheddan immediately shot two out of the sky; the other two managed to escape. The Luftwaffe also launched bombing and strafing attacks in the Petershagen area but these were not as successful.

As casualties were steadily mounting in the bridgehead, not only from the attack from the air but also from the remorseless sniper, mortar and artillery fire, it was decided that 45 (RM) Commando would not wait for the remainder of the brigade to cross but would mount an attack on Leese forthwith in an attempt to relieve the pressure on themselves. The commandos fought their way out of their positions but their attack managed to advance only 150 yards towards the village due to fanatical opposition from the SS youths. With no chance of success, the commandos were forced to break off the attack a mile short of their objective and dig in. The intention had been for the remainder of the commando brigade to cross the Weser during the day and attack Leese on the night 6–7 April but word came from Brigadier Mills-Roberts that 45 (RM) Commando was now to withdraw to 8 RB's bridgehead. This was because the rest of the brigade could not be ferried across since the additional boats had still not arrived. This withdrawal to the smaller perimeter proved fortuitous as a heavy counter-attack, only beaten off with great difficulty, fell on the bridgehead at dawn on 7 April. With such determined opposition on the right bank, Brigadier Mills-Roberts ordered the commando not to mount any more attacks but to hold in their bridgehead until the remainder of the brigade could cross; this however would take time due to the problems with the assault boats.

Despite the Corps' difficulties on its northern axis, the need to continue advancing was paramount and during the night 6-7 April orders were received from 2nd Army instructing VIII Corps to push on at once to the next river, the Leine. The 6th Airborne Division accordingly took up the advance the next day, making excellent progress to reach Neustadt and Bordenau on the Leine by evening. As the armoured division was still unable to cross in the Stolzenau area, it was given use of 6th Airborne's bridges at Petershagen to allow a flank attack to be mounted from the south on the SS battalion in Leese. During the morning of 7 April 159th Brigade Group crossed the Weser; 15th/19th

King's Royal Hussars (15th/19th Hussars) and 1 Cheshire struck north towards Leese, whilst 2nd Fife and Forfar Yeomanry (2 FF Yeo) and 1 Hereford advanced east to Loccum, which they captured after a sharp battle. Supported by 23rd Hussars from the left bank, the 15th/19th Hussars and 1 Cheshire Group initially made reasonable progress but the clearance of the village of Heimsen and continual attacks from Panzerfaust teams cost valuable time and it was not until late afternoon that they neared Leese; however with daylight fading, it was decided that they would not attack, leaving the final battle for the village to the commando brigade.

Whilst these troops were moving forward, events unique to the air war in Europe were taking place far above their heads. Some of the soldiers might have noticed the contrails from bombers high above them and seen the smoke from aircraft crashing to earth, but none would have realised that they were witnessing the launching by the Luftwaffe of its last major effort against the US 8th Air Force. But this was not the only significant fact, for it was also the first, and last, occasion on which the Germans employed the ramming of bombers as a deliberate tactic. In an attempt to inflict mass casualties on the devastating American daylight raids and obtain a better return than normal methods, it had been agreed by Hitler that volunteers should crash their aircraft into bombers. In February 1945 volunteers for special duties were called for from fighter training schools to be taught to fly lightweight Messerschmitt Me 109s at high altitudes and in high speed dives. If the pilot failed to shoot down the bomber whilst in the dive, he would ram it forward of the tail unit with his own wing, breaking the bomber in two; the fighter pilot, if he survived, would parachute to earth. The unit so formed was named Sonderkommando (Special Command) Elbe.

On 7 April, a mixed force of some 1,200 B-17 Flying Fortress and B-24 Liberator bombers, escorted by 800 fighters, was tracking across the North German Plain to attack targets in the North Germany/Schleswig-Holstein region. Whilst over the Nienburg-Husum area they were set on by 120 Fw 190 and Me 109 fighters of Sonderkommando Elbe, escorted by conventional fighters and twin-jet Me 262s. Despite the Americans being taken completely by surprise by the determination of the German pilots to prosecute this new form of attack, the ramming mission was a complete failure with only two B-17s of the 452nd Bombardment Group, one B-17 from each of the 385th and 388th, and a B-24 from the 490th being brought down. Of the 183 German fighters that took off, only 15 returned to their bases; 77 pilots were killed. Many of the ramming fighters were shot down by the American fighter

escorts as they were easy prey during the long climb to their attack alti-
tude of 36,000 feet, whilst others were unable to reach that height due
to severe icing problems. Had the ramming attack been mounted with
the quantity of aircraft envisaged by its proponents it might have met
with more success; the operation was not repeated.

Back on the ground, during the night 7–8 April, 3 and 6 Commando and 46 (RM) Commando crossed the Weser and joined 45
(RM) Commando, who had spent a terrible day in the bridgehead
under merciless artillery fire. For the remainder of the night the complete brigade then conducted a difficult encircling manoeuvre in single file across marshland to attack Leese from the east. By dawn, 6
Commando had reached Leese's outskirts, taking by surprise a 2cm
Flak and its crew. As the commandos began to break into the village
they were joined by the Comet tanks of C Squadron 23rd Hussars
which had crossed the Weser at dawn to support them. Accompanied
by the armour, the brigade moved into the village which was cleared
quickly as the SS companies had evacuated the village some two hours
previously and had withdrawn to the north-east, leaving behind the
four 2cm Flak guns from Batterie 4./871 and a few stragglers. It seems
likely that the SS battalion realised that Leese had become untenable
with enemy armour and infantry on the Weser's right bank to their
south and decided to withdraw to fight another day. The village had
also been subjected to heavy artillery fire, as well as Typhoon attacks,
further convincing them that the time to pull out had probably
arrived. 3 Commando gave chase and tangled with the SS battalion's
rearguards in the woods north of Leese, but the Germans were in no
mood for a fight and continued to withdraw rapidly. 3 Commando
therefore returned to Leese and in so doing captured the heavily camouflaged V-2 factory together with a number of rockets loaded on railway wagons, and the complete scientific staff. Sixty-nine of the Hitler
Youths lie buried in the war cemetery at Leese.

Although Leese was now in British hands and secure from direct
fire, the Germans did not give up the struggle and continued to harass
the bridgehead with artillery fire. It was decided therefore to abandon
the ill-fated Stolzenau bridging site in favour of the Petershagen bridges
and for 15th Scottish Division to build a new crossing site upstream
from Stolzenau at Schlüsselburg. As it would take time for the Scottish
division's engineers to build this bridge, the remaining units of 11th
Armoured Division were ordered to move south and cross at Petershagen, prior to taking up the advance once more on the Corps' northern
axis to secure a bridgehead over the Leine.

During the morning of 8 April, 29th Armoured Brigade crossed the Weser at Petershagen to join 159th Brigade Group on the right bank, and 4th Battalion the King's Shropshire Light Infantry (4 KSLI) with the tanks of 3 RTR began to advance north to get onto the northern divisional axis. It was now that a company of marines from Bataillon I./6 became the first members of 2.Marine Infanterie Division to fire shots in anger. These soldiers had been deployed south from their battalion in Nienburg to occupy the village of Husum and act as a guard force for the main battalion position. Also with the marines in the village were SS youths from Kompanie 5./12 who had joined them to act as a rearguard for their own battalion's withdrawal from Leese. As the British advanced north through the woods towards Husum, they were harried continuously by other members of the SS battalion and it was not until late afternoon that they reached Husum; no white flags were seen to be flying and the British entered the village without a shot being fired. The peace was however illusory and Captain Corbett, who was second-in-command of B Company 4 KSLI, describes the events that followed.

'We entered the village quite peacefully, 12 Platoon going right through without trouble, 10 Platoon on the left had two casualties and reported Germans out on the left. As Company HQ moved to the centre of the village they came under fire from snipers and CSM Baker was killed... After our own squadron and vehicles and the main body of the battalion had passed through the village the snipers, who had kept out of sight, now started to work in earnest and we suffered more casualties at their hands with ten killed.

'Second Lieutenant Bracknell's platoon, which was ordered to clear a street running off to the left of the main street, met stiff resistance and was held up after its platoon commander was mortally wounded. We asked for flame throwers to help us clear the resistance, but even this did not prove successful. During this hold-up I crossed the courtyard in search of the company commander who had gone forward to where Bracknell's platoon was held up and was lucky when a sniper, covering it from several blocks away, only scored a near miss. I took shelter in a house and was trying to locate him when to my horror Major Edwards walked into the courtyard through some double doors at the far end. I shouted to warn him but as he turned his head in my direction the sniper shot him and he dropped like a stone. Believing him dead, I was just debating the wisdom of risking further lives when an armoured ambulance, which had been sent for to evacuate 2nd

Lieutenant Bracknell, drove into the yard. Fortunately we were able to lift Major Edwards in under cover of the vehicle, but it was not until next day that I heard that he was still alive. The ambulance, alas, was little use to poor Bracknell as he died just before it arrived.

'We were extremely grateful to the CO when he sent a troop of tanks to help us and as reports had come in that civilians were also using fire-arms, they had no mercy on the buildings when they did a combined attack with Lieutenant Jimmy West's platoon, and soon many of the houses were blazing as a result of their tracer. Even so, darkness was upon us before we were really sure that we had cleared all the enemy from the village. I established what was left of company HQ in a cafe in the centre of the village and spent a very uncomfortable night, most of which was taken up with visiting the two remaining platoon commanders.

'Next day we were all very glad when the order came to move out of Husum and take up a position on a cross-roads a few miles further on which had just been vacated by D Company. Here a platoon of Hitler Youth had been caught by our tanks when only partly dug in and there were dead Germans everywhere.'

The battle for Husum was a vicious but one-sided affair in which the British burnt most of the village to the ground; 17 German and 12 British soldiers died in the action, with a further 30 wounded. In this their first action, the marines' dogged performance forebode a willingness to fight regardless of the odds.

The threat posed by the north-easterly advance of 29th Armoured Brigade left no option for the Germans but to withdraw other elements of their forces on the Weser. On the night of 8 April, Flak Rgt.122(E) received orders to withdraw its batteries supporting the Weser Line as there was a real danger that the guns would either be cut off or not make it back in time for the main battle on the Aller. The regimental headquarters pulled back from the Weser and established itself in the village school in Vethem, some 4 miles north-east of Rethem on the Aller's right bank. Two days later it was ordered to move to Hamburg and command of the Flak for the battle of the Aller Line was passed to Flakregiment 95. From Nienburg, Batterie 1./521 RAD with two of its 10.5cm guns managed to join Mar.Füs.Btl.2 at Essel and Batterie 3./607 reached Mar.Felders.Btl.2 in the area of Hellberg. Similarly, Batterie 4./117 also received orders to withdraw and during the night this battery left Ahlhusen and moved via Eystrup to occupy positions in the Kirchboitzen area. Here the gunners occupied a number of farms to the west of the village. Due to the lack of prime movers all the batteries had to leave guns behind. Batterie 2./604 RAD lost one 8.8cm Flak, whilst 4./117 lost all of its four 10.5cm Flak 39 and only by using improvised chassis managed to move three of its 2cm Flak 38. The guns which could not be moved were destroyed and the redundant gunners were formed into ad-hoc infantry companies. Although the other batteries had to leave behind many irreplaceable guns, Batterie 4./162 success-fully managed to withdraw with its full complement of four 10.5cm Flak 39 and three 2cm Oerlikons from the area to the east of Hassel to the hamlet of Heithüsen, and the next day it pulled back over the Rethem bridge to occupy positions in the area of the Timpenberg, a wooded glacial sand dune some three miles to the east of Rethem. Hauptmann Hagemeier, the commander of the Flak artillery supporting Mar.Gren. Rgt.5, ordered both batteries to provide indirect and, whenever possible, direct fire to compensate for the lack of anti-tank guns. Not all guns made their withdrawal in time and British accounts report 8.8cm Flak guns on tow behind prime movers being engaged and destroyed.

The companies of SS-Ausb.u.Ers.Btl.12 HJ faced serious difficulties during their withdrawal. On 8 April a thrust by 29th Armoured Brigade nearly encircled the battalion near Lindsburg, but the SS Panzer-grenadiers managed to fight their way out in platoon-sized groups. The officers, who had been attending orders in an inn, were cut off from their companies and had to fight their way through individually or in groups to rejoin their troops. As a result the battalion was without its officers for the next week. It was during the bitter skirmishes of this confused period that the youthful SS troopers were given their nick-name the 'Steel-Eyed Boys' by the soldiers of 11th Armoured Division. The savagery of the fighting against the soldiers of the Hitler Youth is well described in an account in the regimental history of 23rd Hussars which tells vividly of the clash between a squadron and about a com-pany of SS in the village of Steimbke. Having knocked out two 8.8cm Flak 37 being towed by half-tracks as they approached the village, the squadron surrounded it on three sides whilst two companies from 4 KSLI cleared it. After extremely bitter house-to-house fighting, in which G and H Companies 8 RB exacted their revenge for the rough time they had received from the SS at Stolzenau, the young SS soldiers were even-tually forced out of the village and were engaged by the tanks as they tried to reach the safety of the wood to the north. Steimbke was cleared but left a smoking wreck and 150 casualties were suffered by the Ger-mans. No quarter was expected or given in the actions against the SS, whatever their age.

Other SS companies fared better than the young men at Steimbke. Kompanie 3./12 and 4./12 withdrew via Rethem and their exhausted young SS soldiers moved further back to the relative safety of the area between the towns of Walsrode and Fallingbostel to regroup and recover. Further companies withdrew over the rivers Leine and Aller in the Essel area and the SS battalion now came under the marine division's command.

As it was now clear that the British would not be attempting to cross the Weser at Nienburg and that the north-easterly advance by 11th Armoured Division would soon cut off Bataillon I./6, the town's primary defenders, Hartmann decided to withdraw the battalion whilst he was still able. Accordingly, on 8 April the marines withdrew on foot out of contact to the north-east and, having passed through their comrades from Mar.Gren.Rgt.5 who were hurriedly preparing their positions in Rethem, crossed the Aller and moved to the area of the villages of Altenwahlingen and Bierde. The engineer NCO cadets of ROB-Pi.Btl.Nienburg also managed to withdraw with the marines and moved in depth to the village of Kirchboitzen where they joined Mar.Gren.Rgt.6, the divisional reserve regiment; we will come upon these cadets again later in the battle.

The battle for the northern sector of the Weser-Aller line started, however, with a far more severe blow for the Germans than the withdrawal from Nienburg and the difficulties faced by SS-Ausb.u.Ers.Btl.12 HJ. On 8 April, Vizeadmiral Scheurlen left his headquarters in Walsrode to visit the battle positions Mar.Gren.Rgt.5 and 6 were preparing in the Rethem area. He was driven in his open-top Horch staff car and was accompanied by his Army operations officer, Major Wechsmann. As they sped down the tree-lined Route 209, the noise of the air rushing by drowned the noise of the engines of a number of Allied fighters which had spotted the lone car and were closing for a strafing attack. The car had just passed the hamlet of Sindorf when the driver and his passengers were caught totally unawares and although the first burst missed, the emergency stop led to a skid and the car became stuck in a bank. The passengers in the stationary vehicle were now helpless and the second attack killed Wechsmann and left the Vizeadmiral very severely wounded; the driver managed to escape. Scheurlen was evacuated to the military hospital in Walsrode but he died the next day[3]. The commander of Mar.Gren.Rgt.6, Kapitän zur See Werner Hartmann, took over until a new commander from the army, Oberst Graf von Bassewitz-Levetzow, could arrive.

NOTES

1   Coincidentally this brigade had once belonged to 53rd Welsh Division but had been transferred to 11th Armoured in 1942 when the fighting in North Africa had shown that more infantry were needed in the armoured divisions.

2   James Lucas, *Last Days of the Reich*, Arms & Armour Press. 'Leibstandarte' was 1.SS-Panzerdivision "Leibstandarte Adolf Hitler"; an Oberscharführer was equivalent to a sergeant.

3   Scheurlen lies buried in the military section of Walsrode cemetery.

4

53RD WELSH DIVISION
MARCH – APRIL

Let us now look at the 53rd Welsh Division, the XII Corps formation which will soon be committed to battle against the bulk of the marine division. On mobilisation in 1939 the field formations in the United Kingdom comprised some five Regular and 26 Territorial (13 First Line, and 13 Second Line) divisions and for the remainder of the war the largest single entity in the land battle was the Territorial Army. In addition to its divisions, it provided many smaller formations and independent units and was almost entirely responsible for the country's anti-aircraft defence. Territorials fought in all the theatres, from Dunkirk to North Africa and from Burma to the Baltic. As a means of expansion in time of crisis in peace, the Territorial Army was a success, and in war its units became indistinguishable from Regular units with its divisions making history on many battlefields.

The 53rd Welsh Division was the original Welsh Territorial division formed when the Territorial Army[1] had come into being in 1908. It had been mobilised in 1914 and served in the Middle East throughout the First World War, taking part in the Gallipoli Campaign and the Gaza battles. Between the wars, the division along with the rest of the Armed Forces, entered the doldrums of defence spending with dummy equipment substituting for the real thing and the horse remaining unreplaced by motor vehicles. It was only in the late 1930s, with the likelihood of war greatly increased, that the division at last began to receive new equipment and undergo organisational changes to make up for the years of neglect. On 1 September 1939 the order to re-embody the Territorial Army was issued and the division mobilised in its home area of Wales and west central England. The division did not go to the Continent with the British Expeditionary Force and during the early days of the war, the 53rd combined the tasks of training itself, providing assistance to its second line division, the 38th, and anti-sabotage duties. After Dunkirk and the fall of France, it played its part in the anti-invasion preparations and deployed to Northern Ireland on internal security duties. In November 1941 the division returned to England at a time when the threat of invasion had receded and then spent the next two years preparing for D-Day, being particularly involved in experimental work with new organisations, tactics and equipment. On 28 June 1944 the 53rd Welsh Division's long spell of training and waiting ended when it disembarked in Normandy as part of 21st Army Group and thereafter it was almost continuously in action until the German surrender in May 1945.

As a standard infantry division of the time, the 53rd consisted of three lorried infantry brigades, which in 1945 were the 71st, the 158th and the 160th, each containing three infantry battalions. The division was supported by a number of affiliated arms. First the Royal Artillery, which provided the field artillery, anti-aircraft and anti-tank support. The division had three field regiments in direct support, the 81st, 83rd and 133rd, all consisting of three, two-troop batteries equipped with eight of the effective 25pdr field gun (thus 24 guns per regiment). Target information for their guns was fed not only by the forward observation officers, but also by the four Auster V aircraft of A Flight No 653 (Air Observation Platform) Squadron. Anti-aircraft support was furnished by a light anti-aircraft regiment, the 25th, whose three batteries each had 18, towed 40mm Bofors guns. However, as the Luftwaffe now posed such a reduced threat, each brigade was supported by only a troop whilst the rest of the regiment was employed on infantry duties, such as guarding bridges and headquarters. Anti-tank firepower was available from the four batteries of 17pdr guns of the 71st Anti-Tank Regiment. The regiment fielded 48 guns in total with two of the batteries having towed guns, and two with the Archer self-propelled gun. Artificial moonlight for night manoeuvring was supplied by the searchlights of C Troop 344 Searchlight Battery. Recce for the division was the responsibility of the 53rd Reconnaissance Regiment[2] whose three squadrons were equipped with Humber Mk IV armoured cars mounting 37mm guns, and Daimler scout cars. The regiment had a support group mounted in carriers consisting of a mortar troop with six 3in mortars and an anti-tank gun troop with six 6pdrs, whilst each squadron contained an assault troop carried in M5 half-tracks for use as infantry. The companies of 1st Battalion The Manchester Regiment (1 Manchester) provided Vickers machine-gun (A, B and C Companies) and 4.2in mortar support (D Company). The Royal Engineers provided three field companies in direct support, the 244th, 282nd and 555th, backed up by the 285th Field Park, whilst communication to the brigades and rearwards to Headquarters XII Corps was provided by the 53rd Divisional Signal Regiment.

The infantry battalions were each made up of a headquarter company, support company and four rifle companies. Headquarter company consisted of battalion headquarters, the signal platoon and the various administrative elements such as quartermasters, cooks, clerks and so forth. Support company provided the commanding officer with his own integral fire support and a limited engineering and recce capability. The company comprised a mortar platoon, consisting of six 3in mortars transported in Windsor carriers; a carrier platoon of 13 carriers and three Wasp flamethrowing carriers; an anti-tank platoon of eight 6pdr guns each towed by a carrier; and an assault pioneer platoon of 20 men. The rifle companies were each made up of three platoons which in turn comprised three 10-man sections. The total established strength of a rifle company was some 124 men but the manpower barrel by 1945 had been well scraped and few companies would have operated at this strength. The principal weapons of the rifle company were the infantryman's .303in Lee-Enfield Number 4 rifle and the Bren light machine-gun, but each platoon also had the effective but fearsome PIAT to provide short range anti-tank firepower. A 2in mortar was held at platoon headquarters and a number of soldiers would have been armed with Sten sub-machine-guns. The lorried infantry battalion could be carried in 30 3-ton lorries driven by a Royal Army Service Corps transport platoon. The total established strength of the battalion was some 800 officers and men, but most battalions were operating well below this in 1945.

Following its disembarkation in Normandy, 53rd Welsh Division was placed under command of VIII Corps and was in action a few days later helping hold the bridgehead against determined German counter-attacks. The division's infantry brigades all took part in the bitter fighting associated with the south-eastern sector of the Allied bridgehead and the subsequent advance to Falaise. During late August the 53rd took part in the great advance across northern France culminating in the capture of Antwerp on 4 September 1944. In mid-September the division was involved in fierce fighting when, as part of XII Corps, it took part in the ground advance to support Operation 'Market Garden'.

The subsequent failure to capture the Rhine bridges at Arnhem was not however the only setback for the Allies, for by September 1944 they were facing serious logistical problems which threatened their ability to advance further. These problems could only be solved by opening Antwerp, and on 16 October Montgomery issued orders making Antwerp the sole priority for 21st Army Group. Dempsey's 2nd Army now swung westwards to clear the Germans from south of the Maas and, as a key part of the offensive, 53rd Welsh Division captured the town of 's-Hertogenbosch after a hard fought battle. The division was then involved in the fighting to clear the enemy from the west banks of the rivers Meuse and Roer.

On 17 December the Germans launched their Ardennes offensive. Although they initially met with success, their offensive lost momentum and counter-attacks and Allied air support soon began to take their toll. Montgomery, who had been given command of all Allied troops on the northern flank of the 'Bulge', ordered British 2nd Army to send XXX Corps to deploy behind the Meuse. The 53rd Welsh Division, now back with XXX Corps, took part in the subsequent attacks that were launched by the Corps from the north and north-west as part of the general counter-attack to destroy Heeresgruppe B. By 23 January it was all over and the division began to prepare for the next task: the battle for the Rhineland.

The battle for the country between the Meuse and the Rhine saw some of the bitterest fighting of the campaign, fought in appalling conditions against Schlemm's 1.Fallschirm Armee. The 53rd Division, playing a leading part in the battles to clear the Reichswald forest and the capture of the town of Weeze, lost in a four-week period between 7 February and 7 March some 250 killed and 3,448 wounded and sick. Twenty-one per cent of the casualties were psychiatric casualties suffering from battle stress and it was noted that a large percentage of these men had either been wounded before or were young, immature youths in their first action and with poor combatant temperament and often with below average intelligence[3]. The 53rd Division was no different to other formations and by the spring of 1945 was plainly nearing the end of its tether. This description from the regimental history of the 1st Battalion the East Lancashire Regiment describes the state of a typical infantry battalion in 1945.

'Signs of prolonged strain had already begun to appear. Slower reactions in the individual; a marked increase in cases of "battle exhaustion"; and a lower standard of battle efficiency – all showed quite clearly that the limit was fast approaching. And it applied particularly to the more seasoned veterans, whose personal example and steadying influence were so essential. At home there seemed to be a widespread impression that resistance had ceased on the Rhine; and that the sweeping advance across Germany had become just a triumphal procession. How far the idea deviated from the truth requires no emphasis, but what was not sufficiently realised was the fact that experienced reinforcements were no longer forthcoming, so that each new casualty amongst the junior leaders at that late stage threw an ever-mounting strain on the few who remained. There were, in any case, not enough battle-trained and experienced NCOs in the rifle companies.'[4]

Not only did the vast majority of the casualties fall on the division's nine infantry battalions, leading to many gaps in every unit, but also lost were a disproportionate number of experienced leaders, compounding the effects of the attrition. The impact on the division's fighting ability of the losses of these men was to become starkly apparent during the battle that would follow a few weeks later against 2.Marine Infanterie Division.

On 23 March 2nd Army began the operation to cross the Rhine. The 53rd Welsh Division did not, however, take part in the battle for the Rhine crossing as it was tasked for follow-up operations once the bridgehead was formed. On 26 March the division, now operating with XII Corps, crossed the river and immediately commenced operations to expand the bridgehead and assist in the break-out. Bocholt was captured on 29 March and the division then advanced on the corps' left flank to the Rheine area. On reaching the Dortmund-Ems canal during the first week of April, 2nd Army's advance swung from a north-east to an easterly course. The new role for the 53rd was to relieve the 7th Armoured Division brigades in the Ibbenbüren sector leaving one brigade, the 160th, to operate under 52nd Lowland Division in clearing the Rheine area. The 7th Armoured Division was now released for an armoured drive on the Weser, and the 53rd was tasked to finish clearing Ibbenbüren, then advance north and clear the Germans from the area south of the Ems-Weser canal in order to protect the corps axis. The division was then to follow in the armoured division's wake.

On 5 April the 71st Brigade mopped up Ibbenbüren supported by a half-squadron of Crocodiles, the flame-throwing variant of the Churchill tank, and heavy artillery fire, and on the same day 158th Brigade advanced north to the line of the canal. By mid-day on 7 April the area had been cleared. The 160th Brigade had meanwhile been busy with 52nd Division securing the left flank and mopping up resistance. However, in the early hours of 8 April the brigade commander, Brigadier Coleman, was ordered to move his brigade east to relieve units from 7th Armoured Division at Hoya and start preparations for an assault crossing of the Weser. As the situation on the Weser was fluid and the brigade was somewhat out-of-touch with operations in the van of the advance, Brigadier Coleman visited commander 53rd Division, Major General Ross, at divisional headquarters at Westerkapeln to get updated and hear from him the details of the divisional plan for the river crossings. As a preliminary to the operations to cross the Weser and Aller rivers, 160th Brigade was to close up to the Weser at Hoya and take over from units of 22nd Armoured Brigade, with one battalion on the loop of the river at the town and one on either flank of the loop. Recce of the river to the south was to be carried out by B Squadron 53rd Reconnaissance Regiment, which was to join the brigade as it passed through Westerkapeln. Assuming that no intact bridges would be found, Brigadier Coleman was ordered to start planning an assault crossing of the Weser as soon as his brigade reached the river. To assist in this task the brigade was to be joined by 282nd Field Company RE with 45 assault boats. The 160th Infantry Brigade would make the assault crossing of the Weser; 158th Infantry Brigade would be the second brigade to cross and would form the divisional bridgehead; 71st Infantry Brigade would then pass through and press on to Rethem, the next objective.

By daylight on the 8th, Brigadier Coleman's brigade had begun its 85-mile move to close up to the Weser, a move enlivened by the streams of liberated prisoners and displaced persons of many nationalities moving west. Many had captured German vehicles and motor cycles, and some had 'borrowed' farm carts and horses, but by far the majority were on foot. They trudged along, tired but happy. The German population in contrast stood sullen but interested as the Welsh drove through their villages. The weather for the advance was good and the rolling countryside amazed the troops with its beauty and lack of war damage. Hedgerows were beginning to burst into leaf and the faint, green haze of leaves was appearing on the trees. The only signs of war were the occasional road-blocks made of earth revetted with timber and wire, and the white flags, pillow slips and sheets which fluttered from roofs, windows and gates. Most of the villages were untouched by war and the farms appeared rich with livestock and produce. John D'Arcy-Dawson, a war correspondent accompanying 2nd Army, describes the lush countryside through which the advance was passing.

'The countryside was pleasantly green, the fields full of cattle and the corn well forward. Every farmhouse was in excellent condition, and the farm buildings would have delighted a British farmer. With plenty of slave labour it was no wonder the farms were so well tilled. In parts of the country the houses and outbuildings were similar to the black-and-white beamed houses of Cheshire except that the main barn and house formed one continuous building with an immense steeply sloping roof. The soil appeared to be very light and would, I imagine, require careful handling if it were to give bountiful crops. In some places I saw enormous flocks of sheep, while every farm and house had dozens of chickens running about. Except for blown bridges and wrecked vehicles lying in hedges and ditches this part of Germany was untouched by war.'[5]

By dusk on 8 April the battalions of 160th Infantry Brigade were nearing the end of their long advance and were moving towards the areas they had been allocated to hold on the Weser left bank: 2nd Battalion the Monmouthshire Regiment (2 Mons) – the area south of the Hoya loop and occupying the villages of Stendern, Holtrup and Schweringen; 6th Battalion the Royal Welch Fusiliers (6 RWF) – the area from Hoya to Altenbücken; and 4th Battalion the Welch Regiment (4 Welch) – the area north of the Hoya loop and occupying the villages of Hingste, Ubbendorf and Wienbergen.

The battalion selected to make the assault crossing was 6 RWF. When the battalion reached the ridge overlooking Hoya and the Weser it was ominously quiet and the rumour went round the battalion that the war had ended but no-one had bothered to tell them! 6 RWF's war soon began again however, as the noise made by the withdrawing tanks of 1 RTR as they were relieved by the battalion drew heavy shellfire, mostly as airburst, and throughout the remainder of 8 April any movement near the river was met by instant small-arms fire from Germans in buildings on the right bank. These Germans came from the regimental Kompanie 14./5 and they had occupied the buildings as soon as they arrived during the morning of 8 April, having marched from Rethem. Due to the largely unopposed advance of the last few days, some British troops seemed to have forgotten that there was still an enemy to be faced. The 282nd Field Company RE had been allocated the task of bridging the Weser once 6 RWF had secured the bridgehead and the squadron commander, Major Kent, moved forward in his jeep with a member of his company to recce the proposed crossing site. Unfortunately the major was either unaware of the Germans' presence on the right bank, or was somewhat over-confident, as he was shot in the legs by a sniper whilst studying his map in his jeep. The major was fortunate to escape with his life and he was perhaps the first of many to be surprised by a new-found aggressiveness in the enemy.

Planning for 6 RWF's crossing of the Weser continued through the remainder of the day. It was decided that two rifle companies would spearhead the battalion's operation, paddling across in the flimsy assault boats. Once across, the battalion was to establish a bridgehead on the right bank to provide protection whilst a Bailey bridge was built to replace the road and rail bridges which had been demolished by the Germans. Although the intention had been for the crossing to be made during the night of 8–9 April, after the companies had marched back to the assembly area and had drawn the assault boats, the men were very tired and so it was decided to postpone the operation to the hours before dawn on 9 April. Despite the weariness of the soldiers, as all three battalions were on a very extended front and their companies in contact only by radio, a busy patrol programme had to be arranged to give security, recce the lie of the land and discover enemy dispositions on both banks. During its recce of the area to the brigade's south, B Squadron found the going difficult and it was hampered by the many water obstacles in the area. The recce troops discovered that Draken-burg, on the right bank of the Weser, was occupied by the enemy but investigations by the infantry battalions in their areas revealed that apart from a few stragglers, there were no enemy troops on the left bank; the right bank however appeared generally to be strongly held. During the course of 7 and 8 April, 83rd and 133rd Field Artillery Regi-ments were hurriedly deployed forward to take up positions to support the Weser crossing operation. The procedures for such moves were by now second nature and the advance parties had departed to plot in the next gun positions some time before the regimental road moves began. By the time the guns arrived the individual gun positions were marked by marker flags and no time was therefore wasted. The 133rd Field Reg-iment was the first to move and by 2210 hours on 8 April the regiment reported to 160th Brigade that all its guns were in position. In addition to the field regiments, the 53rd Division also had available to it the valuable support of the 5.5in guns of 72nd Medium Regiment. This reg-iment had moved some 85 miles during the course of the day, complet-ing the longest move it had conducted so far in the war. By 1830 hours it was in action with 14 of its guns in the area of Dudden south of Bre-men firing a number of missions in support of 160th Brigade's plan for crossing the Weser.

During the remainder of the night 8-9 April, the battalions of 160th Brigade continued to mount constant patrols and fire mortar barrages at any German movement identified on the right bank in order to make a show of force on what was a very thinly held front. 2 Mons had a minor success when they captured 10 members of the Feldgen-darmerie (military police) who had been cut off on the left bank when the bridge was blown at Hoya. But the engagements were far from one-sided. D Troop of 25th Light Anti-Aircraft (LAA) Regiment RA had allocated two Bofors in the ground role to support 160th Brigade and these guns were moved during the night right up to the bank of the Weser. Unfortunately, with the crossing operation delayed and with dawn breaking, they were caught in the open and could not be withdrawn. The marines were not slow to take advantage of the gunners' predicament and opened fire on the guns and the heaped ammunition next to them from the windows of the houses they were occupying. One of the marines was the 17 year-old Matrose Rolf Fuchs who still remembers this incident.

'The exploding ammunition damaged the gun; we could not believe it and were ecstatic. We then turned our fire on the second gun which we also commenced to destroy. A short while later we came under heavy artillery fire from the other side so we took cover in the cellar.'

A patrol from B Company 4 Welch also met with disaster when it tried to cross the river in assault boats during the early hours of Monday 9 April. The boats were seen and shot-up in mid-stream with all but one officer and three soldiers failing to return from the 17 who had set out. With the rivers nearly in flood, these were the first of many soldiers from both sides who were to die in the swirling waters of the Weser and Aller over the following days.

Despite the difficulties of the night and the coming of dawn, brigade headquarters decided to press on with the operation to cross the Weser as speed was of the essence. To reduce the risk to a daylight crossing, a deception plan was devised to take the Germans' attention away from the crossing site whilst the highly vulnerable assault boats struggled across. This plan duly began at 0900 hours on Monday 9 April and involved a smoke and mortar barrage being fired one kilometre to the south of the crossing site. At the same time the canvas assault boats were launched and A Company, commanded by Lieutenant Dufty, and C Company, commanded by Captain MacHenry, began to cross. Although the banks made entry and exit difficult, both companies crossed with remarkably few casualties and it appeared that the Germans had been distracted by the deception plan. In reality, the marines' inexperience in fighting a land battle was the key to the successful crossing as they had not realised that the quickening of the artillery programme heralded an assault crossing and most were taking shelter in the cellars as the boats crossed. By the time they emerged it was too late. Rolf Fuchs had been one of a party of 13 marines which had taken up positions in the court house. When the artillery fire lifted they climbed out of the cellar in which they had sheltered via a window and began to move to take up fire positions. They did not get far. Machine-guns began to engage them and three were killed immediately. Two marines were taken prisoner and the rest of the party managed to escape. Rolf Fuchs was one of the prisoners and he remembers feeling ashamed to be taken prisoner so early in the battle and before he had fired many shots in anger.

Although the crossing was unopposed, fighting was bitter on the right bank as each house had to be cleared in turn. Having been forced out, some of the marines managed to get away by moving along hedgerows before the area was cleared. The opposition from the troops of Kompanie 14./5 was fierce and to quote from 6 RWF's history they were, 'a very difficult lot of young men, who seemed to have nothing to live for, and who seemed to enjoy dying!' However, these soldiers were too few to hold 6 RWF and by 1100 hours the British were firmly lodged on the right bank having lost four killed and 17 wounded. The commanding officer, Lieutenant Colonel Hutchinson, was ordered by brigade headquarters not to put more troops across and the sappers of 282nd Field Company RE were given the go-ahead to start bridging. Fortunately the Germans' demolition of the road bridge had not been sufficiently thorough and although the first span had dropped, the second was only damaged and the third was intact. The company began constructing a 35-yard Bailey bridge to link the first pier to the left bank, being joined later by 244th Field Company RE who supported them by repairing the damaged centre span. By 2330 hours the bridge was opened to Class 40 traffic and the way was now open for 53rd Welsh Division to exploit to the Aller at Rethem. Despite their successful bridging operation, 282nd Field Company's collective nose was put out of joint the next day by the BBC who reported that 7th Armoured Division had bridged the Weser at Hoya!

During the rest of the day the other two brigades of 53rd Division - 71st and 158th Infantry Brigades - moved forward to the Weser and at 1600 hours 160th Infantry Brigade reverted from 7th Armoured Division to come under command of its parent division once more. The relative ease with which the brigade had crossed the Weser and formed a bridgehead now led to the divisional plan being amended. The 158th Infantry Brigade, commanded by Brigadier Wilsey[6], instead of expanding the bridgehead, was now to pass through and exploit to the Aller. In the early afternoon Brigadier Wilsey held his orders in which he detailed how the next phase would be conducted. The brigade group with 4 Welch under command would cross the Weser at Hoya as soon as the bridge was finished, pass through the 6 RWF bridgehead, advance to Rethem and hopefully capture its bridge intact before establishing a bridgehead over the Aller. The battalion tasks were as follows: 7th Battalion the Royal Welch Fusiliers (7 RWF) would be first across to clear the village of Hassel which lay some three miles to the east of Hoya; 4th Battalion the Welch Regiment (4 Welch) would then follow and clear the village of Eystrup to the south of Hassel and provide right flank security; 1/5th Battalion the Welch Regiment (1/5 Welch) was allocated the important task of advancing through these battalions to seize Rethem and its bridge; whilst the 1st Battalion the East Lancashire Regiment (1 E Lan R) would cross last, clear the Memsen state forest then advance to take the area of the villages of Hohenholz and Hämelhausen which lie roughly half-way between Hoya and Rethem. To beef up the infantry division's advance, XII Corps allocated to it the tanks of 5 RTR from 22nd Armoured Brigade.

As the Weser's right bank had been only lightly held, a speedy follow-up was considered essential to prevent any German reinforcement or consolidation. Prisoners from Mar.Gren.Rgt.5 taken during the battle for the Weser bridgehead revealed not only the presence of a fresh formation but also one prepared to fight. Although this aggressiveness surprised the British, they were wholly unsuspecting of the very tough fighting that was soon to occur and a 53rd Division intelligence summary mentioned that although little had been gleaned on the marine division from the prisoners of war, 'what has emerged so far does not create an awesome picture'. The division's view of the marines was shortly to change. It was not however only 53rd Division who were having some trouble assessing the opposition, as the last entry in XII Corps' Intelligence Log for 10 April reported the presence of a unit entitled '5 Infantry Mining Regiment' in Rethem! Little wonder perhaps that the British were later to be caught unawares.

Whilst the British were planning the next phase of their advance, in Rethem on that Monday morning, Jordan had announced to the frightened population that the town would be defended to the last. The marines prepared their positions with increased vigour as the sound of the fighting to the west during the early hours of the morning had been clearly audible and it was obvious that the war would soon be on them. At 2330 hours the leading battalion of 158th Infantry Brigade, 7 RWF, began crossing the Weser Bailey bridge on foot and the companies spearheaded the advance to the division's next objective, the bridge over the Aller at Rethem.

NOTES

1   Known then as the Territorial Force.

2   The Reconnaissance Corps had been formed in January 1941 to carry out recce for the infantry divisions. In January 1944 it had been absorbed into the Royal Armoured Corps and re-designated the Reconnaissance Regiment. Each unit had a total of 28 armoured cars and 24 light recce cars.

3   F. Crew, *Medical History of the Second World War, Vol IV, North-west Europe*, HMSO.

4   Brig Burden, *History of the East Lancashire Regiment in the War, 1939–1945*, Rawson & Co Ltd.

5   John D'Arcy-Dawson, *European Victory*, Macdonald & Co.

6   Brigadier Wilsey's son is General Sir John Wilsey KCB CBE, at the time of publication Commander-in-Chief United Kingdom Land Forces.

RETHEM AND ITS DEFENCE
5–8 APRIL

The small town of Rethem has occupied its site on the left bank of the River Aller some 12 miles south-east of Verden for 630 years and other than some expansion on its northern side, its layout has changed little. In 1945 the town consisted of two parts: the Old Town, which was close to the Aller bridge, comprised old brick and timber buildings laid out in a tight grid of streets; and the more recent 19th Century red brick developments, collectively known as the New Town, which had spread along the roads radiating out from the town centre, particularly towards the west and the railway. Rethem has always been an important crossing point of the Aller and a number of roads focused onto it, the most important of which being Route 209, the main road linking Nienburg and Lüneburg. The town was connected to the railway system by a branch line and had a small station and sidings. In addition to its importance as a crossing point of the Aller, Rethem was a local centre for the outlying villages on both banks of the river. In 1939 its population was 1,586.

At the start of the war in September 1939 life in the small town initially altered little. Wartime restrictions gradually began to be applied however, the first of which being the issue of ration cards for food and clothing and the imposition of the blackout, and soon the men began to be called up as the country prepared itself for war. In the late autumn of 1939, following the successful conclusion of the Polish campaign, the men called up for service were replaced in the workforce by about 100 Polish prisoners of war who were assigned to work for the farms in Rethem and the surrounding villages. Each night after work the prisoners had to return to their camp which was established in the hall of the Hillmann public house near the bridge over the Aller. In the summer of 1940 the Poles were joined by French prisoners, and following the invasion of the Soviet Union the numbers were further swelled by an influx of Soviet prisoners. The civilian population were given strict instructions not to fraternise with the prisoners and they were even forbidden to eat together at the same table; these orders were however seldom complied with. During the latter years of the war, although the quality and quantity of German household rations declined markedly, in the rural areas there was sufficient food for the population and there was none of the privation experienced by the town dwellers. The inhabitants were however called upon to help the war effort by providing raw materials and on 19 February 1941 the bells of Rethem church became victims to one such drive. Between December of that same year and January 1942 large scale collections of clothing for the Eastern Front were made. During these drives, usually conducted by the Hitler Youth, the young people chanted as they went from house to house, 'Rags, bones, iron and paper. We collect everything, everything.'

The local inhabitants first came into contact with their own army in 1939 when troops were quartered in a hutted RAD camp near the Aller. This camp had been built before the war but the RAD labourers who had occupied it left in 1938 to work on the Siegfried Line, leaving the camp empty for a number of years. In 1940, after the fall of France, the need to re-quarter troops back in the homeland reached a peak and several companies stayed in the camp, whilst others were billeted elsewhere in the town. During the summer of 1942 a 200-strong SS unit occupied the huts and quartering then continued irregularly until 1943 when the need for extra accommodation within the Reich ended due to the huge demand for manpower placed by the Fronts. By 1945 the town's population showed a strong bias towards women, the very young and the old as most of the male inhabitants had been called up for service in the Wehrmacht. Despite the change in its population, the pattern of rural life altered little during the war years, and apart from the loss of friends, relatives and neighbours who had died in the Wehrmacht's ranks, it was the war in the air that had brought the inhabitants closest to the fighting.

The air war had started timidly enough with British leaflet raids in March 1940, but by 1942 the fighting had gathered pace. In the summer of that year the townsfolk experienced their first direct involvement with the war when a British aircraft was shot down over Rethem. The plane crashed near the Fährsee on the Aller's right bank, and the Australian pilot who had baled out was immediately captured by soldiers of the Marine Kraftfahrzeug Abteilung stationed in Hülsen[1], the next village downstream from Rethem. On 9 November 1942 the area suffered its first damage when Hülsen was hit by incendiaries and high explosive bombs. Three houses were destroyed and more damaged by the bombs which were probably part of a jettisoned load. A few days before this incident Sahlberger, the mayor of Rethem who was also an air-raid warden, had issued a timely reminder to the local population who were not sufficiently obedient to air-raid warnings.

'Rethem (Aller), 20 Oct 1942
Subject: <u>Behaviour on Air-Raid Warnings</u>.

It has been noted that a large part of the population behave irresponsibly during air-raid warnings.

Therefore, more severe measures to adhere to air-raid discipline and to protect the population have to be ordered.

The Reichsluftschutzbund (RLD) has explained hundreds and hundreds of times what is both to be done and to be avoided during an air-raid warning, ie. on hearing the alarm take cover, take children to a safe place, clear roads, stop and park vehicles of any kind, close shops until hearing the 'all-clear' signal.

In future anyone met in the streets during an alarm will have to expect to be fined.

After receiving construction material, the completion of slit trenches is to be carried out as fast as possible. Until then you have to look for adequate cover yourself.

The largest part of the air-raid shelter in the Bünte can now be used and is available to anyone who has not got adequate cover.

The orders of the holders of the blue RLD arm-band have to be obeyed implicitly. As of today the security service, wearing a white arm-band, will be on patrol during every air-raid warning and will report anybody who violates air-raid orders for punishment.

Signed: Sahlberger'

By 1943 the air war had increased markedly in intensity. Rethem posted two men, one to the Old Town and the other to the New, to act as air-raid wardens between 2330 hours and 0330 hours and the town received its own anti-aircraft defence when a heavy machine-gun was mounted on a wooden Flak tower built near the Aller. The wardens were tasked to observe enemy air activity and were also expected to check suspicious people. From June 1944 they were supplemented by two Hitler Youths who were detailed to run messages. The inhabitants witnessed in awe on the night horizon the great incendiary fires from the raids on Hamburg and Bremen and watched by day the American bomber streams battling their way to and from targets deep in the Reich. In May 1944 they accepted into their homes the first evacuees from the devastated cities, and during that summer jettisoned incendiaries set fire to the local moors and the children had fun collecting the strips of aluminium backed paper dropped by the enemy bombers to disrupt radar directed Flak and fighter control. From the second half of 1943 the enemy's air attacks began to have a far more direct effect on local life as Allied fighters now began to sweep across Germany attacking opportunity targets. On 2 November 1944 an Allied fighter shot up the Verden to Schwarmstedt train whilst it was passing Wohlendorf, killing one woman and wounding six other passengers. Eight days later another train was treated similarly at Wahnebergen in the Weser-Aller triangle and 20 passengers and station staff were killed and 40 wounded[2]. Throughout the remainder of 1944 and on into 1945 the air war raged overhead and there was a steady toll of shot-down bombers and fighters crashing in the area.

In the late summer of 1944 a V1 launch ramp was built in the woods near Rethem from which about 25 of the weapons were subsequently launched at unknown targets with unknown effect. In November 1944 all men between the ages of 16 and 60 were ordered to join the Volkssturm. However, as there were neither weapons nor uniforms for them and their training negligible, they were of no use at all when the battle came to the Aller. In January 1945 the townsfolk accepted the first evacuees from the territories in the east which had been overrun by the Soviet armies. These people came by rail from East Prussia, Pommern and Mecklenburg and were billeted on the townsfolk.[3]

The first indication of the impending land war was on Friday 6 April when 11 tanks, five Panther Mk Vs and six Tiger Mk VIs, rumbled through the town and headed off to the west. This force had left Fallingbostel that same day and was all that remained of the once powerful Panzer Lehrdivision which had had its home base at the Fallingbostel camp since August 1943. The group of tanks commanded by Major Schulze, a holder of the Knight's Cross with Oak Leaves, was making its way to counter the British threat in the Petershagen area, and later the same day it mounted the attack on the 5th Parachute Brigade bridgehead described earlier. However, it was to be on the next day, Saturday 7 April, with the arrival of the marines at Rethem's railway station, that the inhabitants' role in the war as spectators changed irrevocably and violently to that of participants.

It will be recalled that as soon as Mar.Gren.Rgt.6 arrived at Rethem station on 7 April, Bataillon I./6 was deployed forward to defend Nienburg on the Weser. The battalion was accompanied by Kapitän zur See Hartmann and the regimental headquarters. When the battalion reached the town, one company was deployed to the village of Husum,

four miles to the south, to provide an element of delay and early warning in case the breakout from the bridgehead won by 11th Armoured
Division at Stolzenau irrupted in a northerly direction. Also located in
Nienburg were a number of disparate units which were grouped
together under the Kampfkommandant, or operational commander,
Nienburg: 300 engineer NCO cadets of ROB-Pi.Btl.Nienburg, together
with Landesschützen-Bataillon 1020[4] and Pionier-Baubataillon 211,
each with a further 300 men.

The responsibility for the main defensive position covering Rethem
and its bridge was given to Bataillon II./5, commanded by Kapitänleut-
nant Burkel. However, as the regimental commander was in overall
command of the defence of the Rethem sector, Burkel was to play a
subsidiary role to his superior. To delay the enemy's advance and cause
maximum casualties, Jordan had to create as much depth to his
defence as possible. He accordingly based his plan for the defence of
the town on two layers: an outer layer located in the outlying villages
and hamlets, and an inner layer on the town's perimeter. The outer
layer positions, based on a Flak or anti-tank gun protected by infantry
in platoon or company strength, dominated the approaches to Rethem
and would for a while prevent the villages being used as secure bases
for mounting attacks on the town. These outer positions were located
in the villages of Stöcken and Wohlendorf and the farmhouse at the
multiple road junction half a mile to the west of Rethem. So as not to
weaken Burkel's companies defending the town's perimeter, Jordan
allocated two companies of marines from Bataillon I./5 to provide the
troops for these outer layer positions; one company deployed to the
village of Wohlendorf, half a mile to Rethem's north-west, whilst
another took over the farmhouse and the immediate area of the multiple road junction. This advanced outpost, known as the Strassengabel
strongpoint, had been initially prepared by 65 soldiers from an
unknown unit who had arrived at the farmhouse on 5 April; these men
later moved off to the west towards Hassel, leaving the position for
occupation by the marines.

Apart from perhaps the southern approach, which had some cover
from hedgerows and small coppices, all the other approaches to the
inner layer were table-top flat, largely bereft of cover and provided
defenders on the town's perimeter with excellent fields of fire.
Notwithstanding German doctrine for the defence of towns which held
that the main resistance should be located within the built-up area as
edges were believed to be too vulnerable to artillery fire, Jordan decided
to defend Rethem from its perimeter. Shortage of time to prepare

strongpoints within the town, as well as the excellent fields of fire on the perimeter, probably led him to ignore the doctrine. Unfortunately for Jordan, he had neither the engineers nor the time to construct obstacles to channel and break-up attacks. He had a few Teller anti-tank mines, although far too few to create a minefield.

The most likely direction of enemy approach was from the west and it was on this approach that Jordan concentrated his strength. The approaches to Rethem from the west included the two major roads, Route 209 and the road from Eystrup; both were particularly exposed and attacks using either as an axis would be very vulnerable. Jordan took maximum advantage of this and sited a full company position and three platoon strongpoints to cover these western approaches; Route 209 was covered by a company position dug-in along the railway embankment and in the fields forward of the railway line, whilst the platoon strongpoints covered the Eystrup road. The company had the powerful support of the combined Batteries 1. and 4./125 (E) with five 10.5cm Flak 39 heavy anti-aircraft guns mounted on railway flats sited on the sidings at Rethem station. The battery also had two 2cm Flak, one Vierlingsflak and one Zwillingsflak, in the area of the station. Due to the lack of prime movers and fuel to move wheeled batteries, the heavy railway Flak of the combined batteries 1. and 4./125(E) had been moved during the night of 5 April from Eystrup station, where they had been covering the Weser.

The 10.5cm Flak was a most effective anti-aircraft gun which could also be used in either the anti-armour role or as conventional artillery. Surprisingly, the redeployment of railway Flak in general had not been difficult despite the very heavy air attacks on the railway network. Locomotives were nearly always on time and the fuel shortages that were being experienced by motorised units did not affect the railway Flak. The main advantage of railway batteries was their ability to be rapidly moved and concentrated, preventing accurate plotting on Allied Flak maps. As a consequence they were much feared by Allied bomber pilots. Their main disadvantage was an exposed superstructure which made the guns and crews vulnerable to bomb blast and splinters and, in a land battle, shell and small-arms fire. The crews of the Flak guns at Rethem attempted to reduce this threat to themselves by stacking railway sleepers around the front of the flat-beds.

Jordan allocated the second company of Bataillon II./5 to the defence of the north-west and northern approaches to the town. Here Rethem's perimeter would be defended by independent platoon-strength strongpoints rather than a company position. The platoons were sited in depth of the Strassengabel position and were established to cover the approach to the town down the road from Eystrup and the approach across the fields from the village of Wohlendorf. The first strongpoint was located on the south side of the Eystrup road centred around the farmhouse belonging to the von der Kammer family. In addition to the marine platoon, this strongpoint also contained three Pak 40 anti-tank guns. To its north was the second strongpoint, based on an isolated farm which the marines nicknamed 'Elfriede', probably after a wife or girlfriend. The farm belonging to Heinrich Wohlke lay just to the east of a rivulet, the Wölpe, which flowed sluggishly across the fields to the Aller some 500 yards to the north. From the farm the marines could dominate any attempt to approach Rethem from either the north-west or the north. The third platoon was based in the area of Schumann's Mill on the town's northern edge from which it could cover the Aller's flood meadows to the north; this position was reinforced by a 2cm Flak gun. The third company from Bataillon II./5 was allocated to cover the southern approach. Although this was possibly the least likely to be used by the British in their initial attacks, Jordan allocated a full company with a Pak 40 anti-tank gun to the defence of the town's perimeter in this sector as the relatively well covered approaches could allow an attack to close on the town. Bataillon II./5's fourth company, the heavy weapons' company, distributed its MG42 teams amongst the other three companies and deployed its mortars to a base plate position on the right bank of the Aller.

With the majority of his troops allocated to the perimeter positions, Jordan had few resources left for the interior of the town. A barrier consisting of a Pak 40 anti-tank gun and an anti-tank obstacle made of vertically-set logs was established on a road junction near the town centre to prevent the Aller bridge being rushed. Although these log obstacles were commonplace throughout Germany, they were largely ineffective and were nicknamed 'Sixty-one Minute Barriers' – the enemy would laugh at them for 60 minutes before tearing them down in one. The Aller bridge, a strongly-built steel cantilever set on concrete piers, was prepared for demolition and Jordan established his regimental headquarters in the cellar of the Wehland house on Junkernstrasse in the Old Town near the bridge. Jordan had as his adviser at his headquarters a much-decorated, but unidentified, Oberleutnant from the Army. It is not known where Burkel established his battalion headquarters but it was probably near the area of the railway station.

Although the regiment had a plentiful supply of the hand-held Panzerfaust, it lacked heavier anti-tank firepower and Scheurlen had to rectify this by allocating to its support 1.Batterie of Mar.Pz.Jg.Abt.2 with its effective Pak 40 anti-tank guns. With the divisional artillery regiment still in Schleswig-Holstein waiting for horses to be provided, the only available artillery support in the division's area of responsibil-

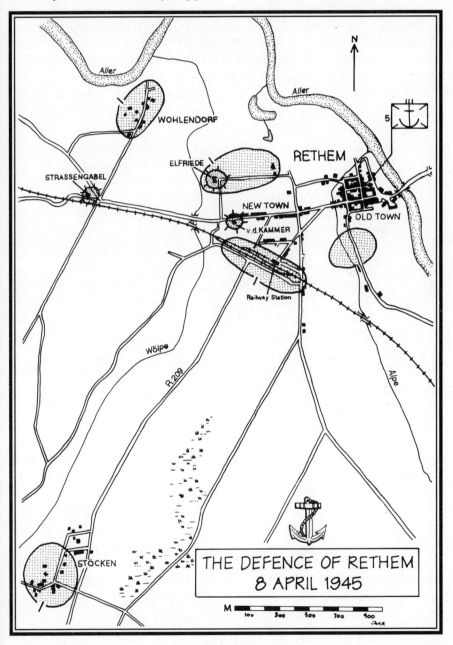

THE DEFENCE OF RETHEM
8 APRIL 1945

ity would be provided by the Flak batteries of Flak Rgt.122(E). These guns could only join the defensive plans for Rethem once they had played their part in the battle for the Weser and had successfully withdrawn across the Aller, where they could then be employed in the direct or indirect roles.

Jordan's other battalion, I./5, now with only one rifle company and elements of the heavy weapons company, deployed on Bataillon II./5's right to defend the villages of Hülsen and Westen and the ground which lay between them. As it had been assessed that Rethem was to be the most likely objective once the British were across the Weser, the majority of Jordan's marines were concentrated in its defence. This left the remainder of the regimental frontage very short of effective defenders, so Jordan allocated to Bataillon I./5 the only additional troops available to him as reinforcements. The first unit was a three-company Hungarian artillery training battalion, entitled Ungarisch Art.Ausb. Btl.7, which had been undergoing training at Verden and was of very dubious quality and reliability. The second was the Marine Kraftfahrzeug Abteilung at Hülsen which had been placed under Scheurlen's command; Scheurlen allocated both these units to Jordan who in turn used them to reinforce the depleted Bataillon I./5. These weak forces were later to prove to be the Achilles heel of the northern sector of the Aller Line.

On 8 April, with the sound of battle audible to the west, Ortsgruppenleiter Meineke ordered the town to be evacuated. Some civilians left Rethem and fled to the forests near Stöcken, to Hämelsee, to Rethemer Moor or to holes they had dug in the grazing land near the river; many, however, decided to stay and see things out. For those who stayed, and in particular the owners of the strongpoints, the following days were to be fraught with danger. The von der Kammer strongpoint was occupied by a very young Leutnant and a number of marines who according to Karl von der Kammer were full of optimism, believing that the bulk of the British forces were still at the Rhine and that they would be facing only light advance guards. A resident of Heinrich Wohlke's farm (Strongpoint Elfriede) was however less sanguine.

'We were christened Strongpoint Elfriede when the first defenders occupied our house. The establishment of the defences telegraphed no good. The house was 300 metres in front of the first houses near the Alpe and we were to experience everything which a strongpoint could experience in war. We were to receive no quarter.'

NOTES

1   This Abteilung was a transport unit which had been stationed in the Hülsen area since 1941. It had been responsible for moving ammunition, primarily mines and torpedo heads from magazines established in old salt mines to the naval bases in the north.

2   By the far the worst local disaster wreaked from the air occurred on 15 October 1944 at Lindwedel station to the south-east of Schwarmstedt. The Soltau-Hannover passenger train and a freight train laden with torpedos from the Hülsen munitions depot were in the station at the same time when they were attacked by fighter aircraft. The munitions train blew up with three massive detonations, killing ninety three people and seriously wounding one hundred and eighty; a further eighty-five were never found. The station was levelled, with the explosion producing a crater 25 feet deep and 55 feet wide, whilst parts of carriages and freight wagons were found 250 yards from the line.

3   In 1953, of the 2,230 inhabitants of Rethem, 450 were evacuees. Their arrival in the town is marked to this day by street names, such as Ostpreußenstrasse and Pommern Weg, in the New Town.

4   Landesschützen battalions consisted of full-time soldiers whose age or fitness had precluded them from joining front-line units. They were employed on internal security duties but were not home guard (Volkssturm).

6

BATTLES ON THE ALLER
10 APRIL

Having crossed the Bailey bridge at Hoya, 7 RWF made good progress during the night advance on the right bank. Opposition from the marines of Kompanie 2./5 and 13./5 was quickly overwhelmed and the village of Hassel was in the battalion's hands by 0300 hours on Tuesday 10 April. In clearing some woods to the north of the village, B Company had a skirmish with about 20 troopers from SS-Ausb.u.Ers.Btl.12 HJ; two of the youths were killed and one was captured, the rest fled. These troopers were probably a leaderless group from Kompanie 5./12 still withdrawing from the battle for Husum. The next battalion across the Hoya bridge, 4 Welch, then moved through 7 RWF and by 0400 hours had captured Eystrup, which had been occupied by Kompanie 3./5, and was now able to provide flank security to the south. So far the operation could not have gone smoother.

The marines from the regimental companies 13./5 and 14./5 which had deployed forward to the Weser and had survived the battle for Hoya, were now forced to carry out a daylight withdrawal using the cover of the numerous pine woods to dodge the ever-present threat from fighter aircraft. These marines were prepared to mount quick ambushes if the opportunity arose and were soon to do so with effect. Whilst this withdrawal was taking place, the small detachments in the outer layer of Jordan's defence, occupying the outlying villages and hamlets which lay on the likely British axes of advance, continued to prepare their defences as fast as possible, in the knowledge that the enemy's first attacks would soon fall on them. Marines supported by a 8.8cm Flak crewed by RAD gunners from Batterie 2./604 RAD, prepared to defend the village of Stöcken on Route 209, two miles to Rethem's south-west, and Kompanie 3./5, commanded by Oberleutnant zur See Jalke, prepared the defence of the farm buildings of the Strassengabel strongpoint which dominated the road junction half a mile to Rethem's west; here they were joined by a Pak 40 anti-tank gun and its crew.

Whilst the Germans prepared for the coming onslaught, during the afternoon of 8 April 1/5 Welch moved to an assembly area near the village of Memsen, some four miles west of the Weser, and here the battalion rested and prepared for the next phase. The companies were called forward to cross the Hoya Bailey bridge during the evening of 9 April and shortly after midnight the battalion crossed the bridge and began the 10-mile advance to Rethem. For the rest of that night the companies threaded their way along sandy tracks through the pine woods and across the moor of the Hämelheide. At 0830 hours, as they neared the end of their advance, they heard the shells of the first friendly artillery bombardment fired by the 25pdr guns of 133rd Field Regiment landing in the centre of Rethem's Old Town. This fire heavily damaged a number of houses and was returned by the railway Flak at the station which fired salvos onto the approaches likely to be used by the British. With these first shells, the battle for the town had begun.

The leading rifle company of 1/5 Welch was C Company. Accompanying the company were a detachment from the anti-tank platoon with two 6pdr guns towed by carriers and a section of assault pioneers. The leading platoon was advancing with its sections in single file on alternate sides of the road followed by company headquarters and the other two platoons similarly deployed. The commander of the assault pioneer section was Corporal Jack Mulhearn.

'As we progressed along the road I noticed on the grass verge on the right hand side what appeared to be land communication cables. I brought this to the attention of the company commander and asked his permission to cut them which he willingly gave. I cut them as per procedure, which involved removing a section of some length to prevent a speedy reconnection, and carried on, still without contact with the enemy.

'My next recollection is of approaching a bend in the road with high hedges on both sides. Just before the bend there was a level-crossing with some form of hand-operated barrier. The lead section had crossed the barrier and were just approaching the bend when we heard the sound of engines, similar to tanks, and the cry of "Tanks!" went up. We immediately sought shelter in the woods alongside the road and we turned our vehicles off the road.

'The anti-tank commander reacted very quickly to get his guns into position. You can imagine how tense the atmosphere was when around the bend came a large enemy charcoal-burning truck! The lead section commander dealt very smartly with the situation and quickly captured the vehicle and its occupants. It was a ration truck delivering food to the enemy forward troops, confirming our suspicions about having crossed into enemy-held territory.

'The situation was secure and we were ready to advance, when again we heard the sound of a machine approaching and around the bend came a German despatch rider. Again the section commander was quick to react, he fired two or three bursts from his Sten gun as the rider tried to turn and escape. As a result of the gun-fire he lost his balance and fell off, he then got up and surrendered unhurt. I have since wondered if his journey was the result of my cutting the cables.'

These minor contacts were followed at 0900 hours with more serious encounters when the leading companies, still about two miles short of the town, were engaged with small-arms fire from marines hidden in the woods. For a while the battalion was able to brush this light opposition aside, but when C Company neared the Strassengabel strongpoint, it was met by a torrent of small-arms fire and the advance stopped in its tracks. In addition to the small-arms fire, the Pak 40 at the strongpoint was fired continuously onto the advancing Welshmen and the Flak guns of batteries 2./604 RAD and 4./117 on the Aller's right bank also joined in. The battle for the strongpoint now raged for most of the rest of the day. One of the first German casualties was the

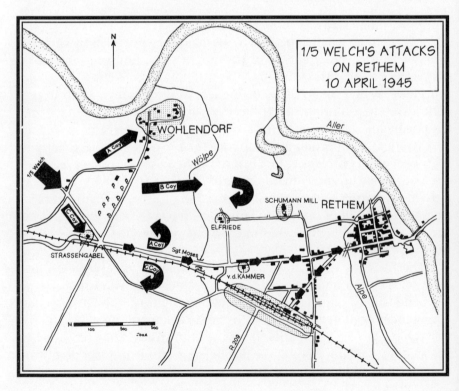

Oberleutnant who was hit in the lower jaw and had to be evacuated to Rethem.

Whilst C Company was attacking the Strassengabel strongpoint, the rest of the battalion closed up and at 1030 hours the commanding officer, Major Bowker, was in a position to order B Company to move around the left flank of C Company and then to enter Rethem from the north. Major Bowker had commanded the battalion since the former commanding officer, Lieutenant Colonel Morrison-Jones, was killed when his jeep ran over a mine near Ochtrup on 2 April. B Company's manoeuvre was made under the cover of a prevailing ground mist which it was hoped would provide a screen. Initially all went well and the company passed to the south-west of the small lake just north of the town. The ground was very flat and open and at the critical moment the mist cleared leaving the company 350 yards short of its objective, without cover and in broad daylight. The marines took full advantage of this turn of events and opened up on B Company with all available weapons, initially from Strongpoints Elfriede and Schumann Mill on Rethem's northern edge but soon with additional fire from marines in Wohlendorf. The company was subjected to a withering cross-fire which was made even more intense by artillery fire from the Flak firing from the right bank of the Aller. The attack was bogged down with the Welsh incapable of either advancing or withdrawing.

With two of his companies committed and little progress made towards his objective, the Rethem bridge, Major Bowker decided to launch a direct attack on the bridge down one of the main roads which lead into the town. At 1100 hours a section of three carriers and two Wasp flamethrowers commanded by Sergeant Moses was despatched on a coup de main attempt straight down the main road. The carriers clattered off down the cobbled, tree-lined road at full speed and reached the perimeter of the town with hardly a shot being fired in their direction. As the force passed the von der Kammer strongpoint, the marines attempted to engage it from the rear with Panzerfausts. They were so inexperienced at handling these weapons however that none hit their targets and some even exploded in the barn, identifying their position to Moses' force. In the subsequent return of fire, the youthful Leutnant commanding the strongpoint, who had been so optimistic the day before, was fatally wounded and the crews of the three Pak 40 killed or wounded.

The force pressed on deeper into the town, firing flame and machine-guns against targets on both sides of the road until they were stopped by the road-block on the Alpe, 450 yards short of their objective. Here one of the Wasps took a direct hit from a Panzerfaust, destroying the vehicle and killing the crew. The Leutnant in charge of the marines on the block had a very lucky escape as he received a direct hit of flame fuel from one of the Wasps but for some reason the fuel failed to ignite, leaving him alive but with a heavily polluted uniform! The remainder of the force managed to swing about but on the return journey two of the vehicles took a wrong turning and found themselves in a dead-end leading to the station. Again they swung about back towards the main road encountering a Pak 40 when they reached it. This they immediately flamed, turned left and headed back to the battalion under heavy fire all the way. To compound the difficulties of their withdrawal, the marines detonated Teller mines tied to trees in an attempt to block the road. Although most of Moses' force regained friendly lines, losses and casualties in this courageous attempt were three men dead, three missing and one Wasp destroyed.

With the obvious approach from the west strongly defended, Major Bowker ordered A Company to clear Wohlendorf as the village would have to be taken before further attacks from the north-west could be mounted and some of the pressure taken off the beleaguered B Company, still marooned in the fields. A Company's attack began at 1330 hours but the marines resisted fiercely here as well and fighting went on in the village until the late afternoon. Even when Wohlendorf was eventually cleared and the battalion left flank secured, the soldiers of B Company were still unable to extricate themselves from their desperate situation caught in the open meadows. Although an attempt had been made at 1330 hours to help them by firing smoke to cover a withdrawal, even with this assistance withdrawal was not possible due to the volume of fire which continued to rake the open fields and they were forced to endure this terrible predicament for many hours to come. Among those caught in the open was Captain Davies, the company second in command, who found cover from an unexpected source.

'On our approach we took a prisoner who then accompanied us during the remainder of the manoeuvre. As we neared the town, the mist suddenly lifted leaving the company in full view of the enemy, with no cover whatsoever and in brilliant sunshine. We were immediately engaged by fire and my prisoner was shot in the arm. Fortunately for me, he had provided me with a measure of protection without which I would have surely been killed.'

As dusk fell, members of the company were eventually able to work their way back to safety under the cover of darkness. When the roll call was taken, it was discovered that only 24 men had managed to return from the attack which had been mounted with such high expectations that morning.

The brigade headquarters of 158th Infantry Brigade also suffered a severe blow during the morning. The DAA and QMG[1], Major Lemon, had been delayed at divisional headquarters when the rest of the brigade headquarters moved to Hämelhausen. A despatch rider, Private Smith, was sent to the old location to meet Major Lemon and escort him to the new. Tragically, for some reason they overshot the junction which would have taken them to the right place and encountered a patrol of marines which had sallied forth from Hülsen. These marines had cut the axis used by 1/5 Welch and Lemon and his driver were ambushed and killed. A Company 1 E Lan R was immediately tasked to re-clear the axis which they accomplished by 1645 hours.

During 1/5 Welch's attacks on Rethem during the morning, other units of 53rd Welsh Division were pushing eastwards from the Weser. 1 E Lan R, from 158th Infantry Brigade, moved by truck via Hoya and Hassel and cleared Hämelhausen to be close behind 1/5 Welch. The battalion spent the rest of 10 April in a concentration area waiting to hear whether they would take part in the battle for Rethem. 7 RWF had spent the day clearing the woods to the north of the brigade axis. During the afternoon the commanding officer, Lieutenant Colonel Tyler, attended orders at brigade headquarters at which he was tasked to advance and capture the village of Hülsen, situated on the Aller downstream from Rethem. The companies subsequently spent the afternoon alternately advancing and establishing firm bases as the battalion moved cautiously toward their objective.

2 Mons meanwhile, from 160th Infantry Brigade, was ordered to capture Nienburg. As resistance on the Weser's right bank seemed weak at best, it was decided to risk a rush down the most direct route, the main road. Every vehicle in the battalion was accordingly filled with troops and the battalion then made a 40mph dash down the road concluding in the town's capture without a shot being fired. This was not surprising as not only had Bataillon I./6 withdrawn from the town, but the town had in fact already been captured by C Squadron 3 RTR, from 11th Armoured Division, the day before. The Bürgermeister had sensibly met the leading tanks and had handed over his town as quickly as he could to avoid any destruction. The soldiers of 2 Mons were however perfectly justified in thinking that they had captured the town as

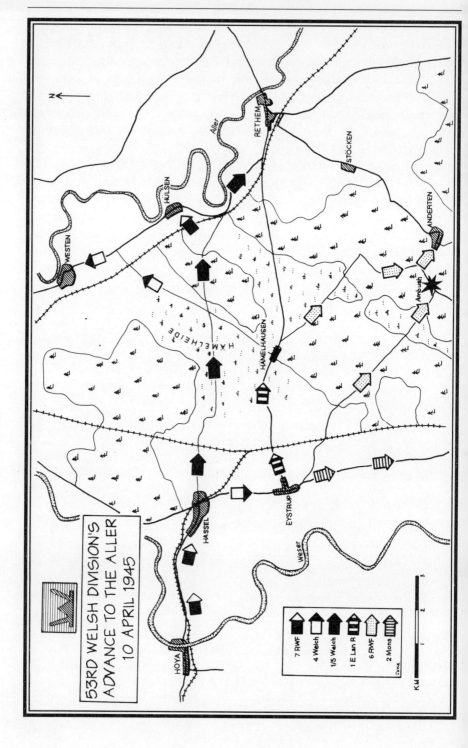

53RD WELSH DIVISION'S
ADVANCE TO THE ALLER
10 APRIL 1945

WESTEN

HÜLSEN

Aller

RETHEM

STÖCKEN

ANDERTEN

Ambush

HAMELHEIDE

HAMELHAUSEN

HASSEL

EYSTRUP

Weser

HOYA

7 RWF
4 Welch
1/5 Welch
1 E Lan R
6 RWF
2 Mons

KM

the squadron had pushed on to the east having accepted the surrender. Once the town was secured, 2 Mons established defensive positions to protect sappers from 7th Armoured Division who began building a Bailey bridge across the Weser.

4 Welch meanwhile, who had reverted to come under command of their own brigade, the 160th, when 1/5 Welch advanced to Rethem, was ordered to advance north and clear the ground between the Weser and the Aller as far as the confluence of the two rivers just north of Verden, about nine miles away. The battalion had been in a concentration area in the woods near Hassel since mid-afternoon and its first task was to clear and occupy the villages of Stedorf and Westen; this would be done with the help of the tanks of A Squadron 5 RTR. B and D Companies were ordered to advance north and capture Stedorf, clearing Dörverden on the way. By 1900 hours they had accomplished both tasks, meeting only minor opposition in the northern part of Stedorf. A and C Companies meanwhile struck off to the north-east as they had been directed on Westen, which it will be recalled was held by Hungarian soldiers reinforced with a platoon of marines from Bataillon I./5. The village was reached without incident and as the companies started to attack the village the Hungarians either immediately surrendered or pulled back across the Aller. The marines, however, resolved to fight it out and in their last ditch stand seven were killed with a further four dying of their wounds in captivity the next day; the remainder were taken prisoner. The capture of Westen now not only drove a wedge between the German troops remaining on the left bank of the Aller but also provided 53rd Welsh Division with a crossing site which could be developed if required.

Meanwhile further south in the Rethem area, an air OP was tasked to check whether the Rethem bridge had been blown. The pilot of the Auster from A Flight No 653 Squadron reported back at 1325 hours that it was still intact. Accordingly planning began for yet another attempt by 1/5 Welch to break into Rethem and seize the bridge. Brigadier Wilsey contacted Major Bowker by radio at 1545 hours and ordered him to launch a maximum effort, direct attack on Rethem, and allocated to him one medium and two field regiments of artillery to support the battalion's attack. Major Bowker planned for the attack to begin in the late afternoon. A and C Companies would assault from the west astride the Eystruper Road under the cover of the artillery barrage, which was expected to neutralise the German defence whilst the attacking infantry crossed the open ground.

However, before any further attack could be mounted against Rethem, the Strassengabel strongpoint, which was still holding out, had to be captured as the Germans holding the farm were able to prevent movement from the west. Whilst the detailed planning for the attack on Rethem was underway, C Company continued during the afternoon to attempt to capture the strongpoint. The company eventually managed to overwhelm the dwindling defenders and capture the position. But its success was to be short-lived, for almost immediately a platoon of marines commanded by Leutnant zur See Wittman counter-attacked in a most determined manner and succeeded in recapturing the farmhouse, the strongpoint's keep, forcing the Welsh to withdraw. Both sides had taken heavy casualties; Leutnant Wittman was hit in the stomach by a bullet and lay where he fell pleading with his men to put him out of his agony, but none were prepared to do this and they were relieved when the poor man eventually died. Despite their success, only 10 men now remained to defend the strongpoint against the next British attack. This was mounted at 1505 hours and the Germans were finally evicted from this position.

With the Strassengabel position finally in friendly hands, A and C Companies' attack could go ahead and H-Hour was set for 1735 hours. The two companies formed up for the attack and made final preparations as they lay waiting for H-Hour and the start of the artillery bombardment. The thunder of the guns signalled the assault to begin and the assaulting platoons got up from their positions where they had lain waiting. But as soon as they revealed themselves they were met with a torrent of small-arms fire, principally from machine-guns, which stopped the attack dead in its tracks before it could even cross the start line. By 1800 hours the commanding officer realised that the attack was doomed and he ordered the battalion to withdraw under cover of the artillery and take up defensive positions for the remainder of the night. 1/5 Welch's war diary recorded that one officer and 47 other ranks were killed or wounded during these actions. The battalion's day however had not ended as shall be seen.

1/5 Welch was not the only battalion to have received an unpleasant surprise at the new-found German aggressiveness. Following the successful assault crossing of the Weser on 9 April, 6 RWF had remained in the bridgehead waiting to hear what the next task for the battalion would be. Although the battalion had been ordered to take part in the capture of Nienburg, the seizure of the town by 2 Mons rendered this unnecessary and the battalion enjoyed a night's sleep. On the morning of 10 April the battalion was ordered to clear the area between the Weser and the Aller south of the line Eystrup-Rethem and the companies were ordered to push on quickly, accepting risks, to prevent the Germans reorganising. As little or no opposition had been encountered between the rivers, reconnaissance was not considered to be necessary. For this operation the battalion had attached to it two tank troops, each comprising three Cromwells and a Sherman Firefly, from C Squadron 5 RTR; this regiment having been detached from 7th Armoured Division to 53rd Welsh Division that morning. No 10 Troop was attached to A Company 6 RWF and 11 Troop to B Company. The task of the two companies was to advance south-east from Eystrup in two columns on parallel routes and capture the village of Anderten. The troop sergeant of 11 Troop was Sergeant Jake Wardrop. This brave and resourceful soldier had joined 5 RTR in 1937 and had fought with the regiment in France in 1940, the Western Desert, Tripolitania, Tunisia, Italy and in Europe from D-Day onwards. Throughout his service he kept a graphic record of his experiences and this diary was later to be edited by Lieutenant Colonel George Forty and published as *Tanks Across the Desert*. The diary not only gives an insight into Wardrop's many adventures with 5 RTR but also serves as a vivid battlefield record of the regiment to which he was so proud to belong.

At 1815 hours the tanks and infantry companies married up and they set off shortly afterwards. The tanks led the advancing columns through the thick pine forests, each tank carrying a section of infantry on its deck. The troop sergeant of 10 Troop was Sergeant George Stimpson, a long-standing friend of Wardrop. In *Tanks Across the Desert* he describes what befell the lead platoon of B Company and 11 Troop.

'At the briefing we were told that the infantry had already patrolled into the wood that morning and that it could therefore be considered as being clear of enemy. With this in mind, the first few miles through the wooded area would be carried out at the double, with the infantry riding on the backs of the tanks... At zero hour, both troops advanced along their allotted centre lines and 11 Troop was soon well inside the wood, while 10 Troop, which had more open ground to cross was still clear of the trees. We suddenly saw a number of friendly fighter aircraft clearly shaping up for an attack with us as their targets, so we took the prudent course of stopping and displaying our recognition panels. 11 Troop, unaware of this delay, continued on into the wood. There was really no reason why they should not have done so, after all, it had already been reported as clear. Eventually they came to a track junction, and slowed down to check the map, when all hell broke loose!

They were right in the middle of an ambush with enemy dug-in all around the crossing. It was later discovered that the enemy were marines.

'The last two tanks in the troop managed to pull back and from their reports it soon became clear that a terrific and bloody battle had been fought at the cross-roads, with considerable losses to our side, including Jake's Firefly... As soon as I was able I went to the squadron commander and asked for permission to go back into the wood to look for the two missing tanks from 11 Troop. This was granted on condition that I took only those members of my own crew who volunteered to come with me. There were no second thoughts given to this and we set off down the road back into the wood. It was rather quiet and frightening, but there were no signs of the enemy and we eventually came to the place where the battle had taken place. The two tanks were still and quiet and there were bodies of British soldiers everywhere. I found Jake's body at the side of his tank which was in the middle of the cross tracks. He had been killed by machine-gun fire. I then inspected the tank and found that it had been hit by a bazooka which had struck the armoured cover over the forward extractor fan, just at the side of the driver's head, but had done very little permanent damage to the vehicle. It was obvious, however, that enough chaos and confusion had been created to make the crew think they had been hit badly and that they must bale out. They were gunned down as they tried to escape.

'It was at this time that I took Jake's diary into safe-keeping. I was well aware where he had kept it. Later I was able to start the tank and we drove it back to the squadron, where a new crew took it over.'[2]

The infantry had a somewhat different perspective of the ambush, particularly the part played by the armour. This graphic account of the ambush from the RWF's regimental history was written by an unnamed fusilier from B Company 6 RWF.

'We set out travelling at high speed, all tanks in sight of each other. The first house was situated at a T junction and as we turned a corner into the village one of the section spotted two of the enemy. He jumped off the tank which pulled round a corner 100 yards away. The tank commander looking through his glasses spotted a road block, and, pulling in to the side of the road, told the rest of the section to dismount. The second tank came along and was knocked out by the enemy. We did not see the third and fourth, but from the noise and explosions in their area it seemed hardly possible that they could have escaped. The enemy fired all he had at us, and we did the same keeping their heads down while we obtained good fire positions. The only support we received was from our tank, which fired one burst as it turned round and retired the way we had come, instead of putting up a fight with us as we had hoped. We were left by ourselves. Underneath the knocked-out tank, was one of the dead crew and another badly wounded.

'We thought at first we might be able to hold Jerry off until support came. No support did come, however, and more of our boys were killed and our platoon commander, Lieutenant Castles, was wounded in the face, shot through the shoulder and again through the wrist. He was bleeding badly as was the fellow by the tank, but we could do nothing for them. Anyway they held on, the platoon commander telling me to take charge if anything else happened. Luckily nothing did and he kept us under control. The enemy crept around us on all sides. Knowing we did not stand a chance, we decided to surrender, which I think was the best thing for otherwise we would all have been shot up.

'The Jerries took us into a wood, stripped us of all equipment, turned out our pockets and all the while we still thought we would be liberated by the other two platoons in the company. If only they had come then. We were marched on through the wood, being joined by another company of Jerries who were pulling out in some sort of order. As we came out into the open some more Typhoons came overhead, so we were made to go back into the wood until they had passed over. When we pulled out again we ran into one of our artillery barrages and it was anything but pleasant to be on the receiving end this time.'

Another fusilier present during the ambush was Fusilier William Haley, aged 19, who was a Number 2 on one of the sections' Bren guns.

'My main memory is of travelling very fast and grimly hanging on on top of the light, fast tanks through the forest road. We stopped briefly to question a civilian walking towards us. Everything appeared to be OK so we travelled on. When approaching a T junction I observed movement on the right-hand side of the junction but it was not possible to communicate to the tank commander due to all the noise.

'We turned left at the junction and up ahead we could see a tree blocking the road about 100 yards away, maybe less. We approached slowly, still aboard the tanks. We dismounted – I was on the right-hand side of the tank – and moved up to the obstruction following in line.

Suddenly a lance corporal doubled back towards me saying, "There are Jerries up there," and kept going. Then the action started. Panzerfausts knocked out the second tank, blocking the first against the obstruction; this tank must also have been hit, as I immediately dropped flat in the shallow, roadside gulley and was joined by the first tank's crew. My first reaction was alarm that I appeared to be the only one armed in this little group. I took up a firing position and the face of a young German popped up just a couple of yards in front of me. I fired and didn't see him again – if I had had a grenade I would have made sure.

'My position in the shallow gulley was not conducive to observe and fire without showing my position. I cleared the empty round and bolted another, ready to fire, but then my rifle jammed and I was unable to clear this without exposure. In the meantime, the noise of action was all around, sniper fire from the tree tops was "pinging" about while I'm worrying about being separated from the rest of the platoon and having the spare barrel and ammo for the Bren gun, which was somewhere with my mate Norman Kent, the Number 1, on the other side of the road.

'After a while – it seemed an eternity – I heard our officer shouting, "Kamerad, Kamerad." I shouted to the tank crew in the ditch, "Get up, it's all over," then walked down the road where the remainder of the platoon and our wounded officer were gathered. The Germans took over. They seemed a mix bag; young and old; some sailor types, possibly marines. We were taken through the forests and one wounded tank crew member was left in a forest cottage to be looked after by civilians. After a few rests we eventually came into a small town (Rethem) where we received the usual hostile welcome for POWs. After a few kicks etc we were told to empty our pockets into our helmets and wait for interrogation.

'I went in before two officers, one of whom spoke good English. Having taken some of my personal bits and pieces he told me my division's number and said, "Why are you fighting?" and I replied, "For freedom," but I must admit I felt a little foolish. He got angry and said, "Bloody Englishman, get out!" We were then marched to Stalag XIB.'

The other two platoons and the surviving Cromwell did in fact re-attack the ambush site forcing the marines to withdraw, but the riposte was not mounted sufficiently quickly to recapture the prisoners. This ambush was probably laid and commanded by Oberleutnant zur See Helmut Vollmers. It would seem likely that he and his marines had been making maximum use of the woods during their withdrawal to

Rethem to provide cover from the ever-present threat of Allied fighters, and that Vollmers laid an immediate ambush when he heard the noise of 11 Troop's tanks. German accounts state that he personally knocked out a tank. The 6 RWF reported five killed, three wounded and 15 missing as a result of this short but bloody incident. The two tanks which were abandoned in the ambush, Sergeant Jake's and the Cromwell, were included in a survey of casualties among armoured units in North West Europe compiled by two captains from the Royal Army Medical Corps[3]. In their survey they examined not only the fate of the crews but also the mechanical and structural damage done to the tanks. They duly recorded that Sherman Vc WD Number 212700 was struck at a range of 30 yards by a hollow-charge warhead, which damaged the fan cowl on the hull top just behind the co-driver's hatch. The explosion caused no internal damage, although the driver, who had his head out, was wounded by fragments. The driver moved the tank out of the action but the turret crew, comprising the commander, gunner and operator, were all killed by small-arms fire once they had dismounted. The survey recorded that a small fire had started in the Cromwell V WD Number 121768 as a result of a hollow-charge explosion on the road wheels. The smoke caused the crew to abandon the tank except for the gunner who stayed firing the machine-gun until all ammunition was expended; sadly the identity of this brave crew member is not known. Trooper Hennessey was shot in the head after escaping from the tank.

The death of Jake Wardrop was keenly felt throughout his regiment and the formal recording of the fate of Jake's troop in 5 RTR's tank casualty log, an excerpt of which is reproduced overleaf, conceals the sadness that existed

By the time the ambush was over it was almost dark and 6 RWF was in a dangerous situation in thick woods containing many Germans. Lieutenant Colonel Hutchinson therefore ordered A Company to close on B Company and to push briskly on into Anderten. The village was captured by 2215 hours, but as the battalion with its squadron of tanks was now out of physical contact with any other British troops, all-round defence was taken up and vigorous patrolling continued throughout the night. A patrol from C Company went as far as the village of Stöcken, some two miles to the north-east, and reported it to be held and that an 8.8cm gun was covering the likely axis of advance from Anderten.

Whilst 6 RWF was involved in the south, its sister battalion 7 RWF had made good progress in its advance towards the Aller and by about

Excerpt from 5 RTR Tank Casualty Log, 10 April 1945

Date	Location	Tank Type/No	How Lost	Crew	Cas	Remarks
10 Apr 45	Stöcken	Sherman 212700	Hit by bazooka but did not brew and is a runner	Sjt Wardrop	KIA	By MG fire on evac
				Tpr Wood	Missing	Believed PW
				Tpr Forrest	KIA	By MG fire on evac
				Tpr Colton	OK	
10 Apr 45	Stöcken	Cromwell 75 188494	Undamaged	Lt Crocker	OK	
				Tpr Skidmore	KIA	Hit in head by sniper
				Tpr Smart	OK	
				Tpr Orpwood	OK	
				Tpr Rands	OK	
10 Apr 45	Stöcken	Cromwell 75 121768	Hit by bazooka in road wheels and explosion in turret. Did not brew and is a runner	Cpl Richardson	Missing[1]	Believed PW
				Tpr Wilson H	Missing	Believed PW
				Tpr Butler	Missing	Believed PW
				Tpr Kinvig	Missing	Believed PW
				Tpr Hennessey	Severe head wounds: evac to RAP RWF. Since DOW.	

1 Corporal Richardson and his crew were the ones who joined William Haley in the gulley; all four were captured. It is assumed that it was Trooper Hennessey who was the wounded tank crew member left with the civilians. Richardson's crew spent only six days in captivity as they were released from Stalag X1B at Fallingbostel by 8th Hussars on 16 April. They reported bad treatment, assumingly at the camp, and that Trooper Wood from Sergeant Wardop's tank was in hospital. The relief of this camp and Stalag 357, also at Fallingbostel, is described in Chapter 16. Tragically, Corporal Richardson was to survive only a few days beyond the war's end. He was in a party disposing of arms and ammunition from a ship, when an anti-tank mine hit the deck and exploded; on 14 May he died of the wounds he received.

2200 hours was ready to attack Hülsen, with B Company tasked to mount the initial assault. The attack was allocated substantial artillery support and 81st and 83rd Field Regiments and 72nd Medium Regiment fired 50 rounds per gun in pre H-Hour bombardments. Despite this fire, German reports mention that it caused relatively little damage as it was concentrated away from the built-up area and fell instead onto the area of the railway station to the south-west of the village. The rain of shells was added to by the railway Flak at Rethem station which fired harassing missions in an unsuccessful attempt to break up the assault. As B Company began to enter Hülsen the platoons were met with staunch opposition from the marines, who had deployed many snipers. Fighting from house-to-house, the momentum of the attack began to flag and A Company had to be ordered forward to assist. The village was finally cleared by 0300 hours on 11 April and 28 prisoners were taken. Many Germans attempted to flee by swimming the Aller and there were losses among these men not only from shell and small-arms fire but also due to drowning and exposure. The graves of 40 soldiers who now lie buried in the cemetery in nearby Westen bear testimony to the difficulties of this withdrawal.

Meanwhile in Rethem, Jordan took advantage in the lull in the fighting to visit his marines in their forward positions. He did this riding on the back of a motorbike which belonged to a marine named Hermann Pieper. Pieper had been a member of the Marine Kraftfahrzeug Abteilung holding Hülsen but had managed to escape on his bike to Rethem when the village was attacked by 7 RWF. When he arrived in Rethem he was immediately placed at the personal disposal of the regimental commander. That night he drove Jordan around the positions, weaving through the debris that was now strewn across the town's streets. He had particular difficulty negotiating the many severed cables hanging from the telephone poles, not made any easier by Jordan shouting at him to go faster. Pieper completed his mission with his commander but his bike was to be written off by shell splinters the next day. Pieper himself was later captured by the British but managed to escape and make his way to his home town of Papenburg near the Dutch border.

Battle had also been joined on 10 April on 2.Marine Infanterie Division's left flank, which was held by Mar.Füs.Btl.2. Whilst Korvettenkapitän Gördes had deployed with his own headquarters and two marine companies forward to the Leine in the Bothmer/Schwarmstedt area, his remaining marine company, Kompanie 1./2, and the other forces under his command remained on the right bank of the Aller to prepare positions there. The two 8.8cm Pak guns were in Eickeloh, Leutnant zur See Kohlmorgen's Kompanie 1./2 was in the village of Hademstorf and Festungs Pak Kompanie 11 in the woods between the rail and road bridges. However, since his battalion's arrival on 8 April, Gördes had received some important reinforcements. Three companies from SS-Ausb.u.Ers.Btl.12 HJ had managed to reach the safety of the Aller's right bank, following their confused and bloody withdrawal from Stolzenau, and had moved to the woods in the area of the villages of Eickeloh and Hademstorf to recuperate and gather in stragglers. RAD Batterie 1./521 had also managed to reach the Aller's right bank with its two 10.5cm Flak guns. The guns were sited in direct fire positions to cover the meadows and the approach to the road bridge on the left

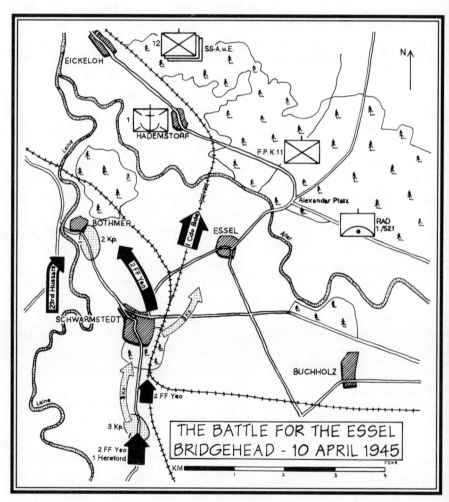

bank, whilst the RAD gunners who no longer had guns to serve dug a linear position covering the river.

During the course of 9 April 159th Infantry Brigade Group, consisting of 15th/19th Hussars, 2 FF Yeo, 1 Cheshire and 1 Hereford had crossed the Leine using bridges built by 6th Airborne's engineers at Bordenau and Neustadt and had advanced north up the right bank of the Leine. On the morning of 10 April, 2 FF Yeo and the Herefords began the final advance to the confluence of the Aller and the Leine with their objectives the capture of the villages of Schwarmstedt and Essel and the clearance of the enemy from the area. The 2 FF Yeo led the advance but as it neared Schwarmstedt the leading tank was knocked out by a Panzerfaust, indicating that a stiff fight was to be expected. Kompanie 3./2, commanded by Leutnant zur See Schröder, established in positions in the village and the wood to the east, put down heavy fire whilst the British attack was organised. One of the tank squadron leaders and an infantry company commander of the Herefords were wounded in this exchange and the leading troop of tanks was forced to withdraw. Progress then stopped for a while until the armour discovered a route alongside the railway that ran parallel to the eastern flank of the village. With the tanks able to dominate the village with covering fire, the infantry were able to sweep in and clear the enemy from their positions. The marines of Kompanie 3./2, who had managed to delay the advance until early evening, pulled back and withdrew via Essel to the road bridge and thence to the right bank. The company then took up defensive positions in depth of the bridge in the woods around the area of the road junction known locally as the Alexander Platz.

Leutnant zur See Pampel's Kompanie 2./2 fared less well however. The company's battle from its position south of Bothmer had started promisingly enough and the marines had put down a heavy weight of fire at any targets that presented themselves on the left bank of the Leine. This won time for the two nearby bridges to be demolished and successfully prevented 23rd Hussars from seizing a crossing or even closing up to the river. The 7.5cm Pak in the company position managed to knock out a tank belonging to B Squadron 23rd Hussars before it too was knocked out. However, the advance by 2 FF Yeo and the Herefords up the right bank clearly threatened to cut off the company's withdrawal route and trap the marines against the Leine so the company was ordered to withdraw. Although the order was issued, it never got through in time and the marines were caught in the flank by the tanks of 2 FF Yeo emerging from the northern edge of Schwarmstedt.

The tanks did not close with the position, but launched instead a withering enfilade fire supplemented by artillery, killing or wounding many marines whilst they tried to escape. Using the cover of the wood to the north of Bothmer, some did make it back to the right bank of the Aller and these marines joined Kompanie 1./2 in Hademstorf; the majority of Pampel's company was however either killed or captured.

Although 159th Brigade Group had cleared the main German positions from the ground between the Leine and the Aller, it was decided not to move up and clear them from their final positions in the village of Essel as this would inevitably lead to the demolition of the road bridge over the Aller, which it was hoped might be captured intact. It was the existence of this bridge which had tempted Major General Pip Roberts, Commander 11th Armoured Division, away from his allocated axis which should have taken the division towards Winsen some 10 miles to the east. Although the German defence of the Leine had been overcome quite easily as 159th Brigade Group had been able to roll up the defence from a flank, this tactic would not be possible for the defences on the Aller which would require a direct assault. Even when the Aller had been crossed, the heavily wooded country beyond the river was ill-suited to armour and it was clear that the next phase would be primarily an infantry battle. General Roberts, recognising that there was insufficient infantry for this task in 159th Brigade, asked the Corps commander for more and was immediately allocated 1st Commando Brigade for the forthcoming action; the commandos had been resting in a concentration area near Aremsen following the tough battle for Leese and were trucked forward to the Aller. Whilst his commandos were moving up, Brigadier Mills-Roberts went forward to the Aller to recce the ground and assess how he would tackle the river crossing. His recce convinced him that a direct assault by the commandos on the road bridge was most unlikely to succeed as it was the only crossing for some miles and would be prepared for demolition and closely watched. The brigade plan focused instead on a night infiltration across the railway bridges which lay about a mile to the north. As the divisional commander was keen to capture the road bridge if at all possible, Brigadier Mills-Roberts agreed to cut round behind it once he was across and attempt to seize it from the rear. His top priority however was to secure a bridgehead.

At 2300 hours 3 Commando led off, silently following the line of the railway track toward the bridge. When still short of the objective there was a massive explosion as the Germans detonated demolition charges on the first span. Despite the blast, the second span remained intact and a party of commandos rushed across in stockinged feet and destroyed two machine-gun positions at the far end. A patrol was then immediately despatched to report on the Germans' defence of the road bridge, later reporting back to say that it was very strongly held. Because it looked as if the brigade would have to fight for its bridge-head, Brigadier Mills-Roberts spent the rest of the night pushing forward the remainder of his brigade so that they would be ready for the inevitable counter-attacks the next morning. Although at the time the commandos were not to know it, the battle for the Essel crossing was to be the most bitter and bloody in the whole of their fighting experience.

Tuesday 10 April thus came to a close. For the British it had been a mixed day. Although in XII Corps' sector, the Weser bridgehead had been established with ease, Nienburg captured with no loss and the Aller reached in places, all attempts to capture the bridge at Rethem had been soundly repulsed. In VIII Corps' sector the Germans' defence of the Leine had been defeated, the Aller had been crossed and a bridgehead formed, but there were indications that the next day would be tough. The 2.Marine Infanterie Division had shown that it was going to offer staunch resistance wherever it was confronted and the Germans' defiance did not bode well for the morrow.

On 10 April the Germans yet again changed the command of their forces facing the British 2nd Army. On Hitler's orders, Student and Blumentritt now swapped commands with Student taking over 1.Fallschirm Armee, still hotly contesting XXX Corps' advance on Bremen, and Blumentritt taking over Student's Armeegruppe, which was then retitled with Blumentritt's name. The reason for this swap is not known but perhaps Hitler felt that Student[4] was better suited to the fighting withdrawal being conducted on the German right flank. Blumentritt had enjoyed a distinguished war record and he had built a reputation as a thorough planner. From 1941-42 he served as Chief of Staff of 4.Armee during the early years on the Eastern Front, and this had been followed by a two-year tour as Chief of Staff of Heeresgruppe D where he served von Rundstedt, and then von Kluge and Model during the Normandy battles and the retreat from France. Appointments then followed fast and furious with him commanding XII.SS Armeekorps in the Aachen area during the winter of 1944, 25.Armee in Holland during February and March 1945, and then 1.Fallschirm Armee for barely two weeks before taking over Student's new Armeegruppe. Despite his skills, this command was to be Blumentritt's last.

The situation facing him could not have inspired much optimism. In the Bremen area on his right flank was Korps Ems, a numerically relatively strong and as yet uncommitted formation, but made up of low-grade troops of very suspect effectiveness. His centre was held by 2.Marine Infanterie Division, thinly spread over a wide frontage; whilst his left flank was virtually undefended between Celle and the Harz mountains. As it was obvious to Blumentritt and his superior Busch that the British VIII Corps and the Americans to their south would have a virtually unopposed advance to Magdeburg and thence Berlin, Busch ordered him to redeploy forces southwards to seal this gap thus releasing Wenck's 12.Armee to move to defend Berlin. Blumentritt ordered Panzer Division 'Clausewitz' to move from its concentration area near Soltau to effect this, and the division consisting of two to three battalions of infantry, eight guns and 20 tanks duly set off. As the infantry in this woefully small force had to move on foot with horse-drawn transport, it is hardly surprising that this counter-move was totally non-effective with it taking some five to six days to cover the distance. Blumentritt was further hamstrung by his inability to find out where the enemy was as air reconnaissance was no longer available and ground recce units and their vehicles non-existent. He was reduced to the humbling tactic of 'Fernsprech-Aufklärung' or recce by telephone call, which involved him telephoning village postmistresses or officials and asking them whether the enemy had arrived with them! Furthermore his command and control system was in tatters with only one signal site between Bremen and the Harz and his headquarters supported by one weak signals company. He was forced to find his commanders by touring in his staff car, in itself not a healthy act in 1945, and giving them orders when and if he found them! Despite his abilities as a commander, Blumentritt was in a quite hopeless position as the battle for the Aller got underway.

NOTES

1   'DAA and QMG' stands for Deputy Assistant Adjutant and Quartermaster General. This officer was responsible for personnel matters within the brigade and for the provision of combat supplies. In today's NATO staff nomenclature the appointment is called Deputy Chief of Staff (DCOS).

2   G Forty, *Tanks Across The Desert*, William Kimber.

3   'A Survey of Casualties Amongst Armoured Units in North-west Europe' by Captain H. B. Wright and Captain R. D. Harkness. These two officers belonged to a Medical Research Council Team attached to No 2 Operational Research (OR) Section and their report analysed the data obtained on three hundred and thirty three armoured fighting vehicle casualties and seven hundred and sixty nine personnel casualties sustained by nineteen armoured regiments between 24 March and 5 May 1945.

4   Student was to experience one further change of command before the war ended. On 28 April he was ordered by Hitler to take over Heinrici's Heeresgruppe Weichsel, falling back in disorder from the Oder, and organise the defence of Mecklenburg; he was never to reach this last command. Captured by the British in Schleswig-Holstein he was later charged and tried at Nürem-

burg for condoning atrocities in Crete; he received a 5-year sentence which he never served. Student died in 1978 having been preceded by his wife and his only son, who was killed in 1944 whilst serving in the Luftwaffe. How ironic it must have been for Student, who had played such a key pioneering role in the use of airborne forces, to have to combat the Allied airborne forces in 1944 and 1945 with his grounded 1.Fallschirm Armee.

THE ATTACKS CONTINUE
11 APRIL

Having failed to crack Rethem's defences in daylight, Brigadier Wilsey planned that 1/5 Welch should attack during the night of 10-11 April. At 2300 hours he called Major Bowker to brigade headquarters and ordered that the battalion should mount a further attack at 0445 hours on Wednesday 11 April. The attack would be supported by the divisional artillery regiments reinforced with two platoons of 4.2in mortars from D Company 1 Manchesters. The plan, if successful, would then involve 7 RWF and 1 E Lan R making an assault crossing of the Aller and securing a bridgehead opposite Rethem for the division.

In the early hours of Wednesday morning Major Bowker gave his orders for a two-phase night attack with the first phase silent, which meant that the fire support would not be automatically used but rather left 'on call' until the enemy, hopefully caught by surprise, became aware of the attack. Major Bowker's plan was based on A and C Companies attacking the town from the north-west. The companies would break-in, overcome the perimeter defences allowing D Company to pass through them to mop up the opposition in the remainder of the town. Although it was an identical plan to the one that had so signally failed the previous afternoon, it was assumed that the cover of darkness would give the attacking companies the advantage. But by now the men of 1/5 Welch were far from fresh and were feeling the strain of battle acutely having been in constant action and without sleep for 48 hours. The casualties and the lack of success had done little to bolster their resolve.

At 0345 hours the companies moved to their forming up point for the attack which was in the area of the Strassengabel strongpoint. Both companies then infiltrated forward under cover of the darkness to the Wölpe, the stream on the western edge of the town, which was to be the start line. All initially went well, the stream was crossed on H-Hour at 0445 hours and the attack achieved surprise with both companies reaching the town's outskirts without the Germans realising that yet another attack was being mounted. Their success in reaching the outskirts was however short-lived for the marines in the two strongpoints -

Elfriede and the von der Kammer farm - suddenly becoming aware of the attack opened up on the Welsh with every weapon which could be brought to bear. In addition to the fire from the marines occupying the strongpoints, withering fire was poured onto the Welsh from other marines in buildings on the town's fringe. The strongpoints now became rocks around which the battle ebbed and flowed with both sides well aware that their positions were keys to the perimeter's defence. Whilst the marines fought above ground, civilians were sheltering in the cellar of the von der Kammer farm. One of the civilians later described the frightening ordeal through which they went.

'Over twenty civilians were huddled together in the cellar which was only 3 metres by 3 metres. Our labourer - a French POW - and a comrade from another farm arrived in the cellar and said, "We have come to stay with you - we'll help when the Tommies come". This they later did. On Wednesday 11 April firing commenced onto our property and at 0500 hours the English (sic) attacked again. It came to hand-to-hand fighting - we could tell by the noise. Ownership of the house changed on several occasions. The house had been hit many times. Dust and dirt had made us unrecognizable and we could hardly identify each other. During a quiet period I crawled out and saw a mountain of bodies. The pig sty was being held by about fifteen Englishmen and near the barn were several German soldiers. I heard the German sergeant say, "Get the Panzerfaust here". The English must have understood since they found a white flag and surrendered. We were subjected to German and English artillery fire. Only by some miracle was it that only property was damaged. Later, when a cellar window barricaded with sand bags was ripped open by a shell burst we could see that the house was burning ... we wanted to leave for Stöcken to my brother-in-law so the English, who had re-taken the ground floor, let us go. At the next strongpoint (Elfriede) the German soldiers prevented us from going further and told us we had to turn back as they were concerned we would betray their position. We had to return and hid under a dung-heap near the house. Here we were subjected to heavy small-arms fire from Germans in the Schumann Mill even though our house had been retaken by other German soldiers. One of our Frenchmen had been wounded in the meantime as he brought back some wounded.

'Heavy fire forced us to leave our hide in the dung-heap and we crawled through the plough furrows to the Wölpe. The children gave us the most trouble. Even though we must have been recognised as civilians we were fired on by German soldiers. One of the women had a pram with her which was pierced by a bullet but luckily the baby was not hit. I dragged a child on top of a pillow behind me. At the Wölpe the women were so terrified that they stood in the cold water as they believed that they were safer there.

'On the Friday we were able to move back to our house, bury the animals and tidy up. A little bit of joy was however left - a pig had given birth to fifteen piglets.'

The bitterest hand-to-hand fighting took place around the von der Kammer farm leaving seven soldiers from C Company dead and many more wounded and captured. During a lull in the fighting, the marines moved the captured wounded to a neighbouring house for their protection, and it was here that one of the soldiers who died was found to have on him 400,000 Reichsmarks from the Bocholter Sparkasse. The fortunate finder soon ran out of luck as the cupboard in which he hid the money went up in flames when the strongpoint was later consumed by fire.

Whilst C Company was fighting to capture the von der Kammer farm, the men of A Company managed to gain a foothold in the area of Elfriede. Their success was however only temporary and they were unable to eject the marines who fought tooth and nail for this key point on Rethem's perimeter and the strongpoint remained in German hands.

As both companies had failed to break the town's outer defences due to the marines' ferocious defence, at 0545 hours with dawn breaking, Major Bowker ordered the reserve company, D Company, to be committed in the hope that it would push the scales in the attacker's favour. However, this company fared no better than the others and so he ordered all companies to withdraw. Unfortunately the onset of daylight made withdrawal far from easy and the men had a difficult time crossing back over the Wölpe whilst under heavy small-arms fire. Smoke and HE barrages had to be laid by 83rd Field Regiment RA at 0630 hours to try to assist the forward elements to break clean, which they eventually managed to accomplish by 0740 hours. The withdrawing companies concentrated back in the area of the crossroads and the decision was taken to reorganise as the companies had become so depleted. The survivors of A Company were distributed among the other three rifle companies and the battalion took up defensive positions.

The soldiers of 1/5 Welch were totally taken by surprise by the strength of the resistance. Leslie George, who was a corporal in the anti-tank platoon, recalls the soldiers' reaction.

'I remember it was a total shock, especially for the younger intake who had not until then encountered heavy action. As can no doubt be appreciated, some of the lads were used to bloodshed and various set-backs and took things as they came. I myself was known as a "bad bas-tard" as I was the first man in the battalion to gain an award (DCM in Normandy). I was looked upon as mad and, thinking back, I did do some bloody stupid things but they had the desired effect of keeping the lads from panicking at times.'

The casualties reported at the time from the two companies were 20 wounded and 60 missing believed killed. The fate of 15 of the missing became the subject of an unfortunate affair. Private Parry, the only sol-dier from those who had fought to capture Elfriede who had returned, made a statement alleging that a massacre of prisoners had occurred at the hands of the SS. The Times newspaper reported the incident in its issue of 17 April 1945.

BRITISH PRISONERS SHOT BY GERMANS

EYE-WITNESS ACCOUNT
From Our Special Correspondent
OUTSIDE RETHEM,APRIL 11

The shooting of a number of British prisoners of war, probably about 15, after they had surrendered outside a house on the edge of this town this morning, was described to-day in a sworn statement by an eye-witness, Private Ivor Parry.

Private Parry has made and signed the following statement:- "On the morn-ing of April 11 we were attacking the village called Rethem, we being members of a company of the ..... Regiment. We were slowly pushing our way into the village against heavy concentrations of shell-fire. The major who was leading the party made for a big house. When the party had occupied the house the Germans opened up with a 20mm gun, which is commonly used against air-craft, setting it on fire. Then they closed in on the house and entered it. They dragged our troops outside and set them up against the slowly burning wall and shot them with one of our Bren guns. I myself was 25 yards away and heard the screams of our men. Seeing what happened to them I shammed dead and when our 25-pounders laid a smoke-screen I took the opportunity of getting back to our own lines."

Talking to correspondents afterwards, Private Parry said that the shooting took place between 5 and 6 o'clock this morning. In the half-light he was not able to distinguish how many of our men were brought out of the house, but he thought there were 15. One German held the gun and swept up and down the line, firing until they were dead. Then he walked towards Parry, laughing and kicked him to make sure that he too was dead. Parry managed not to betray any sign of life. It is not clear what German unit was responsible. The bulk of the resistance in this sector has come from a naval division, but there have also been reports of SS troops in the town.[1]

The Illustrated London News' war artist, Captain Brian de Grineau, drew a disturbing picture on the basis of the testimony, and news of the incident spread rapidly throughout 21st Army Group, generating widespread bitterness. The 7th Armoured Division's Intelligence Summary for 13 April provided the following additional information on the massacre.

'Nice Fellows When You Get To Know Them
'Interrogation has revealed that the responsibility for the murder on 11 April of 15 PW from 53rd Welsh Division rests with 4 Company 12 SS Training Battalion.'

'TAILPIECE
Matrose BRAUNART, 8 Coy 5 Marine Grenadier Regt
'PW a smart and well-disciplined youth knew nothing about the murder of British PWs. It was impossible, he said, that such a thing could occur as no German was capable of such an unchivalrous act. Asked about the SS, he replied that they were normal German boys just like the Navy.'

After the fall of Rethem an investigation into the massacre was immediately mounted and the civilian occupant of Strongpoint Elfriede describes his experience of the British investigation.

'We were burying our animals when a group of English officers came toward us. They searched the house and property. Suddenly one of them picked up a round, pointed to it and said in broken German, "You comrade killed. Go away." I had to submit to the anger of these men. The next day saw more high ranking officers arrive and they too conducted a search. One of the officers who spoke perfect German accused me of shooting fifteen English soldiers. I naturally denied this. Interrogations and interviews commenced but fortunately our Frenchman came forward and proved my innocence.'

The rumours that prisoners had been massacred not only further dented the flagging morale but also led to some ugly scenes after Rethem eventually fell, as Leslie George witnessed.

'I came across a group of about three dozen German POWs who were being searched by a warrant officer of the Field Security Police. He was a cocky little so-and-so who had his lance corporals scattered around the immediate area. The POWs had been some of the defenders of Rethem and quite a few had English cigarettes in their possession. The warrant officer had got to one of the POWs who was about 40 years old and a bit portly. On finding a packet of "Players" in his pocket, he threw them on the ground then told the German, using sign language, to pick them up. As he bent to pick them up he kicked him in the backside; as he straightened up he gave him a rabbit punch to make him bend down again. This treatment went on four or five times.

'By now, apart from his NCOs, my gun crew and myself, several other soldiers had gathered to the scene and I was becoming very angry. I placed a magazine on my sten gun, cocked it, pointed it at the warrant officer and said to him, "If you touch that man once more, I will pull this trigger." He ordered his NCOs to arrest me. My gun crew looked into my eyes, saw a sign that they now knew and told the NCOs not to go near me or the warrant officer would be a dead man. The warrant officer was by now screaming at his men, but when he looked into my eyes, as I told him to, he realised how close he was to death. I said quite quietly to him, "I have been fighting bastards like you (meaning SS and Nazis) and unless you do your job properly, I shall treat you the same way as I would treat them, and if you take it out on the prisoners because of what I have just done to you, I shall find out and will trace you all over Europe and kill you. I have at least three dozen witnesses to what you were doing to that POW."

'My gun crew assured his NCOs that I meant every word I had said and that the best thing they could do was to treat the POWs according to the Geneva Convention and to convince their warrant officer to do the same. Although I doubt if the Germans could speak English, they realised what I had done and I shall never forget the look in their eyes as they were loaded into the trucks, particularly "fatso" who had been on the receiving end.'

The massacre however never took place and it was later found that the Germans had treated the wounded, evacuated them to the military hospital in Walsrode and had scrupulously observed the rules of war. Another 7th Armoured Division Intelligence Summary, dated 17 April, provides the probable truth behind the story.

'TAILPIECE
'Not So Atrocious After All
'The tale of 15 PW alleged to have been murdered has now been discounted by the recapture of an officer from the party.

'The enemy formation involved was 2 MID and NOT 12 SS. They took our men prisoner and marched them away and apparently treated them quite correctly.

'Several buildings in the neighbourhood were brewing, and some of these contained pigs and cows which were shot by the Germans with a Bren gun to put them out of their pain. The squeal of the animals no doubt accounted for the gruesome stories put forth. In actual fact therefore, the enemy seem not only to have behaved correctly, but also to have trespassed on the prerogative of the Island Race – Kindness to Animals!'

Why Parry made the statement is not known but it is probable that with the poor light and his state of battle fatigue, his imagination got the better of him.

1/5 Welch lost a further four officers and 139 other ranks, killed, wounded and captured, during the attacks of 11 April. The battalion war diary records that the battalion strength by now was reduced to 26 officers and 696 other ranks, a loss of some seven officers and 186 other ranks in 48 hours. These were extremely heavy losses for any period of the war, but were particularly so for this stage when the advance was virtually unopposed and mopping-up actions the order of the day. These must have been two very hard days and no-one in the battalion had expected to meet resistance of this type as the Germans had seemed completely at the end of their tether. The battalion's lack of success in bouncing the Germans out of Rethem and the casualties and the missing must have come as a particularly bitter setback. Some official histories attempt to explain the lack of success on the presence of SS elements amongst the defenders of Rethem. They allege that the SS had been placed there not to take part in the battle themselves, but had been given the special task of ensuring that the marines fought and denied Rethem against all odds. This certainly happened elsewhere and the SS's reputation for awarding draconian punishment to the faint-hearted was well known, but it is not however correct in Rethem's case and the only SS in the area were some of the exhausted young men from SS-Ausb.u.Ers.Btl.12 HJ who had withdrawn via the town during the preceding days.

The frontal attacks mounted by 1/5 Welch over open ground were doomed to failure. With the benefit of hindsight, it is clear that over-confidence coupled with the pressures to get on were major factors in the battalion's rebuttal, and the ease with which the Weser had been crossed must have further encouraged this confidence. The presence of fresh and determined troops would have been totally unsuspected. With the battalion's initial attacks firmly repulsed, it would seem that lack of resolve became a significant factor and the high proportion of soldiers captured by the Germans would appear to bear this out. Sir David Fraser's words quoted earlier which referred to men not wishing to court death if risk could be avoided probably have relevance here.

With Rethem proving to be a much tougher nut to crack than had been expected, divisional planning now began to concentrate on employing the other two brigades to unhinge the defence. Plans were produced based on two scenarios, both employing 160th Infantry Brigade to attack Rethem as 158th Infantry Brigade's battalions were likely to be either exhausted or maldeployed for an assault. The scenario for Plan A was based on 160th Infantry Brigade successfully capturing Rethem. Once the town was secure, 7 RWF and 1 E Lan R from 71st Infantry Brigade would then form a bridgehead over the Aller opposite Rethem whilst 1/5 Welch acted as reserve on the left bank. Plan B was based on the failure by 160th Infantry Brigade to capture Rethem. In this case 158th Infantry Brigade would move north, assemble south-east of Westen, which was already in the hands of 4 Welch, and then for 1 E Lan R and 7 RWF to cross the Aller and form a bridgehead. This could then allow subsequent operations to be mounted in a south-easterly direction to cut off the marines in Rethem or force their premature withdrawal to the right bank. So that Plan B could be implemented as rapidly as possible if the need arose, Brigadier Wilsey and Lieutenant Colonel Allen, commanding officer 1 E Lan R, visited the Westen area at mid-day on 11 April. Their recce revealed that although a bridgehead at Westen could sustain operations up to divisional level, it was unsuitable for a Corps axis. Encouraging though the recce was, there was clearly no alternative to the bridge at Rethem and the town would still have to be captured at some point in the near future.

On the southern divisional axis, 6 RWF continued to make progress on Wednesday 11 April. In the early morning the patrol from C Company had reported that the village of Stöcken was held by the Germans with an 8.8cm Flak and an attack was planned for later that morning. At 0900 hours D Company assaulted the hamlet, using the north-west edge of the woods as an axis. The company was shot in by the Shermans and Cromwells of C Squadron 5 RTR and the fire from both medium and field artillery and 4.2in mortars. As the last 350 yards were dead flat and bereft of cover, smoke was used to protect the assaulting infantry who were consequently able to reach the houses with little difficulty. Most of the houses were burnt to the ground during the short fight and the 8.8cm Flak from Batterie 2./604 RAD and a few prisoners from Bataillon I./5 were taken. C Company 6 RWF, supported by two troops of tanks from A Squadron 5 RTR, then exploited to Rethemer Moor, an area dotted with farmsteads to the south of Rethem, which they captured by 1315 hours. The battalion then spent the remainder of the day consolidating its gains and mopping-up, which resulted in a further 39 prisoners-of-war. The capture of the Stöcken area was important as it provided a firm base for the attack to be mounted on Rethem by 160th Infantry Brigade from the south-west.

NOTES

1   © Times Newspapers Limited, 1945.

'SHOWERS OF PANZERFAUSTS'
11 APRIL

The battalion warned by 160th Infantry Brigade to carry out the next attack on Rethem was 2 Mons. At 0800 hours on 11 April the commanding officer, Lieutenant Colonel Brooke, was called to brigade headquarters to receive details of the attack from the brigade commander, Brigadier Coleman. Colonel Brooke was told that his battalion was to attack Rethem that afternoon and that he would be supported by four troops of tanks from B Squadron 5 RTR and would have the fullest artillery and air support. He gave his orders at mid-day and set H-Hour for 1600 hours.

The decision to allocate 5 RTR to the infantry division had not been a popular one with the tank crews. Although it was extremely experienced, the regiment was war-weary and its members not keen to rush into an assault without the fullest preparation and support. 5 RTR was equipped with the light but fast Cromwell rather than the heavier infantry support tank the Churchill, and although the squadrons were accustomed to working and fighting with infantry, this had been with their armoured brigade's own motorised battalion whose members were well experienced in tank-infantry cooperation. The mismatch between regiment and battalion was exacerbated by the troop leaders only meeting the battalion's officers shortly before H-Hour. Why this happened is not known as time had been available for discussions about tactics and cooperation. Additionally, when the Regiment was fragmented to support the various 53rd Division battalions, they lost the decisive leadership of their own first class commanding officer, Lieutenant Colonel Ray Leakey. But there were other reasons for their misgivings as well. They had lost the support of their own armoured recce regiment, 8th Hussars, and the 25pdrs of D Battery 2 RHA. The positive effect on the morale of soldiers about to go into combat that they will be supported by known and trusted men and units should not be under-estimated, and their sudden removal did little to boost B Squadron's. However, one aspect did prevent the officers and troopers feeling totally without confidence: they had an exceptional squadron leader in Major Dennis Cockbaine who, with his headquarters team, was unflappable and known to be very careful of the men under his command.

The commanding officer of 133rd Field Regiment RA prepared the artillery fire plan - codenamed 'Hatton' - for the 2 Mons' attack. For the first 20 minutes after H-Hour a barrage fired at the slow rate would creep forward of the assault and fall on targets progressively closer to

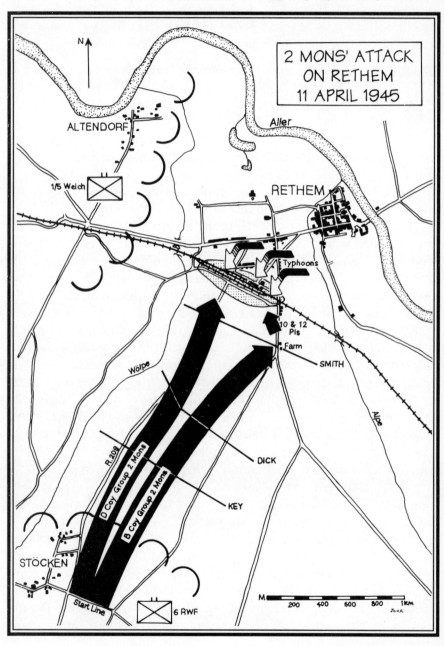

the railway line. Between H plus 20 and H plus 30 minutes, three targets in depth of Rethem on the Aller's right bank were to be engaged before fire suddenly shifted for the last 15 minutes of the advance to re-engage, with normal rates of fire, targets on the western edge of the town. At H plus 80 two smoke screens would be fired onto the right bank to mask enemy OPs and interfere with enemy direct fire weapons. The targets would be engaged with concentrations fired by 83rd and 133rd Field Regiments RA, thickened at various times by the 5.5in guns of 72nd Medium Regiment RA. The artillery fire plan would be preceded by a pre H-Hour attack by Typhoons.

The Typhoon 1Bs from No 137 Squadron, took off from the newly-repaired B-106 strip at Twente at 1424 hours and married up with others from No 182 Squadron. At 1511 hours red smoke was fired at Rethem to mark the target and some 14 minutes later the 24 aircraft, commanded by Wing Commander Webb, were over the town. The heavy aircraft peeled off from 8,000 feet and at full power dived steeply towards the target area. The 2cm Flakvierling in the area of the railway station unleashed an intense barrage of fire and the crews of the 10.5cm Flak guns furiously elevated the barrels to engage this new and lethal threat. As the Typhoons neared the end of their dive the pilots opened up with their cannons to suppress this ground fire and allow them to hold the aircraft steady during the rocket firing sequence. The pilots reached the point of release at about 1,500 feet and launched their rockets either as pairs or as complete salvos of eight, with the aircraft momentarily seeming to hang in the sky with the effect of the explosive launch. The attack appeared to the watching troops to have been made with customary devastating effect, with the salvos of 60lb rockets throwing up clouds of smoke, dirt and rubble, shaking the whole town and surrounding area. Many buildings were destroyed, a large explosion was seen from the rear of the town and numerous fires were started.

One of the marines in the defensive positions forward of the railway station was Otto Pfister. Pfister recalls the ferocity of the Typhoon attack.

'The whole day we were attacked by artillery fire, Jabos (fighter-bombers) and so forth. It was terrifying. The moans and screams of the injured still ring in my ears, but there was nothing we could to help them.'

The Typhoons flew away to the west after their rockets were exhausted and by 1606 hours had returned to their bases without loss. Despite the ferocity of this air strike, neither the marines' forward positions nor the railway Flak in the sidings at Rethem station would appear to have suffered. Although divisional headquarters were well pleased with the mission and described it as 'highly successful and accurate', photographs of the station area and the railway Flak taken after the capture of the town clearly show that these exposed and obvious targets had not been destroyed by the rocket attack. How these obvious targets, which were on the immediate objective for the 2 Mons attack, escaped destruction at first sight seems very odd[1]. For the Welsh, the fact that the company position on the railway line had been unaffected by the apparent fury unleashed from above was soon to become all too apparent.

Whilst the Typhoon attack was in progress, 2 Mons moved up to the start line. The plan involved a phased attack from the south-west on a two-company front: B Company right supported by two tank troops; D Company left, likewise supported by two troops. The two assaulting companies' tasks were to capture the railway embankment and to establish a breach in the town's outer defences. Once they had achieved their objectives, C Company was to pass through to clear the remainder of the town. In his briefing, the Brigade Intelligence Officer had estimated that the town was held by between 500 and 1,000 marines supported by railway guns. Even on the lower figure, the combat ratio was hardly favourable to the attackers and quite how one company was expected to be sufficient to clear the town is unclear.

On H-Hour at 1600 hours the artillery fire plan began. At the same time the soldiers of the assault companies of 2 Mons got to their feet, crossed the start line and were at once in full view of the German defenders as the approach was so extremely flat and open. The ground over which the attack was to take place is described by Edward Wilson who was a troop leader in B Squadron.

'The terrain was laid out more for a medieval than for a modern set-piece battle. The road we were on ran roughly north-west – south-east, which meant it was approximately parallel to and about 1,200 to 1,500 yards from the railway embankment which was so important a feature of landscape, and so important a part in the battle for Rethem. The main part of the town lay on the far side of this embankment, the bridge and most of the houses being completely obscured by it. In front of the embankment, bounded by a straggling wood on the left and a substantial hedge on the right, was an almost completely flat and open stretch of country. It was across this huge arena, 1,200 yards or so long and perhaps 600 yards wide and devoid of all cover, that we had to advance. The most sinister feature of the embankment was the presence on it of the railway-mounted 10.5cm pieces of artillery.'

Despite the openness of the ground, the advance was initially without incident. Both companies and their accompanying tanks advanced cautiously with the infantry following the tanks in single file and using whatever cover from view was available. Although good progress was being made under the protection of the artillery fire plan, neither arm felt at all at ease during the advance; the close presence of the tanks made the infantry feel that they would draw fire, whilst the tank crews manoeuvring at a walking pace felt very vulnerable in their lightly armoured Cromwells. The complete inability of either arm to be able to communicate with each other further added to the advance's difficulties. By 1630 hours both companies had reached report line Key and line Dick was similarly reached 15 minutes later. But when crossing line Smith, and whilst still some 450 yards short of their objectives, both companies came under heavy and accurate fire from machine-guns and the light Flak, whilst the tanks were engaged by the railway Flak and Pak 40 anti-tank guns. From the time of this initial engagement the infantry and armoured attacks developed separately, particularly on the left, with inevitable results. Every time there was a burst of fire the infantry went to ground whilst the tanks, indifferent to small calibre weapons and as yet out of range of Panzerfausts, continued to advance unaware that the infantry were no longer with them.

The gunner of 4 Troop leader's Cromwell tank was the aptly named Trooper Joe Cannon who from his position in his tank gained a very close impression of the attack.

'We formed up just in front of the crossroads about a mile from Rethem and moved out down the road to the town. A short distance down the road and the ground opened up to fields on both sides of the road. On the right of the road were some allotments with sheds. Some Germans came out from there and were shot up. The Troop Leader's tank went to the right of the road, the other two Cromwells to the left with the Firefly on the edge of the road behind us. To our right were small heaps of hay in lines which had been cut, heaped and left to dry and here we spotted further Germans in the open, not dug in behind the hay. We took them out. By this time the forward infantry were trying to reach the railway embankment that ran in front of the town and were clearly in trouble. The enemy were dug-in in front of the embankment in holes with all the topsoil removed so they were flush with the ground and hard to spot. The enemy were also behind the embankment and on the railway line were a hell of a lot of 88mm (sic) Flak guns all pointing down the line.'

On the right of the attack B Company initially made reasonable progress. The company had advanced in the order 11 Platoon, 5 Troop, Company Headquarters, 10 and 12 Platoons. No 11 Platoon's task was to seize a group of farm buildings 300 yards short of the railway and to establish there a firm base for the final assault by 10 and 12 Platoons who were to move forward, under cover of smoke if necessary, to establish themselves on the railway embankment. No 11 Platoon was 90 yards from the farm buildings when it came under effective fire. However, by moving in short dashes the whole company managed to establish itself in the area of the farm buildings. Supporting the attack were the tanks of 5 Troop. The gunner of the troop's Firefly was Lance Corporal Harry Ireland.

'What a field day of a shoot we had that day. There was a certain amount of hate at this time as we had been informed that Rethem was being held by fanatical marine troops from Hamburg and that they were shooting all prisoners captured the previous day.

'We took up position facing the railway line and set about engaging targets. The marines had brought up mobile 88mm (sic) guns mounted on railway flats and were firing HE at the infantry position. For hours we engaged and appeared to knock out the guns but the determination of the Germans amazed us. If it hadn't been such a life and death business you could say it was like being at a fair ground for as fast as I machine-gunned and HE'd the target, up sprang another crew to take the place of the dead around the gun. However, after numerous attempts to crew the guns, we managed to knock them all out.'

Although B Company had successfully reached its initial objective, the slightest movement outside the buildings brought a hail of fire from marines on the railway embankment and casualties began to mount. A request was made for smoke to screen the advance by 10 and 12 Platoons to the railway embankment. The platoons left the uncertain safety of the buildings and advanced, covered by the fire from 11 Platoon's Bren guns. The smoke proved ineffective however and both platoons were forced back by the weight of enemy fire; casualties included Lieutenant Mackenzie, one of the platoon commanders, who was stunned by a shot through the helmet. Smoke was again called for and this time was much more effective. Under its cover the platoons repeated their attack and were soon engaging the marines in slit trenches in the field between the farm and the embankment. While these localised actions were being fought, the smoke again drifted away leaving the platoons both exposed and short of their objective. Some of the enemy left their trenches but the majority fought bitterly. The platoons were silhouetted against the smoke and were fought to a stand-still 40 yards short of the embankment where the marines were well dug-in. The only cover available were a few shell craters, and the marines' accurate fire pinned the soldiers down; any movement attracted a burst of fire from all sides and casualties were repeatedly hit by snipers. Lieutenant MacKenzie received five more wounds - two in the arm, and one each in the back, chest and face - but continued to encourage his men. Sergeant Williams, the acting Company Sergeant Major who had taken over command of Lieutenant MacKenzie's platoon when he was first hit, was killed and about a third of the company were casualties. Lieutenant Evans, the other platoon commander and now commanding both platoons, found a volunteer in Private Brock to take a message to company headquarters in the farm buildings telling them what had happened, as they seemed unaware of events due to the smoke and general confusion. Whilst the infantry fought and died at the railway embankment, the gunners of one of 72nd Medium Regiment's batteries also had their share of misery when a 5.5in gun had a premature explosion killing the gun's Number 1, Sergeant Tomlinson, and wounding another gun number.

Whilst B Company struggled to get forward to the embankment, D Company on the left was also in difficulties. The armour and infantry attack was by now totally uncoordinated and the infantry, pinned down by small-arms fire, were unable to move up to support their tanks. As the armour was unable to advance further without the infantry to clear the Panzerfaust firers, the tanks stood off and attempted to pick off the enemy positions, as Joe Cannon describes.

'At about 1,000 yards from the railway in front of Rethem the Monmouths came under fire from weapon pits both on and in front of the embankment. We halted at 800 yards out and returned fire to enable the forward elements of the Monmouths to withdraw back to the main body. We engaged the enemy on the right of the road down by the railway line and took them out firing HE on delay. By this time all our infantry had moved to the left of the road and so we joined them, but were then asked to go back to the right. We went back and were firing on the embankment when we were hit by a heavy machine-gun, about a 20mm I think. We were really plastered and found later that he had nearly penetrated the turret. The Troop Leader spotted him just on the left of the road where it crossed the railway line and we finished him with a 75mm HE round. We then went back to the left of the road by what looked like a small electrical sub-station which was some 800 yards from the embankment.

'The Troop Leader had just said words to the effect, "Thank God those guns are all pointing down the line," when one turned round and fired at us. He was bang on for line but short. At this all the Cromwells opened up with HE and AP and began to take out all the guns on the embankment. This went on for some time and we made sure that they were out. By this time I was getting low on ammo and had to re-stock from under the turret floor and get Besa ammo from the lap gunner. We then concentrated on the enemy pits on the left of the road firing HE on delay for air bursts over the pits, watching for him to fire and then firing the machine-guns when he was exposed; we had fair success with this. Suddenly the Troop Leader spotted an anti-tank gun on the left of the road, down by the level-crossing. The gun, a 7.5cm I think, was side-on so I aimed an AP round at the thick part of the barrel and put a hole right through it. Range was 800 yards, it was one of my best shots and I'm still proud of it! Some time late in the afternoon a train engine to the right of the road and the signal box was getting up steam and I was told to destroy it. I fired an HE into the cab and an AP through the boiler. I could hear our other troop firing at times but never saw them as they were busy with their own bit of front. We were very short of ammo by now and we tried to conserve as much as possible but there were too many targets.'

The battalion attack was now bogged down and Captain Eric Wilde, who was then in B Squadron Headquarters, was clearly frustrated at the lack of headway in the battle.

'...The attack started in the late afternoon and was directed on the village from the south-west. There was a railway embankment just south of the village and the ground was very open in front of it. On the embankment there were a number of 10.5cm guns which were manned but stood out very markedly. Two 7.5cm anti-tank guns opened up from the east and gave some problems, but they were knocked out. It may well be that these guns were manned by inexperienced gunners, certainly they should have given our tanks more trouble than they did. In the meantime while the tanks were advancing and dealing with these guns, the infantry also advanced until they came some 400-500 yards short of the embankment. Then the enemy opened up with MG and rifle fire and the infantry went to ground - and that was virtually the end of the infantry attack. The enemy infantry were very well positioned. Some MG posts were on, or dug into, the embankment and these the tanks could observe and knock out. But the main enemy positions were sited in front of the embankment in flat fields. They were individual foxholes with no parapets to give away their locations. The excavated earth was scattered around so there was no indication of a foxhole till you were almost on top of it. The enemy infantry hid in these foxholes, popping up to fire their rifles, MGs and Panzerfausts and then dropping down again. It was extremely difficult for the tanks to deal with them. It was hard to identify the positions and difficult to get a HE round into them. Great care had to be taken of the Panzerfausts. We tried to get the infantry to close with the enemy, but somehow nothing was achieved and everything petered out. The infantry never seemed to come up with the tanks. One troop of tanks actually managed to get onto the embankment but came under a shower of Panzerfausts - luckily badly aimed - and had to withdraw. After two hours of fighting the tanks had virtually run out of ammunition, the two leading troops had none left and they were relieved by two troops from C Squadron. The tanks continued to give maximum fire support and engaged every sign of enemy activity, but the infantry were able to make no progress ...'

A gunner in one of the C Squadron Sherman Fireflies which relieved the B Squadron tanks was Trooper Huett.

'During the late afternoon my troop drove up the road towards Rethem. About halfway we stopped and the roofs of the houses, which ran across our front were machine-gunned and set alight. As we got nearer to the level crossing - it was getting dusk now - we stopped again. During this stop an English casualty was helped onto the back of our tank and laid down across the back. We also had two German prisoners, uninjured I believe, on the back. I always remember an incident at this point. As one of the prisoners bent down towards the injured chap, our radio operator, Mike Parker, gave him a sharp knock on his arm with his Sten gun apparently thinking the Jerry was going to harm the casualty. The Jerry looked up with a very hurt look as he was only bending down to take a cigarette out of the casualty's mouth as he couldn't do it himself and was about to get burnt. I felt a bit sorry for this Jerry as he was only doing something to help.

'As it got dark we were ordered to return back down the road towards our startpoint - we didn't mind this! We therefore drove back, dropped off our casualty and prisoners and looking back could see the town still burning fiercely.'

As it was clear to Lieutenant Colonel Brooke that the battalion's attack had failed he ordered the companies to break off. To assist the break clean and withdrawal, the artillery were asked for yet another smoke screen which would be thickened by fire from mortars and tanks. The speed of the general advance resulted in smoke rounds being in short supply and two screens had already been demanded that afternoon, however a screen was fired 25 minutes later - the gunners using up their last shells to provide it. Immediately it was down, B Company's carrier, driven by Private Wild and commanded by Lance Corporal Dawson, dashed forward conveying the order to withdraw as radio communications had broken down. Many of the wounded were piled into it for the return journey while others were carried by their comrades.

By this time the town was well alight and the dark evening was lit by roaring flames. Despite this, Dawson and Wild volunteered to take the carrier forward again to pick up any other survivors. Covering fire was given by the tanks, and although the carrier was clearly illuminated by the flames they managed to drive within 35 yards of the enemy positions. Here Dawson and Wild dismounted and examined every casualty for signs of life, bringing the living back to safety. Meanwhile 10 and 12 Platoons had retired through 11 Platoon, which had also suffered casualties. Both these soldiers were awarded the Military Medal for their courage; Lieutenant MacKenzie was awarded the Distinguished Service Order for his gallantry during the battle.

Edward Wilson's account of the withdrawal sadly reflects how complete was the breakdown of cooperation between the infantry and their armour.

'At twilight, when we got the orders from squadron headquarters to pull back troop by troop, I looked around for our supporting infantry, only to find that they were no longer there. We met up with them again later, because both tanks and infantry only pulled back overnight to the other side of the road from which we had started. Here we lay up for the night: ourselves snug in our tanks; the poor 2 Mons very much out in the open. We took pity on them, as we took pity on our own divisional infantry, by sharing the brew up which we quickly got going in the tanks. They came in relays for their brew and, during one relay's visit, I had the only laugh of the day. While one of the platoon commanders and some of his men were with us, our A Echelon arrived with much needed replenishments. The platoon commander asked me who commanded the A Echelon: I replied it was the RSM. I then heard an awed, sotto voce comment from the ranks. "Christ", the voice said, "You wouldn't find our fucker this close to the sharp end".'

By 2100 hours the companies and tanks had withdrawn half a mile from the railway embankment and awaited a decision from higher levels as to what was to happen next. The order to break-off all further action was confirmed at 2200 hours by Major General Ross himself who had been at Headquarters 160th Infantry Brigade throughout the 2 Mons' attack. He ordered no further attacks to be mounted on Rethem for the present and stated the town would not be re-attacked until dusk the following day, and then only if a major air effort and Crocodiles were available. The battalion was ordered to pull back and concentrate in the area of Stöcken and the start line of their attack. That night the battalion despatched a fighting patrol to discover whether any gaps existed in the enemy defences; the patrol reported back in the early hours of 12 April that the line of the railway was strongly held and that no gaps were evident.

Although all of 53rd Welsh Division's attempts to capture Rethem had been repulsed, Jordan had suffered serious losses in men, ammunition was in short supply and he knew that he would not be able to hold off attacks for a third day. Jordan was aware that the British had been in Westen since the day before and that they would attempt a crossing there before long. Any such crossing would inevitably lead to his regiment being cut off and so he ordered a withdrawal to the right bank to take place that night. Jordan was however faced with a problem regarding his withdrawal route, for during the afternoon's Typhoon attack the demolition charges on the Aller bridge had blown up in some form of sympathetic detonation. The ensuing explosion had killed and wounded a number of marines in the immediate area and dropped the bridge into the river, effectively and prematurely removing the regiment's withdrawal route. Alternative methods and points for crossing had to be found. While a weak rearguard provided cover for the withdrawal, during the course of the night 11-12 April he and 100 of his marines crossed the Aller in small boats which had been gathered together. As soon as the main body had safely reached the right bank, the regimental rearguard, commanded by an Oberleutnant, withdrew in a south-easterly direction in the early hours of 12 April and crossed the Aller using the Eilte ferry, which was scuttled once they were safely across. The remnants of Bataillon II./5, only numbering some 200 men of the original 600, withdrew to the cover of the woods between the villages of Nordkampen and Südkampen, and here they regrouped and recovered from the ordeal of the past three days. In the cellars of Rethem they left behind them those, both German and British, who were too seriously wounded to have survived the withdrawal and there they were tended by the townsfolk and Rethem's doctor, Doktor Hoffmeyer. This 70 year-old had been involved throughout the battle offering first aid and his heroism was talked about long after the war's end.

It was obvious to General Ross that the town could not be taken without many more casualties, but it was also clear that for the future advance of XII Corps, a crossing site at Rethem would have to be captured to carry the Corps' main supply route. It was therefore decided to implement Plan B and establish the bridgehead opposite Westen with 158th Infantry Brigade. A Class 9 bridge would then be built across the Aller to enable 71st Infantry Brigade to cross and clear the right bank, thus cutting off the Germans who were still thought to be in Rethem. Rethem would then be reduced on 12 April by Mitchell medium bombers from the RAF's No 2 Group and anything that survived would be captured by 160th Infantry Brigade assisted by Crocodiles; work would then begin on a Class 40 bridge to open up the axis for 7th Armoured Division to exploit to Soltau. In preparation for this, on 11 April the armoured division had been relieved from the fighting on the approaches to Bremen by Major General Whistler's 3rd Infantry Division and had moved to a concentration area south-east of Nienburg. However, in the unpredictable way in which events unfold in war, Rethem's capture did not come about in this way and as we shall see later, the town's deliverance from total devastation was directly attributable to a tank becoming bogged during 2 Mons' attack.

Fierce fighting was also taking place elsewhere on 11 April on the left bank and 4 Welch in particular was encountering stiff opposition as the companies set about clearing the enemy from the Weser/Aller triangle. An especially bitter little action was fought in Barnstedt, another river-side village similar to Westen and Hülsen, where the Carrier Platoon got into difficulties when it was encircled in the village by

Kompanie 3./7. A Cromwell from A Squadron 5 RTR was knocked out by Panzerfausts whilst attempting to relieve the platoon and two more became badly bogged trying to move across country. The buildings the platoon was occupying began to burn, and it was only with the help of a second troop of tanks and a further platoon of infantry that the besieged platoon was extricated, leaving behind the dead, two carriers and the village uncaptured.

Whilst the 53rd Division battalions were fighting hard in the Rethem area, equally ferocious fighting was going on to their south-east where 11th Armoured Division was still attempting to secure the bridgehead over the Aller gained by 1st Commando Brigade the night before. Brigadier Mills-Roberts had planned to launch 46 (RM) Commando to take the road bridge from the rear but his plans were thwarted by the marines of Kompanie 1./2 launching a fierce counter-attack against them. At the same time 3 Commando was attacked by marines from Kompanie 3./2 who used the cover of the thick pine woods to work their way forward in short, sharp rushes despite the heavy small-arms fire that was directed at them. This attack was only beaten off by the artillery fire of 1st Mountain Regiment RA bringing down barrages immediately to the commandos' front. With pressure mounting on his bridgehead, Brigadier Mills-Roberts realised he had to gain the initiative with some form of offensive action. No 6 Commando, commanded by 24 year-old Lieutenant Colonel Tony Lewis, was in reserve within the bridgehead and was the obvious choice for this task. Colonel Lewis describes the events that followed.

'I had been listening to the command net and had gathered that the enemy was proving to be a very ferocious form of opposition. Eventually I received the order I expected from the brigade commander himself, whose radio procedure was non-existent, "Tony – take the bridge – Out!". Although the bridge had been blown by the Germans, there was no doubting the clarity or intent of this order, but where exactly 3 Commando was in the thick pine woods I did not know! I decided that they were not within 300 yards of the Aller's bank and that the best course of action was therefore for me to rest my right flank on the river bank and to move towards the bridge with the unit at right angles to the river. I decided to use the bank of a deep drainage ditch, which was marked as a canal on the map, as a start line and to secure it immediately with 6 Troop. Meanwhile, as that troop moved off, I gave orders to the remaining five troop commanders. I had decided not to use artillery support as I did not know 3 Commando's position and as we would be moving quickly it would be difficult to co-ordinate any fire support. As a morale substitute I placed my section of Vickers machine-guns – old favourites with the men – on the right flank.

'I could see the troop commanders' faces looking a little doubtful about the lack of artillery support. The war was showing every sign of coming to an end and most infantry units were leaning on the use of guns to save casualties at so late a stage in the war. We then moved swiftly, crossing a bridge over the ditch and ducking down behind the bank on the east side. As we settled down, girded our loins and fixed bayonets for the charge, 6 Troop commander returned from the direction of the river to say that he had been held up by a strong group of

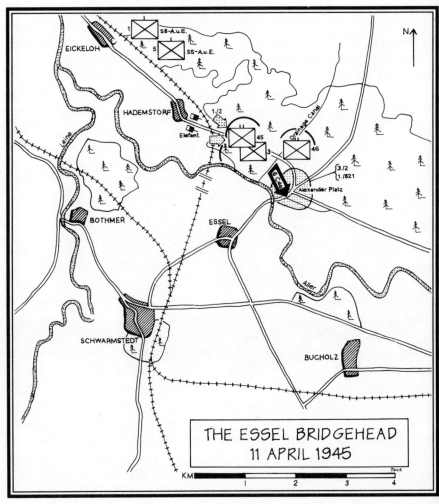

THE ESSEL BRIDGEHEAD
11 APRIL 1945

ght: Major General Ross,
mmander 53rd Welsh
vision.

low: Brigadier
rington, Commander
st Infantry Brigade,
en here with
ontgomery.

Above: Brigadier Wilsey, Commander 158th Infantry Brigade.

Above: Brigadier Coleman, Commander 160th Infantry Brigade

Below: Vizeadmiral Scheurlen, Commander 2.Marine-Infanterie-Division

Below: Kapitän zur See Jordan, Commander Marine-Grenadier-Regiment 5

Top: Kapitän zur See Hartmann (second
from right), Commander Marine-
Grenadier-Regiment 6.

Above: Korvettenkapitän Gördes,
Commander Marine-Füsilier-Bataillon 2.

Above: Kapitän zur See Neitzel,
Commander Marine-Grenadier-
Regiment 7.

Above: Infant
from 53rd We
Division pause
a typical tree-
lined road dur
the advance to
Weser.

Left: Young
members of 7.
Kompanie SS-
Ausb.u.Ers.Bt
HJ pose for a
group photogr.
before battle is
joined.

Left: The Bail
bridge built ov
the Weser at
Hoya. The
damaged build
ings in the
background we
occupied by R
Fuchs and the
marines of
Kompanie 14.

op of page: 10 April. Soldiers of 1/5 Welch
ancing towards Rethem through the
rning mist.

ove: Sergeant Jake Wardrop (second from
t) with his Firefly and crew.

ght: The ventilor on Sergeant Wardrop's
efly showing the Panzerfaust penetration.

Above: Captain Bryan de Grineau's drawing in *The Illustrated London News* of the massac[re] that never happened (ILN).

Below: The road down which Sergeant Moses advanced into Rethem. The ruined house [on] the right is the von der Kammer strongpoint.

ght: 11 April. A Welsh
lier examines German
itions after the capture of
Elfriede strongpoint.

low: 11 April. A dead
i-tank gunner from
r.Pz.Jg.Abt.2 lying next to
Pak 40 on the outskirts of
hem. Note the unused
izerfaust by his side.

Above: 11 April. M14 half-tracks from 58th LAA Regt RA and infantry of 4KSLI crossing t
Aller near Essel. Note the thick pine forest on the far bank. (IWM)

Below: 12 April. The fall of Rethem. A blurred view of the destroyed town taken from the
turret of a 5 RTR tank.

...ht: 12 April. 10.5cm Flak
...atterie 1. and 4./125(E)
...he sidings at Rethem
...ion. The Welsh launched
...r attack from the right of
...photograph. Note the kill
...s for Allied aircraft on the
...barrels. (IWM)

...ow: 12 April. Sergeants
...rge Stimpson (sitting
...and Ted Lines (right)
...e on the Pak 40 in the
...tre of Rethem. 'Cold-
...l' Pearson is in the leather
...in centre rear.

Left: 12 April. Cromwells and a Stuart from 5 RTR i Rethem town centre.

Left: 12 April. Captured marines in Rethem are marched away past Captai Braddel and Major Crickn (right) of 5 RTR.

Left: German civilians bur ing fallen marines under British supervision. The ra way line can be seen in the background and a truck trundles past on Route 209 (IWM)

ove: 13 April. Frazen's knocked-out Tiger F02 blocking the path of an advancing Comet
n A Squadron 3 RTR. Note the huge difference in the width of the tanks' tracks.

ow: 13 April. Vickers machine-guns of 1 Manchester supporting operations on the Aller's
t bank. (IWM)

Left: The Class 9 folding boat bridge over the Aller a Westen.

Left: 14 April. 4.2in mor of D Company 1 Manches in action during the Germ counter-attacks.

Left: 14 April. Kangaroos carrying 6 RWF and Shermans of the Greys wai in the centre of Rethem for the order to cross the Baile bridge over the Aller. (IWM

ove: The centre of Rethem taken from the remains of the demolished road bridge. Part of Bailey bridge over the Aller can be seen in the right hand corner.

ow: 14 April. A Sherman of the Greys crossing the floating Bailey bridge at Rethem.

Left: 15 April. A German mother and her two daughters wheel away their remaining possessions after their house has been destroyed in the battle for Gr.Eilstorf. (IWM)

Left: 15 April. Soldiers of 1/5 Queens mounted in Kangaroos during the advance to Walsrode.

Left: 15 April. Burning buildings in Rethem following the night air attack

ve: Stalag XIB with its Appel-platz in the centre. Groups of prisoners can be seen centre
t and in the background.

ow: Prisoners, among them a number of paras captured at Arnhem, enjoying their first
e of freedom following the relief of Stalag XIB. Camp huts and a 'goon' tower can be seen
te background. (IWM)

Left: May 1945. Die Stunde Null. Dejected German soldiers with a motley collection of transport congregate at a collection point. (IWM)

Left: April 1992. Ex-Members of 2.Marine-Infanterie-Division at Rethem's war cemetery.

Left: Becklingen Commonwealth War Graves Cemetery

the enemy firing Panzerfausts at his forward section. I told him to leave a small party to occupy the enemy and to protect the Vickers teams. He returned to his troop and let me know when he was ready to move forward. I then ordered the Vickers to start firing; when I heard their friendly chatter, I said over the radio to the troops, "OK, let's go!".

'Four hundred and fifty men rose to the top of the bank shouting and hallooing at the tops of their voices and our two horsy men – one a racehorse trainer and the other a polo player – blew their hunting horns, achieving fame for this 5 days later on the front page of the *Daily Mirror*. Only I knew it was still 500 yards to the bridge! After about 100 yards we passed brigade HQ on our left. They all stood up and cheered and threw their berets in the air. We must have been an impressive sight, so many men on a narrow front, and therefore in deep column, all with their bayonets flashing and shouting fit to burst.

'About now, the enemy woke up from the shock of seeing us bearing down on them through the wood. I was sad to see Sergeant Virgo, our intelligence sergeant, go down at this stage. On we went and I was beginning to feel the exhilaration similar to that I had experienced only once before when riding a motor bike at 90 mph; a sort of nirvana crept over me, which protected me from the fear of death.

'The closer we got to the bridge the more intense became the enemy's fire. Some of the enemy machine-gun teams had a bad habit of firing at us until the last moment and then dropping their weapons and putting their hands in the air. Our soldiers cured them forever of this bad habit. After about the 300 yard mark, the enemy fire suddenly ceased, as if by order, and they broke and ran for the woods to the north. It was now that we inflicted the highest number of casualties with men using the standing firing position as if at a hare shoot. The right flank wheeled on to the bridge's approach road while the left swept across the road to the forest on the opposite side.

'We then dug-in around the bridge and in the woods nearby. I had difficulty in calling back the Troops who had crossed the road as they were chasing a number of enemy who were trying to get away. There was a momentary lull in the battle whilst those enemy who had not been concerned with the charge put in a series of small counter-attacks from the north, but each time we turned them back with casualties. It was during this phase that I decided to walk round our Bren positions in order to make sure that our men were taking on proper targets and not shooting up brigade HQ by mistake. I regretted this move as I realized that I might walk into our own fire from behind as well as the enemy's from in front. After about two hours the enemy withdrew.

'Our record of casualties assessed that we killed some 55, wounded 30 and took 74 prisoners during the charge, for a loss of nine dead and 26 wounded. I believe that this is the last occasion the British Army mounted an assault solely using small-arms and the bayonet, unsupported by any other forms of fire. I was lucky with my plan as I had not realised that 3 Commando had cleared the area of the bridge over the drainage ditch earlier that morning and that its bank would provide such a suitable and safe start line.'

No 6 Commando's charge gained a respite for the right flank of the bridgehead and drove Festungs Pak Kompanie.11 and Kompanie 3./2 from their defensive positions in the area of the north end of the bridge, with the guns of Batterie 1./521 RAD also being subsequently captured. The Füsilier battalion suffered a severe set-back when Korvettenkapitän Josef Gördes, who had moved up to be with his men in the forefront of the action, was killed by a grenade splinter whilst fighting with them in the area of Alexander Platz.

Meanwhile, on the left flank of the bridgehead 45 (RM) Commando was attacked by Kompanie 1./2 supported by the two Elefant self-propelled guns of Panzerjäger Abteilung 71. These vehicles posed a great threat to the bridgehead as there were no tanks across yet and the only counter to them was medium artillery fire. Two fire missions were called for which initially had no effect as accuracy against the lumbering vehicles was not easy to achieve. However, the weight of fire of the 5.5in shells eventually proved too uncomfortable for the self-propelled guns and the commandos were much relieved to see them retiring. The reason for their withdrawal was in fact more as a result of casualties among the accompanying infantry, without whose protection the vehicles were very vulnerable to close-quarter infantry attack. Throughout the rest of the day the fighting was both bloody and confused in the bridgehead, although the Germans were unable to dislodge the British. Whilst the commando brigade and the armoured division were fighting it out on the Aller in the Essel area, 15th Scottish Division had continued the eastwards advance, making good progress, and by nightfall had closed on the town of Celle, with 6th Airborne Division following in its wake clearing the woods.

NOTES

1   The effectiveness of rocket-firing, Typhoon close-air support has been over-estimated and news-reel film footage, no doubt selectively chosen, has reinforced the image of devastating power. After D Day Typhoon support became the subject of much study by No 2 Operational Research (OR) Section, which served with 21st Army Group from June 1944 to July 1945. A joint Army

and Air Force OR report written in the autumn of 1944 and entitled Joint Report No 3, "Rocket Firing Typhoons in Close Support of Military Operations," found that three hundred and fifty rockets, involving forty-four sorties would have to be fired at a small gun position to obtain a 50% chance of a hit, and that rockets were at their most effective reducing enemy morale and raising our own. In the light of this, perhaps it is not so surprising that the railway Flak and the station area escaped unscathed.

THE CAPTURE OF RETHEM
12 APRIL

Compared with the noise and confusion of the preceding days, Thursday 12 April dawned curiously quiet in the Rethem area. Other than the occasional round of harassing artillery fire hitting the smoking rubble, no activity was evident elsewhere and even many of the fires had burnt out. Despite the eerie calm, the British were still unaware that the town had been evacuated and made no attempt to close on Rethem.

Stuck in a field in front of the railway embankment lay the immobilised Firefly. Belonging to 10 Troop commanded by Sergeant George Stimpson, it had bogged in when it had moved forward with the rest of C Squadron the previous afternoon. The squadron had withdrawn with the 2 Mons' companies when the action was broken off and the tank had to be abandoned by its crew. George Stimpson describes the events that followed.

'When it got dark we were told to pull out (including the infantry) as a large bomber raid was to be laid on. While doing this, the tank in my troop commanded by the corporal got bogged down. It was not possible to get it out without a lot of noise and light so we took out the firing pins of the guns, locked the tank up and left it. Next morning (12 April) after breakfast I asked if we could go back and recover the tank - this we were allowed to do. At this stage we were four tanks on our own about 200 yards from the level-crossing. I had a talk with my other sergeant, Ted Lines - we had been together since early in the desert - and we agreed that there did not seem to be many enemy about so we did what we had done so many times before. We took the hull-gunners from a couple of tanks and we started to walk into the town, Ted with his man on one side and me on the other. We soon reached the level crossing with no trouble and were able to have a closer look at the dead soldiers still lying in the field, there must have been a whole company of them and I don't think I have ever been so saddened as I was that morning. I called the tanks forward and we continued. Just around the corner we were met by a party of civilians with a white flag led by the Bürgermeister. He let it be known that the town was prepared to give in and I said that this was OK provided all arms were laid down and the remaining troops formed up on the road. Failing this we would shoot the lot! At about 0930 hours all this was passed to our CO Lieutenant Colonel Leakey - who came up quickly.'

In fact prior to this, Lieutenant Colonel Leakey had come forward that morning to talk to C Squadron commander, Major Crickmay. Colonel Leakey takes up the story.

'When I arrived at his (Major Crickmay's) HQ I was told that he had gone forward to see if one of his tanks which had been abandoned had been `brewed-up' by the Germans during the night. I went down the farm track he had taken, and sure enough I came across this lone officer walking towards the main Rethem defensive line. He jumped onto the back of my small scout car and we continued on our way. It was the driver who called our attention as to where we were. "Blimey", he said, "what a lot of dead Boche about and look at them large railway guns." We were passing through the outer defences which had been abandoned during the night. I called up the Adjutant, Captain Dixon, on the radio and told him to order B and C Squadrons to move as fast as possible into Rethem. I also asked him to inform 53rd Welsh Division of the situation and suggest that the Monmouths might help us to clear the town of the inevitable enemy rearguard.'

Whilst his commanding officer was coming forward, George Stimpson was being taken to a large cellar beneath a public building.

'One of the Germans asked me to follow him to the basement of a large building where a hospital had been set up by some German nursing sisters. They explained to me that they urgently needed medical help and when I looked around the basement I estimated there was something like a hundred cases on the floor and at least half of them were British. I promised them all the help they needed and as soon as I got back to the Troop I reported it to the Squadron Leader who had by now joined us. Ted and I then continued to the river where we found the bridge blown and another anti-tank gun abandoned.'

Their somewhat unconventional role in the final act of the battle for Rethem over, Ted Lines[1] posed with George Stimpson and his crew for a photograph on the abandoned 7.5cm Pak at the barricade on the Alpe. Seen sitting on the gun shield in the rear of the photograph is

George Stimpson's hull-gunner, 'Coldsteel' Pearson, whose main contribution to the war effort was to shoot George in the leg in Normandy!

Whilst Lieutenant Colonel Leakey was moving toward the centre of the town he was called up on the radio by his Adjutant, Captain Dixon.

'He told us that divisional HQ had sent a message to say that five hundred bombers were on their way to flatten Rethem and we were to get out immediately. This was one of several orders in my career I refused to obey! Thanks to Dixon's efforts the RAF were able to recall their aircraft - but only just. We were listening for them and did hear them. The town of Rethem owes Dixon a debt of gratitude.

'As the lead tanks approached the centre of the town an incident occurred which I shall never forget. I happened to be behind the leading troop of B Squadron. It was commanded by Lieutenant John Gwilliam, a large, powerful Welshman. When his tank came up to a T junction he rightly dismounted and poked his nose round the corner to see if there was an anti-tank gun covering this approach. A rifle shot whistled past his head and Gwilliam disappeared round the corner, reappearing moments later carrying a small German soldier, rather like a cat with a mouse. I asked Gwilliam if this was the soldier which had so nearly shot him and he replied that it was. "Then why didn't you shoot him?" I asked, and back the answer came, "Oh no Colonel, he's much too small!". After the war, Gwilliam went on to captain Wales at rugby.'

Whilst Lieutenant Colonel Leakey and C Squadron were entering Rethem from the south-west, 5 RTR's recce troop, operating from Rethemer, had entered Hedern and then advanced north-west to the outskirts of Rethem. Several Panzerfausts were fired at the leading Stuart but the Germans were in no strength and by 0950 hours the troop was half-way into Rethem. The 2 Mons was ordered into the town at 1120 hours and some two hours later Rethem was at last secured. C Squadron investigated the area of the railway line position where such fierce fighting had occurred the day before, and here were found five knocked out 10.5cm railway Flak, two 7.5cm Pak, several 2cm Flak and many dead Germans with equipment scattered about. In this final phase of the battle, 120 prisoners were captured and 42 German dead were counted in the town and on the southern outskirts. The road bridge, of course, was found demolished and lying in the Aller, and the bridge over the Wölpe on the western edge of the town had also been demolished.

At 1415 hours A Company 2 Mons despatched a recce patrol across the Aller to check the condition of the next two bridges on Route 209 and discover the whereabouts of the enemy. The patrol reported back at 1715 hours that both bridges had been blown and at 1800 hours a platoon established itself in a defensive position on the right bank of the Aller to protect the construction of a Class 40 Bailey pontoon bridge by 53rd Division Engineers. The last entry in 2 Mons' War Diary for 11 April concluded somewhat ruefully that the Germans had fought with great energy and spirit regardless of their heavy casualties and the fire support directed on the town.

The battle for Rethem was costly for both sides. For the Germans it resulted in the loss of some 73 soldiers. Of these men, the youngest was only 17 and the oldest was 53; 11 were unidentified. Fifteen inhabitants also died during the fighting and many more were wounded and injured. The small town was devastated, 65 houses were totally destroyed and a further 64 badly damaged. In the streets, houses, gardens and surrounding fields lay the debris of war: bodies, weapons, items of equipment and ammunition. Although the bodies of the marines were swiftly collected by work parties of local men and buried in an orchard next to the railway crossing, the rest of the battlefield took much longer to clear and an unexploded munition claimed the life of a child nine days after the capture of the town.

Kapitän zur See Jordan's dogged defence was of no strategic value and it only served to forestall the inevitable. The delay did not make any material difference to the creation of Wenck's 12.Armee, which eventually sallied forth in a vain attempt to relieve Berlin. It is of course impossible to determine how many soldiers and civilians managed to escape to the left bank of the Elbe as a consequence of the 48 or so hours of delay imposed on XII Corps by Jordan and his marines. The performance of the marines once again demonstrated the formidable fighting qualities of the German fighting man. The highly spirited defence was conducted by men with minimal infantry training, using inferior weaponry, led by officers with little or no experience of a land battle and fighting in the knowledge that the end of the war had to be only days away; despite this they fought with immense courage and tenacity.

However, it is interesting to note the role played by inter-service rivalry in the marines' mental approach to the battle. The 1b, or Operations Officer, of Divisions Kommando 2.Marine Infanterie Division said to his captors after the battle, 'The marines have fought so well because they wanted to show the German Army what the Navy could do if tested!'. Although the defence of Rethem was operationally futile and resulted in death and much suffering to the soldiers of both sides, as well as the inhabitants, the courage shown by the marines is beyond dispute and is poignantly described by Captain Eric Wilde.

'When I inspected the area after it was all over, I was struck by the large number of infantry dead in the foxholes. They had almost all been hit in the head, showing that they had been hit as they stood in the hole engaging us. They could so easily have just crouched at the bottom and would have been safe from everything except airburst. And they all seemed so young. I was myself a week from my twenty-third birthday but they seemed boys to me. I should think they must have been in the sixteen to eighteen age group. The war was hopelessly lost for them, but they fought so bravely. Even then, when one was pretty hardened to death and suffering, we all, I think, felt pity for such young lives being sacrificed.'

For the inhabitants these were grim times. The face of Rethem in April 1945 was ruined streets, no lights, little food, curfew and of course the wounded and dead. The people were relieved to find that the enemy was humane as the wounded were treated, the homeless cared for and medical supplies provided. Looting was minimal and support was provided to rebuild Schumann's Mill.

For the British the battle at Rethem was a most unpleasant surprise. It must have appeared that the Germans facing XII Corps were incapable of mounting a cohesive defence, and this impression would have been reinforced by the relative ease with which the Weser was crossed. Whilst I would wish to avoid being accused of wisdom through hindsight, it is nonetheless difficult to understand why the Welsh persisted in mounting this series of single battalion, frontal attacks against what was so clearly a strong defence. What is puzzling is not the confident way in which the advance to the Aller was conducted, nor 1/5 Welch's first attempts to roll over the enemy, for these actions can be explained by the over-riding need to push on and the initial lack of intelligence about the enemy, but rather the subsequent fixation for frontal attacks. The knowledge of how to assault an enemy-held town should not have been lacking as the division had cleared 's-Hertogenbosch in a most successful operation the previous autumn. Although the operation against the Dutch town was a much bigger undertaking and had employed the completed division, the principle of multiple attacks to probe the perimeter for weak points could still have been employed at Rethem.

German accounts of the battle describe the attacks being mounted using tactics based on irritation and are critical of the British failure to employ armour and infantry correctly, with a preference for mounting attacks over exposed ground. Perhaps the British persevered with these tactics because they had become so accustomed to the rapid advance and overcoming German forces displaying little or no determination. Such tactics, acceptable in a fluid advance against a weak and withdrawing enemy, are inappropriate against an enemy in a reasonably well-prepared position and with high morale. The failure at Rethem was a bitter reminder to the British that despite the appearance of collapse, the fighting qualities of the German soldier could never be taken for granted.

Little would seem to have been learnt from the succession of 1/5 Welch's failed attacks and this battalion's repeated frontal assaults, all from the same general direction, have a flavour of the First World War. Once this battalion was exhausted and the battle handed to 160th Brigade, the subsequent attack still employed a single infantry battalion, using an obvious approach over open ground and attempting to break into Rethem in an area where the defence was strongest. None of 1/5 Welch's bitter lessons seem to have been heeded and no attempts were made to probe or reconnoitre the German defences to determine any weak points. The length of the approach used by 2 Mons dissipated the shock effect of the fire support, particularly from the Typhoon attack, and the Germans were allowed time to recover. As the strength and determination of the enemy was quite apparent, it is puzzling why Brigadier Coleman did not make more use of his available infantry either to attack Rethem from more than one direction or to add greater weight to the attack. Additional infantry were available in the presence of 6 RWF, conveniently placed in a concentration area near Anderten. Whilst this battalion had conducted the assault crossing of the Weser and had suffered some losses in the subsequent advance, it was in no way exhausted and was in an ideal position to take part in a brigade attack. The capture of Westen, allowing Rethem to be outflanked, serves to make many of the attacks appear even less necessary.

The employment of Crocodile flame-throwing tanks would undoubtedly have had a tremendous impact on the Germans' willingness to fight it out. Time and again these terrifying weapons had broken defences with a few squirts and they would have been ideal for clearing the marines from their foxholes and trenches on the embankment. Why they were unavailable to a division in the assault is not known. Half a squadron of Crocodiles from B Squadron 7 RTR had been allocated to 53rd Welsh Division on 7 April but the 7 RTR War Diary shows them suddenly being re-allocated on 10 April to 52nd Lowland Division, the day that 53rd Welsh crossed the Weser and struck off into the unknown. They were returned to the division on 11 April but too late for them to play a part in the battle for Rethem. It is also not known why Wasps were not employed by 2 Mons in place of the Crocodiles. It can only be assumed that they were either considered too vulnerable, or were thought to be superfluous due to the presence of 5 RTR's tanks.

The lack of tank/infantry cooperation has been mentioned and it is interesting to note that at no point in B Company 2 Mons' account of the battle to capture the railway embankment was a tank referred to, despite there being a troop under command. It seems that the tanks and the infantry fought separate battles and the attack foundered as a consequence. Despite some gallant acts, both battalions' attacks lacked resolve. The stimulus to push home the attacks was not there and it is likely that there were more casualties as a consequence. Although military history is studded with examples of attacks pressed home with determination against seemingly impossible odds[2] resulting in very low casualty rates, the loss of leaders due to the savage fighting in the Reichswald the previous winter and the natural concern of every soldier not to become a casualty with the war's end so close, were undoubtedly contributory factors in the failure of the attacks.

General Dempsey in an address to the division after the Surrender said these words about the battle for Rethem.

'You fought like tigers and by winning the battle as you did you opened the way for the 2nd Army to get straight through to the Elbe and so to the Baltic. I have placed this last battle of yours very high; it was a most decisive victory.'

The capture of Rethem and the eventual securing of a bridgehead on the Aller right bank certainly opened the way for the 2nd Army, but it would appear that the real victors of Rethem were the marines of Mar.Gren.Rgt.5 who repelled all attacks, achieved 48 hours' delay and withdrew in good order with the bridge blown. It was however a Pyrrhic victory for the regiment had suffered severe losses. The final words on the Rethem battle belong to Sergeant Stimpson.

'When I walked into Rethem with Sergeant Ted Lines, I saw by far the largest amount of dead and wounded British soldiers that I had ever seen. As a Regular soldier I was in a tank crew in C Squadron 5 RTR from the day the war started to the day it ended and I never left the Regiment for a single day, so the significance of that scene is all the more terrible. I thought I had seen it all.

'Although it can never be compared with the larger battles of the war, a fair sized battle involving heavy fighting took place but it never made the headlines; in fact it has hardly warranted a mention.'[3]

The two Welsh battalions lost over 230 men killed, wounded and missing during these two April days, with the vast majority coming from 1/5 Welch.

Although Mar.Gren.Rgt.5 had been forced out of Rethem, further south the marines were still fiercely resisting 11th Armoured Division's bridgehead on the Aller's right bank. During the night of 11-12 April a squadron of Comet tanks from A Squadron 3 RTR had been ferried across the river on a Class 40 raft, together with 4 KSLI who were ferried across in assault boats by the commandos. The rifle companies of 1 Cheshire also crossed the river, upstream of the Essel road bridge, when they found some lock gates combined with a footbridge which had remained undemolished. The battalion then took up defensive positions in the area of the hamlet of Engehausen where it blocked any possible attacks on the bridgehead from the east. Whilst these forces reinforced the bridgehead, the Sappers began to build a bridge as quickly as possible to allow the remainder of 11th Armoured to cross when the time was ripe.

The Germans had also taken advantage of the cover of night to bring up new forces to continue to seal the bridgehead. These forces were moved forward from Hademstorf to blocking positions to cover the left flank and the central sector of the bridgehead. To seal the left flank and the road leading north-west out of the bridgehead towards the village of Hademstorf, the Germans returned to ground previously held by the commandos and began to dig in. Kompanie 1./2 moved from Hademstorf, where it had retired the day before after the abortive attack with the self-propelled guns, to reoccupy positions along the railway embankment south of the road; whilst Kompanie 5./12 of the SS battalion, last met in the action at Husum and which had been recuperating in the woods north-west of the bridgehead, was brought forward to hold a blocking position on a knoll on the north side of the road. The other two SS companies, 1 and 7, moved into the thick pine forests to block the northern sector. Responsibility for blocking the main road leading to the north was given to a lone Tiger tank. This tank, F02 commanded by Unteroffizier Franzen, had been part of Major Schulze's force of tanks which had mounted the counter-attack on the Petershagen bridgehead some six days before. Franzen had managed to return to Fallingbostel after this action to have a new clutch fitted to F02 and had then been ordered to move to the Essel battle.

Three members of 3 Commando were fortunate to escape being murdered by the SS on this day. CSM Macnaughton, Lance Sergeant Hill and Trooper McPhilbin had gone to a house 60 yards forward of their company's position to make tea for the wounded. When they were in the building they heard German voices and looking out saw that the house was surrounded; they hid their weapons and hoped their presence would be overlooked. This was not to be as a burly SS sergeant and two soldiers burst in, captured them and took them to an officer. One of the party understood German and heard the officer order them to be taken away and shot. They were led away by a single

140

escort. Fortunately they walked into a friendly artillery barrage which so unnerved their young escort that they were able to convince him to surrender to them instead. The party then sneaked back through the woods to the British positions, with the escort retaining his rifle, unloaded for appearance sake.

In the early morning of 12 April, 45 and 46 (RM) Commandos were ordered to sweep back through the woods as far as the railway bridge to clear the enemy who had reinfiltrated into this area. No 45 (RM) Commando advanced on the right of the road and 46 between the road and the river. Whilst still short of their objective, both commandos came under very heavy fire and their advance bogged down. For two hours a bitter fire-fight raged with the commandos finding it extremely difficult to engage the Germans effectively due to their excellent camouflage uniforms and the thickness of the woods. Despite an attack by Typhoons on the German positions, it was clear that without more detailed information on their defences further advance was hopeless and the brigade commander ordered both commandos to withdraw to the line of the drainage canal.

Whilst the two commandos fought it out on the left flank, A Squadron 3 RTR with A and D Companies 4 KSLI prepared to break out of the bridgehead up the axis, the main road which led away to the north-east. Initially their advance went well and the group secured their first objective. However, Unteroffizier Franzen and his Tiger had now reached the battle and it suddenly emerged to rumble down the road and engage and destroy the static British forces. An A Squadron Comet and the scout car belonging to 4 KSLI's commanding officer were knocked out in quick succession and the British were forced to scatter into the woods for cover. A PIAT party stalked the Tiger and managed to hit it twice, but the armour was too thick and Franzen and his crew, after prematurely abandoning the tank, returned on board and drove it back to safety. With the German defence strong in this direction too, the British armour withdrew to leaguer for the night near the river whilst the infantrymen dug in to hold the perimeter. The British were still unsure of the whereabouts of Mar.Gren.Rgt.6 and VIII Corps felt that the resistance at Essel was greater than could have been expected from Mar.Füs.Btl.2 alone and that the grenadier regiment was probably also involved; there was also continuing uncertainty about the whereabouts of the Hitler Youth battalion. Despite the problems at Essel, VIII Corps achieved success on 12 April with 15th Scottish Division's capture of Celle and the completion of a Class 40 bridge there over the Aller.

In marked contrast to all this activity, a seemingly unimportant event took place on 12 April in 11th Armoured Division's area which was soon to lead to an event of worldwide notoriety, totally overshadowing the military operations. An Oberst Schmidt, who was the liaison officer at the Hungarian armour training school at Bergen, arrived at the Aller bridge at Winsen bearing a flag of truce. Schmidt had been despatched to act as an emissary from Himmler to negotiate a neutral zone around the concentration camp at Belsen which contained some 60,000 inmates, amongst whom typhus had broken out. Schmidt was despatched back to Headquarters VIII Corps to present the German terms. As these were deemed unacceptable, the Brigadier General Staff of VIII Corps, Brigadier Fitzgeorge-Balfour, went across the lines to the headquarters of Armeegruppe Blumentritt to present counter-proposals which required, inter alia, for the Germans to withdraw about five miles north of the defined neutral zone. It was now the turn of the Germans to reject the proposals as they pointed out that such a withdrawal would force them to withdraw from Rethem since their position there would be completely outflanked. Although the Germans were tactically correct for the Rethem area as a whole, it reveals how poor the passage of information for them had become as the town had already fallen by the time these discussions took place. Modified proposals were finally agreed and the true horror of the camp would be discovered three days later.

NOTES

1   Ted Lines had a narrow brush with death a week after this photograph was taken when his Sherman was hit and brewed by three anti-tank rounds near the village of Bispingen. Ted escaped unhurt but the three other members of his crew all received burns to the face and hands. The details of this action were also recorded in the survey by the two RAMC captains. The entry for the attack on Ted Lines' tank recorded that there was one oblique penetration into the extreme left-hand side of the front final drive which disintegrated the gear box; a similar penetration on the top of the hull front just below the hinge of the driver's hatch; and a scoop on the turret roof. The tank burst into flames and the crew promptly abandoned it.

2   For example, 2 Para's attack on the Argentinean forces at Goose Green in 1982.

3   In Montgomery's book *From Normandy to the Baltic*, the fighting on the Aller was described in two and a half lines thus: 'There was further resistance east of the river (Weser), where SS elements with 88 millimetre guns on railway mountings temporarily checked 53 Division at Rethem.'

10

ACROSS THE ALLER
12–13 APRIL

On the evening of Wednesday 11 April Lieutenant Colonel Frisby, Commanding Officer of 4 Welch, was ordered by Brigadier Wilsey to establish that same night a small bridgehead on the right bank of the Aller in the Westen area with a view to a possible crossing in strength the next day. A platoon-sized force despatched in assault boats made its way across with some difficulty as the swirling flood waters made navigating the cumbersome craft a less than easy operation. The current was very powerful and the platoon commander advised that a guide rope would be needed as crossing under paddle-power alone was too hazardous an operation. Once safely on the enemy-held bank the platoon pushed patrols forward which met no opposition and the platoon commander was able to report back that all was clear. Armed with this encouraging information, Brigadier Wilsey now ordered 1 E Lan R to be prepared to move from Hämelhausen to Westen and then to conduct an assault river crossing during the remainder of the night. At 2215 hours General Ross confirmed that Plan B was to be implemented and soon after the battalion started a night march across the open heathland of the Hämelheide. Although it was not an easy move, with the night pitch black and the tracks inadequate and nearly invisible, the battalion arrived at Westen at 0100 hours on Thursday 12 April in good order despite the night's difficulties.

The quality of the German forces which would have to counter a crossing of the northern reaches of the Aller was far from uniform. Vizeadmiral Scheurlen had allocated his main combat strength to cover the likely crossing points at Rethem and Essel, and he had committed his third regiment to defend the town of Verden. Whilst Verden had not formally been given Festung (Fortress) status, as a major town and crossing point he would have been compelled to defend it. The force allocated to its defence was known as Kampfgruppe Verden. The Kampfgruppe was commanded by Kapitän zur See Neitzel, Commander Mar.Gren.Rgt.7, and the majority of its strength was found from the two marine battalions of his own regiment and a regiment of artillery recruits from 480.Division, Art.Ausb.u.Ers.Rgt.22, also known as Regiment Schaffer after its commander. Regiment Schaffer was supposedly the provider of 480.Division's artillery support but it would appear that as it either had no guns or no ammunition it was deployed as infantry. It consisted of two battalion-sized units – Abteilung 11 (Kampfgruppe Tebener) of four companies, and Abteilung 22 (Kampfgruppe Hornemann) of three. Schaffer's regiment had been detached from the remainder of 480.Division located in the area between Verden and Bremen, and moved to join Neitzel's forces in Verden. Additional strength for Kampfgruppe Verden was provided by a number of miscellaneous units: the remnants of the Hungarian artillery training battalion Ungarisch Art.Ausb.Btl.7, which had performed so dismally at Westen two days previously; a Luftwaffe battalion of three companies entitled Btl. Blinzler; a Flak Abteilung with the name Hundertmark; and a 120-strong tank destroyer company of Hitler Youth with the imposing title HJ Pz.Löwe (Tank Lion) Kompanie 3. This last group had only been in existence for a day or so and was formed from Hitler Youth from the Hannover region.

Neitzel's Kampfgruppe was numerically strong, being the equivalent of 28 infantry companies, and had the support of 20 8.8cm and 20 2cm Flak guns. However, despite this strength, Neitzel was hamstrung by the requirement to hold the bulk of his Kampfgruppe in the area of Verden, where lack of mobility would prevent prompt reaction if the British threatened to cross the Aller anywhere else.

By 11 April the British points of main effort at Rethem and Essel had become clearly defined and Kapitän zur See Hartmann now ordered a number of redeployments to counter the even stronger enemy attacks that were likely to follow at these points. In Divisional Operation Order No 6 he ordered Mar.Gren.Rgt.7 to assume responsibility for the right bank of the Aller sector as far south as Hülsen, as well as retaining responsibility for the defence of the Verden area. For the former purpose a Kampfgruppe Aller was to be created from Neitzel's forces in the Verden area. The Kampfgruppe to be despatched was based on Hornemann's Abteilung 22 with the following under command: Ungarisch Art.Ausb.Btl.7; companies Bergholz and Bormann (from Hornemann's own command); Kompanie 13./7; a cyclist platoon from Mar.Gren.Rgt.7; and half of HJ Pz.Löwe Kompanie 3. The Kampfgruppe was given written orders by Kapitän zur See Neitzel to defend the line of the Aller between Barnstedt and Hülsen so that, 'any enemy crossing the river will be attacked and destroyed'. As the Hungarian battalion was already in place on the right bank opposite Westen, Hornemann ordered it to, 'hold the position at all costs'. This order was somewhat over-pitched as the Hungarians were very low quality troops, with one German account contemptuously describing them as 'peasants'; and empty exhortations such as this were a familiar cliché to the German soldier of 1945. With the area opposite Westen likely to be a point of enemy main effort, it seems puzzling why the worst troops, who had already fled once from battle, were not reinforced earlier. In a half-hearted attempt to speed the thickening of the defences opposite Westen, a troop from Abteilung 22 was deployed ahead of the main body to join the Hungarians. The divisional order required the regrouping to be started at once and completion had to be by 0400 hours on Thursday 12 April.

Back on the left bank, British preparations for the assault crossing continued through the night. On their arrival in Westen, the 1 E Lan R company commanders were due at battalion headquarters at 0130 hours to check up on details of the plan. It was so dark however that companies had some difficulty in finding their appointed assembly areas. There was also some delay in assembling the assault boats and to allow for this H-Hour, which had been fixed for 0200 hours, was postponed until 0300 hours. As the Aller at Westen was about 90 yards wide with a very strong current, the crossing was not expected to be without some difficulty and it was therefore planned that initially the assault would be on a narrow front and silent - at least for the first two companies. A very tight bridgehead was to be secured and held for the remaining hours of darkness after which the battalion would advance at first light to its objective, the village of Otersen. The rifle companies were to cross in the order A, B, C then D, with battalion headquarters crossing with A Company. Support Company with rear battalion headquarters under the second-in-command, Major Griffin, was to provide the defence of the crossing site and the administrative arrangements. The operation eventually got underway and the first boats from A Company were successfully launched and began to cross, carrying guide ropes to be fixed in position on the far bank. The current was very strong and when the boats were a few yards away from the bank they were rapidly swept downstream. The crews had great difficulty in handling their boats in the darkness and made quite a lot of noise, but after a while they succeeded in reaching the far bank undetected and only 110 yards off their intended course. A further long delay now occurred owing to difficulties in establishing ferry posts and the guide ropes. This took so long that when the first streaks of dawn came, the boat party began to look very exposed and the two platoons which were safely across, very vulnerable. Luckily there was no reaction from the enemy as the Hungarians had presumably failed to establish patrols to observe the river. Fortunately for 1 E Lan R, the decision to implement Plan B during the night of 11-12 April allowed them to secure an initial bridgehead before the bulk of Hornemann's Kampfgruppe arrived.

When B Company began to cross just after dawn, the Hungarians who by now had become aware that something was afoot, started to snipe at movement on the launching site, although evidently still not realising that there was a full-scale crossing under way before their eyes. Their initial weak reaction allowed A and B Company plus the advanced battalion headquarters to tuck themselves away into a small bridgehead on the far bank. C Company was next to cross, and Lieutenant Arthur Sutton, who was then commanding 15 Platoon, describes the difficulties experienced both crossing the river and in the bridgehead.

'Our turn came and I was in the leading boat of C Company. The men had loosened their belts and pack straps, had unslung their rifles and were kneeling in the boat. I took a firm hold on the guide rope and hung-on for dear life. The current was very strong. When we reached half-way we were fired on by rifles and machine-guns, but the aim was high and the bullets cracked above us. Our luck held and we landed safely and took up position under the river bank. It was a very tight little bridgehead and now that the enemy was well alerted a very nasty spot to be in. Movement of any sort was impossible without drawing fire and we knew it was not going to be easy to get out of this muddy hole. First light was also coming fast which added a further hazard and we deployed as best we could along the bank in support of A and B Companies.'

The ground on the far bank was generally flat with open fields and hedgerows. As there were slight undulations and therefore some cover on the right flank, A Company, commanded by Major Whiteside, was able to make progress. Fairly stiff opposition was met but the company succeeded in getting forward along the path leading to a cross-tracks about half a mile from the river. There the platoons were pinned down by fire and superior numbers and although Major Whiteside tried several times to start a new attack, A Company could do little until B Company could come up later on their left. B Company, commanded by Major Storey, had been held up by a series of mutually supporting machine-gun positions on the left flank. It took some time to deal with them and the company lost Lieutenant Merills, a platoon commander, and the CSM, WO2 Potts, in so doing. Whilst A and B Companies were trying to advance, D Company started to cross at 0700 hours and it was now that disaster struck. With the crossing site under continuous enfilade fire, Lieutenant Kershaw and two sections of 18 Platoon embarked on the first boat and began to cross. Arthur Sutton describes what took place.

'D Company started to cross and it was then that I had a "worms eye" of a most tragic event. Suddenly the lead D Company boat lost contact with the guide rope and was swept past us in mid-stream. As some occupants stood up the boat capsized and in seconds the entire crew were in the water and went down at once. Only two soldiers managed to reach the bank on our side. I can only surmise that the party had not been prepared as we had been for such an event and had been dragged down by the weight of their equipment. This was most demoralizing for us all, but we had our own worries!'

Despite this disaster, in which 13 drowned, the remainder of D Company crossed safely. C Company then started to move forward behind A and B Companies and after a short time the Hungarians in the cross-tracks area were sufficiently subdued to enable A and B Companies to advance south-east towards Otersen. C Company then took over and held the cross-tracks while D Company worked forward on the extreme left flank clearing away the enemy still holding out there. By 1200 hours A and B Companies had fought their way forward to Otersen, where their advance was then halted by a heavy weight of fire from the village's defenders. The remainder of the battalion followed, mopping up and capturing some 65 Hungarians in the process. Whilst 1 E Lan R expanded the bridgehead, Brigadier Wilsey ordered the next battalion, 7 RWF, to cross the river and it subsequently made rapid progress during the early part of the morning, leap-frogging the companies past each other as they advanced towards their objective, the village of Wittlohe, experiencing only isolated sniper fire whilst they did so.

With 1 E Lan R and 7 RWF fighting to enlarge and secure a bridgehead, the sappers of 555 Field Company RE began building a 360-foot Class 9 folding boat bridge. This type of bridge was composed of canvas and wood boats, which could be folded for transportation, with a trackway superstructure. The equipment was rather delicate and could expect to be out of action for 8 hours in every 24 for maintenance. Notwithstanding these limitations, they were effective bridges and were quick to construct. The Westen bridge was completed by 1230 hours and seven minutes later the first Wasp crossed. The Germans, realising that a full-scale crossing was in progress, and that it threatened to split the forces in the north from the rest of the division, now began to move reinforcements to the area in an attempt to contain the bridgehead. Kampfgruppe Tebener's Abteilung 11, the second Abteiung from Regiment Schaffer, was now moved to seal any breakout to the north whilst other reinforcements, from 480.Division, also began to move from further afield. Gren.Ausb.u.Ers.Rgt.22 with two of its four battalions, 16 and 489, Gren.Ausb.u.Ers.Rgt.269 with its battalions 47 and 65 together with Pi.Btl.34, were all ordered to move towards the bridgehead.

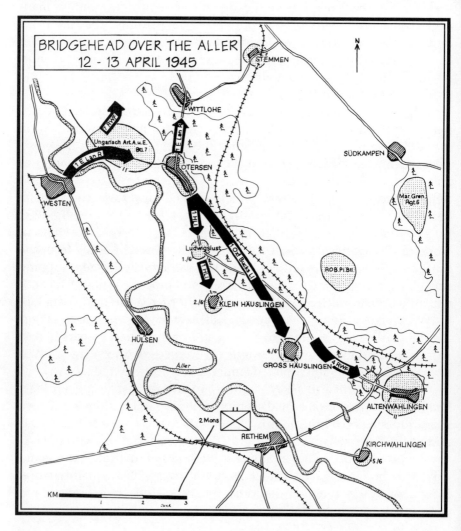

Whilst the Germans were redeploying, A and B Companies 1 E Lan R fought their way into Otersen. The village was held by approximately a platoon of artillery recruits from Abteilung 22./22, commanded by an Oberwachtmeister, and marines from the regimental company 14./7 who had moved on foot from Verden to the village during the night. Major Whiteside led A Company in the house-clearing operations and established a firm base in the northern end. B Company then cleared to the southern exits. Eleven Germans and one Hungarian were killed during the battle for Otersen, with the remainder withdrawing to the north.

The near total collapse of the German reinforcement system by April 1945 is illustrated by the experiences of an artillery Hauptmann named Richard Lange. Lange had been the regimental adjutant of an artillery regiment in Russia until being badly wounded in June 1944. He was evacuated to a hospital in Germany and was then sent to convalesce in his home town of Verden. As the front drew nearer he reported to Regiment Schaffer and was ordered on the morning of 12 April to take over command of one of the batteries. Neither Lange nor the regimental headquarters knew where the battery was so he set off on foot towards the Aller to find it. He eventually reached Otersen only to see groups of British soldiers where Hungarians should have been and narrowly avoided capture. Back-tracking, he found his battery in the southern part of Hohenaverbergen and thereafter fought with the gunners until being captured a few days later when Verden fell.

Both the 1 E Lan R companies involved in the capture of Otersen had battled forward continuously since dawn and had received many casualties in overcoming a numerically superior defence. Whilst they consolidated in Otersen, D Company moved up the road which led north from the northern exit of the village and placed itself in position half-way to the next village, Wittlohe. Sniping was still widespread and the commanding officer's scout car was shot up on this road, fortunately without loss. During the early afternoon D Company 7 RWF passed through the 1 E Lan R companies to assault Wittlohe. This village was held by a platoon of recently arrived artillery recruits of Kampfgruppe Teberer, who had hastily prepared defensive positions in the farms, houses and gardens. A brisk engagement ensued which was observed by Arthur Sutton.

'A lot of sniping and noise, there were some casualties and the enemy were dashing about the village blazing away at everything. The place finally was cleared and we when we later made ourselves secure in the village, in the house I occupied I found a map of the Bremen area marked by the enemy with the German positions during the battle.'

Although there was still some sniping from isolated groups along the main roads and tracks, organised opposition in the area had ceased by mid-afternoon on Thursday 12 April and the Aller bridgehead was firmly established. At 1430 hours 1/5 Welch, which was still reduced to three companies, began to cross to occupy positions in defence of the bridge and by 1830 hours had formed a defensive arc from west of Wittlohe to the Aller's bank. The 7 RWF companies spent the remainder of the day expanding the northern flank of the bridgehead, but not without loss. D Company sent a platoon to investigate a road-block on the main road to the north of Wittlohe, as they approached the platoon ran into a volley of machine-gun and small-arms fire which left two dead and three wounded.

During the course of the afternoon B and C Squadrons of 53rd Recce Regiment crossed the Aller and began to push out into the wooded country beyond Otersen and Wittlohe. The crossing of the Class 9 bridge at Westen was no easy matter for the recce troops as Norman Mitchell, who was the gunner/radio operator in 3 Troop commander's armoured car, describes.

'As I recall there was considerable delay prior to C Squadron being able to cross the Class 9 Bridge at Westen due to the difficulty of the bridging operation. It was only a pontoon type bridge and only one vehicle at a time was allowed to cross. The heavy armoured cars had to proceed extremely carefully and with only the driver on board. The Assault Troop, with its International half-tracks, was left behind as the vehicles were too heavy to cross the bridge.'

The task of the Recce was now to move up to the bridgehead line and then probe forward to discover the enemy's whereabouts. By nightfall they had pushed forward to the outer edges of Otersen and Wittlohe but as nothing more could now be observed and there was a real risk of being caught by enemy patrols in the wooded country, the squadrons went firm for the remainder of the night. As we will be frequently encountering the Recce in this chapter it might be useful to describe how the recce squadrons were organised and operated. The recce squadron had three scout troops, each consisting of two elements – armoured cars and carriers – and an assault troop. In the scout troop besides the troop leader's Humber armoured car, there were two patrols, each of a Humber and Daimler armoured car and both commanded by a sergeant. The seven carriers were commanded by a subaltern whilst the assault troop was carried in M5 half-tracks and was, in essence, an infantry platoon. In the advance a scout troop would normally operate initially on one road with the cars moving ahead of the carriers. The carriers would form a strongpoint as a base for the cars and would then move by bounds from firm base to firm base. The squadron could operate with its three troops on separate roads, or with two up and one in reserve. The assault troop would be used for reconnaissance on foot where cars could not go or for other special tasks. By night the carrier crews would dismount and lead the advance supported by the cars moving closely behind them. Squadron headquarters would usually be some miles behind the lead troops but the squadron leader would normally be found forward in his Daimler.

Operations on 12 April closed for 158th Infantry Brigade with the divisional bridgehead successfully secured, with 1 E Lan R defending its eastern flank from the villages of Otersen and Wittlohe and 7 RWF, which had pushed round to the open country to the north, defending the northern. A total of 331 prisoners had been taken, mainly well-armed Hungarians who protested emphatically that they always shot high to indicate their distaste for conscription into the German Army. Despite their claims, nine soldiers of 1 E Lan R were killed and 26 wounded by small-arms fire during the course of the day. The last word on these Hungarian soldiers should go to the author of XII Corps' War Diary who scathingly dismissed them by noting that, 'these gunners in theory appear to have been pioneers in fact, a not inappropriate fate for the representatives of a kingless kingdom until recently ruled by a fleetless admiral'.[1] Notwithstanding these words, the infantry brigade was lucky that the crossing was achieved whilst Kampfgruppe Hornemann was still arriving. Even though the majority of the troops in the area were Hungarian, had there been time to organise counter-attacks then even these low-quality troops could have made the success of Plan B a far tougher proposition.

Whilst 158th Infantry Brigade fought to secure the bridgehead, 71st Infantry Brigade, commanded by Brigadier Elrington, had been moving up to execute Phase 2 of the divisional plan, the advance south down the right bank of the Aller. Although 158th and 160th Brigades had been heavily committed during 10 and 11 April, the uncommitted 71st Infantry Brigade had been moving up to the Weser so that it would be correctly placed for any subsequent exploitation. Brigadier Elrington's orders for operations on the right bank involved the brigade waiting for

158th Infantry Brigade to secure the Aller bridgehead before crossing and advancing south down the right bank. Although this manoeuvre had been originally designed to outflank the marines in Rethem and force their withdrawal, by 12 April Jordan's force had of course already pulled back to the right bank during the previous night.

On 12 April divisional headquarters ordered the brigade to cross the Weser at Hoya and at 1215 hours the lead elements of the brigade group began to cross to move to a concentration area near Westen. During the late afternoon of Thursday 12 April, led by A Squadron 53rd Recce Regiment, the brigade crossed the Class 9 folding boat bridge at Westen in the order 1st Battalion the Oxfordshire and Bucking-hamshire Light Infantry (1 Oxf Bucks LI), 1st Battalion the Highland Light Infantry (1 HLI), followed by 4 RWF. The brigade advance was initially on a two battalion frontage with 1 Oxf Bucks LI on the left, and 1 HLI on the right. Having crossed the river, both battalions began to move southwards following the axis of the road. The brigade plan was for 1 Oxf Bucks LI to capture Gross Häuslingen and 1 HLI to capture Klein Häuslingen, to allow 4 RWF to pass through them to capture Altenwahlingen. With the right bank opposite Rethem securely in British hands, bridging operations to re-establish Route 209 over the Aller could start.

Up until 11 April, the German forces located on the Aller's right bank opposite Rethem had been widely dispersed. Mar.Gren.Rgt.6 as the divisional reserve had been given responsibility for the area and its companies had been spread between Klein Häuslingen and Böhme, a frontage of some 10 miles. To give it additional manpower the engineer officer cadets of ROB-Pi.Btl.Nienburg had been placed under regimental command and positioned in depth on Route 209 at Kirchboitzen. On 11 April Divisional Operation Order No. 6 ordered the regiment to concentrate and hold itself in readiness in the area between the Häuslingens and Altenwahlingen to destroy any enemy forces attempting to bypass Rethem, as it was clear that a British breakthrough was likely in this area. Bataillon I./6, commanded by Korvettenkapitän Melzer, held the area of the twin villages of Gross and Klein Häuslingen whilst Bataillon II./6, commanded by Korvettenkapitän Meincke, held the Altenwahlingen area. Melzer's marines were deployed with Kompanie 1./6 at Ludwigslust, Kompanie 2./6 at Klein Häuslingen, Kompanie 3./6 in the area of the crossroads to the north-west of Altenwahlingen and Kompanie 4./6 in Gross Häuslingen. During the early hours of 12 April, these companies were joined by the battle-weary marines of Mar.Gren.Rgt.5 who had pulled out of Rethem during the night. With the British forces across the river, the marines on the right bank braced themselves for the next phase of the battle of the Aller Line.

Led by A Squadron 53rd Recce Regiment, 71st Brigade's advance initially went well and no opposition was met until the recce troops hit positions held by marines armed with Panzerfausts near the hamlet of Ludwigslust. A short but vicious skirmish to eliminate these men from Kompanie 1./6 then began. Whilst this action to clear the axis was in progress, 1 Oxf Bucks LI bypassed Kompanie 1./6 and A and B Companies, the leading companies, made good progress until they were about a mile from the village of Gross Häuslingen when they came under intense if inaccurate machine-gun fire. The village and surrounding area was held by marines from Kompanie 4./6 who had taken up defensive positions in the houses and surrounding woods. It proved very difficult to locate the enemy positions in the broken scrub country and for a time the situation was obscure. A Company attempted to outflank the opposition by manoeuvring to the left but this was unsuccessful and the battalion's advance came to a halt. The battalion was by now strung out along a narrow sandy track surrounded by thick pinewoods and with very little knowledge about the enemy's whereabouts. With darkness falling and visibility vanishing fast, the position was very precarious and so the commanding officer, Lieutenant Colonel Howard, decided that the companies should hold firm where they stood and for the battalion to await the arrival of 1 HLI, which would provide a certain amount of flank security to the right.

Whilst 1 Oxf Bucks LI was experiencing problems advancing on the left flank, 1 HLI on the right had no such difficulties. The battalion had moved to a concentration area near Westen during the early afternoon and crossed the bridge later that evening, tasked to capture the hamlet of Klein Häuslingen and a prominent knoll to its south-east. The battalion plan was to attack with two companies up, A Company right, C Company left, with D Company passing through to capture the high ground; B Company was to clear the main road. The advance started at 1830 hours and although more opposition was encountered near the hamlet of Ludwigslust, the companies went forward largely unopposed to secure their objectives by 2330 hours. The battalion captured a total of 35 Hungarians during the course of the operation.

Throughout the advance both battalions received invaluable support from the Vickers machine-guns of 1 Manchester. The ground on the right bank was flat and open and was ideal for medium machine-gun fire missions. Instead of allocating the machine-gun companies to the brigades, Major General Ross placed the machine-gun companies under the centralized command of their own commanding officer, Lieutenant Colonel Crozier, to provide coordinated support for the operations to be mounted by 71st and 158th Brigades. It was clear to Lieutenant Colonel Crozier that the best support could be given by remaining on the left bank, but moving to keep pace with the flanks of the advance and shooting across the front. A Company supported the advance from positions in the Hülsen area, whilst B Company with two mortar platoons from D Company was ordered to do so from positions in Rethem. The plan worked extremely well. The companies were in position well before the advance began and surprised large numbers of Germans from Bataillon I./6 who found themselves cut off between the river and the road and had started to withdraw south. It was a perfect setting for machine-guns and it was estimated that the companies inflicted 200 to 250 casualties during the day. One of the most striking features was the clear inability of the Germans to identify the direction from which the fire was coming with the result that they continued to withdraw in the open.

With 1 Oxf Bucks LI fighting to clear its area, 1 HLI held onto the right flank in the area of Klein Häuslingen spending the day mopping up the few enemy that remained and waiting for 4 RWF to pass through it to capture Altenwahlingen, which was expected to be achieved at first light on 13 April. The 4 RWF had been detached from the brigade to secure Nienburg on 11 April but had been relieved of this task by 6 HLI and had subsequently moved by transport to concentrate in the woods a mile or so to the west of Westen. Although a lone Fw 190 dropped a single bomb in the area of battalion headquarters, the remainder of 12 April passed uneventfully. At 2320 hours the battalion began to move across the Aller, preparatory to advancing south to follow the other two battalions of the brigade. Once across, the first mile or so was covered fairly rapidly, but the advance was then held up due to the problems 1 Oxf Bucks LI was experiencing clearing the marines of Bataillon I./6 from the Gross Häuslingen area, which straddled the axis.

NOTES

1   This refers to Admiral Horthy the ex-leader of Hungary, Germany's less than reliable ally. Following his proclamation of an armistice with the Allies in October 1944, the Germans replaced Horthy with Szalasi, the leader of the ultra-nationalist 'Arrow Cross'.

11

'BRAVE AND RECKLESS FIGHTERS'
12–13 APRIL

Despite the progress that had been made on the right bank, heavy fighting now broke out again on the triangle of ground between the Weser and the Aller. It will be recalled that 4 Welch had been tasked to clear this area which was still held by marines from Mar.Gren.Rgt.7. However, the battalion's efforts to advance further north from Westen and Stedorf, which it had taken on the evening of 10 April, met very stubborn resistance from Kapitän zur See Neitzel's marines who attempted to seize some of the initiative by launching a series of small scale but violent attacks. These attacks were also designed to cover the withdrawal to Verden of other marines from Mar.Gren.Rgt.7 on the Aller left bank. A captured set of Neitzel's orders, entitled 'Regrouping of the Defences of Verden and the Aller Sector', have an air of desperation to them, not to mention a somewhat intriguing objective.

'From now on and all through the night the enemy will be attacked in his positions by small assault forces (20-30 men). During the night 12-13 April the following attacks will be carried out:
1. By assault troops of Bataillon II./7 on Stedorf.
2. By assault troops of Kompanie Klemm on Barnstedt.
3. By assault troops of Bataillon Hornemann on Wittlohe.
'The object is to deprive the English of the pleasure of sleeping at night with honourless German women and to ensure that they live in a constant state of danger and uncertainty in the villages they have occupied. No assault troops without anti-tank weapons! Vehicles, guns etc are to be blown sky-high! Anything that is found belonging to the enemy must be destroyed. Weapons: MG42, MP44, MP40, Panzerfaust and grenades. All packs will be left behind. Be as manoeuvrable and silent as possible. H-Hour approximately 0230 hours.'

This account by Major Bell, commanding D Company 4 Welch, illustrates the ferocity of the small but bitter actions that ensued against Neitzel's troops.

'On 12 April I was ordered to capture the village of Geestefeld with my company, supported by a troop of tanks. After the enemy had lost only a dozen killed they made a hasty retreat. We dug all-round defensive positions and prepared to hold it for the night. We were now some miles in front of the remainder of the battalion and the section and platoon positions could only be tied up with fire owing to the limited number of men available. Our strength was becoming slowly depleted. Night came and complete darkness fell upon the village.

'All went well until about midnight when a runner came into my headquarters with the rather shattering news that a number of the enemy had penetrated our position unseen. Half the company were on duty at the time while the other half rested in the house. The enemy had entered these houses after overpowering the sentries and had awakened the occupants with the order to put up their hands. With their weapons removed my men had no option. The situation was serious. By this time company HQ was covered by spandaus and any move brought a burst of fire. Before any action could be taken there was a series of loud bangs as the enemy started shooting up the transport and company HQ with Panzerfausts. The explosions in company HQ were deafening and the whole building was shaking and burst into flames as the assault continued. I gave instructions for company HQ to make a dash for it across an open stretch to a building 100 yards away from where we could organise one platoon not involved and attempt to restore the situation. Just at that moment the reserve ammo went up with a roar and the building started to collapse around us. We could not stay a second longer, so through the hole where a window had been we dashed to our new positions. By the light of the flames I saw my Sergeant Major dash past. He turned his head and shouted, "And I was going on leave tomorrow, Sir!".

'The situation was now getting very involved and it was difficult to tell which were enemy and which were our own men. A general free-for-all started and the enemy found themselves being attacked by unarmed men with flying fists and feet. There is no etiquette in war. It was a display of guts and courage. Simultaneously, all those who had been taken prisoner turned upon their armed captives. One private soldier, shot through the lung in getting away, turned round and re-entered the house and set upon the enemy again, paying with his life. Before long the enemy dead included their two officers, neither of whom had a bullet wound upon them, and all the enemy were learning by experience what the British soldier can do with his fists and hands. Unarmed combat instruction had not been in vain. Before long the enemy melted away leaving their dead and undoubtedly bearing many reminders of the fight. They had failed to take a single prisoner. I will not belittle them, however. They were German marines and had fought with real guts.

'At first light the Carrier Platoon arrived to give us assistance but by that time the fight was over and we had re-organised ourselves. Not a brick of my former HQ remained standing. All the transport and equipment was destroyed with the exception of the three tanks and they were only saved by beating out the flames at great risk during the fighting. The stretcher bearers had a busy time binding up the injured fists. I found myself left with only that in which I stood up. A later claim from the Army realised nearly a tenth of the value of personal kit that I had lost. It was equivalent to my having fought for some months with no pay at all. An expensive night's fighting! As far as we could ascertain, two enemy patrols each about twenty strong had slipped through our defences in the dark from two different directions.'

Members of A Squadron 5 RTR were also heavily involved in this action and the marines managed to enter the house where two crews from the tank troop supporting D Company were sleeping. Hand-to-hand fighting took place and order was only restored when Lieutenant Jones, the troop commander, killed the marine officer leading the patrol. The marines involved in this fierce action were from Bataillon II./7 who had been ordered to attack Stedorf. It is assumed that they attacked Geestefeld instead either as an opportunity target or perhaps as a result of the fog of war. Notwithstanding the lively time being experienced by 4 Welch, the other two battalions of 160th Brigade had a relatively quiet day on 12 April. In the early hours of the morning 6 RWF had been warned to move two companies to take over the positions held by 1/5 Welch to the west of Rethem so that battalion could move up to the Westen area to support 158th Brigade's operation. At 0327 hours A and B Companies set off from the Anderten area arriving at their new locations at 0840 hours, having had to divert via Eystrup due to a blown bridge.

Meanwhile, back in Rethem, the Brigade's third infantry battalion, 2 Mons, had been mopping up the town and its environs with the support of 5 RTR and at 1240 hours the battalion was able to report that the town was clear. At 1415 hours 2 Mons despatched a second recce patrol across the Aller to report on the state of Route 209 and the whereabouts of the enemy. The patrol had a busy time. Accompanied by some sappers, it first visited a culvert which passed under the road some 200 yards from the river. This they found to have been thoroughly demolished and a 50 foot gap created. The patrol next checked a bridge where the road crossed a large pond; this was found to be intact. The last task was to check the bridge over an ox-bow lake at Rethemer Fähre; not only was this bridge found to be demolished, but the patrol was also engaged with machine-gun fire from the marines of Kompanie 3./6 who were in the nearby woods and buildings. From their final position, the members of the patrol had been able to see activity and possible defensive positions in the fields south of Gross Häuslingen and on the return journey they were shot at from Kirchwahlingen and the fields north of Route 209. It was clear to the divisional planners that due to the two demolitions, Route 209 in the immediate bridgehead would not be able to support the advance once the Aller was crossed and that an alternative axis would have to be found. Bridging operations at Rethem had however already started during the early evening of 12 April when 2 Platoon of 244th Field Company began to prepare the home bank for bridging. At 2000 hours 1 Platoon offloaded the bridging equipment with 3 Platoon joining them at 2200 hours. However, the bridgehead had not been secured on the far bank and this naturally made the sappers vulnerable to enemy interference. At 2300 hours the lack of security was remedied by 2 Mons who despatched a platoon across the river. The need for security was fully justified, for in clearing the house which overlooked the site, an officer and six marines were captured. During the night the site was shelled but fortunately the accuracy was very erratic, probably due to the capture of the party of marines who were controlling the fire, and no casualties or damage were caused.

Whilst the marines of 2.Marine Infanterie Division had been fighting and dying in bitter and desperate battles to hold their ground, on 12 April the bizarre world of the Führer conferences had been continuing. On this day Admiral Wagner, Dönitz's representative, received a report from Reichsleiter Bormann concerning alleged insubordination from members of the division when it was in Itzehoe. The unspecified complaint had been made by the Landrat of Itzehoe. Wagner replied that the report had proved invalid and that Dönitz wished Bormann to take steps against the originator of the report. With their soldiers dying in futile battles, the petty point-scoring between the leaders of the Third Reich in its death throes continued unabated.

We had left 1 Oxf Bucks LI trying to clear the enemy from the brigade axis so that 4 RWF could move through to attack Altenwahlingen and complete 71st Brigade's operation. The companies of 1 Oxf

Bucks LI eventually began to overcome the opposition from Bataillon I./6 in the Gross Häuslingen area and by midnight had been able to start moving forward once again. During the early hours of Friday 13 April, A Company attempted to capture the small pinewood which lay to the east of the main road. This attack was unsuccessful against the marines of Kompanie 4./6 and so the company outflanked the wood by moving round to its left and established itself in another small wood to its south-east. C Company meanwhile had secured the area of the triangle of roads between the main road and Gross Häuslingen allowing D Company to pass through and capture the village unopposed by 0045 hours. B Company completed the final manoeuvre of this phase by moving up through C Company to secure the houses which straggled along the main road. This resulted in a certain amount of small-arms fire from the marines holding the houses but they were quickly subdued by calling down a concentration of artillery fire from 72nd Medium Regiment RA. During the rest of the night there were no signs of enemy activity and the companies consolidated in the positions they had gained.

However, the remainder of the night's relative peace in 71st Brigade's area soon ended as dawn broke on Friday 13 April. Although it had been thought that the enemy had been cleared from the area, small pockets of marines and isolated snipers were found scattered throughout B and C Company 1 Oxf Bucks LI's positions and a strong-point of platoon strength was discovered near C Company's headquarters in the centre of a triangle of roads. The 4 RWF, which was supposed to have taken Altenwahlingen by first light, was now again held up by the confused fighting in the Gross Häuslingen area. Confusion reigned for much of 13 April as both battalions attempted to clear the opposition. At 0730 hours the leading 4 RWF companies were ordered to push on towards their start line, the crossroads half a mile to the west of Altenwahlingen. To do this B Company 4 RWF, with C Company following up behind it, had to mount an attack to force its way forward. The area of the crossroads was held by Kompanie 3./6 and as soon as the two companies came within range the marines opened up immediately with intense machine-gun fire and the attack ground to a halt. With mounting casualties, the soldiers of B Company were pinned down by fire from both flanks, despite some of the battalion's carriers moving forward to provide a measure of protected fire support. The battalion's problems were exacerbated by a split developing between the two lead companies and the rear companies which were still back in the area of Gross Häuslingen and caught up in renewed fighting in that area. The attack to clear Kompanie 3./6 from the area of the crossroads lost momentum and the ensuing delay forced an indefinite postponement of the attack's H-Hour on Altenwahlingen. Although the attack had been delayed, the village was not spared and during the course of the morning it was subjected to harassing fire as a preliminary softening-up. At 0900 hours 60 4.2in mortar bombs were fired at it by 13 and 15 Platoons of 1 Manchester followed by a shoot by the Vickers guns of B Company. In the early afternoon Typhoons from No 184 Squadron, flying from B-110 strip at Achmer, also attacked the village to ensure that the marine defenders from Bataillon II./6 were given no respite.

Whilst the battalions of 71st Infantry Brigade battled to clear the right bank, 244th Field Company, reinforced with two platoons from 555th Field Company, was still engaged in bridge-building operations at Rethem. By 1430 hours all the equipment necessary had been offloaded and two rafts and 60 feet of a 110-foot Bailey pontoon bridge had been built. This type of Bailey bridge consisted of standard Bailey equipment, carried on pontoons, with special landing bay arrangements to carry the bridge from dry land to the floating bays. It was a highly versatile bridge and could be constructed to carry loads from Class 9 to Class 70 by varying the number of pontoons and girder arrangements. However, the site was now subjected to well directed artillery and mortar fire and work had to cease. Whenever the sappers started again, the Germans opened up and this eventually forced bridging operations to stop altogether. Further delay was caused when shellfire sunk one of the rafts and progress was only made after four flights of Typhoons had been called in to attack the area from where the fire was thought to originate. This brought a measure of relief for thereafter the fire was erratic and progress could be made.

During the remainder of the day B and C Companies 1 Oxf Bucks LI, supported by S Company (the support company), fought hard to mop-up the marines in the houses and woods in the Gross Häuslingen area. This became an expensive business and the battalion lost Captain Hawley, who was killed when his carrier was hit by a Panzerfaust, and Major de Warrenne Warren, 2nd Lieutenant Norris and Lieutenant Hedges who were all wounded. As so little progress was being made on the main axis, 1 HLI was ordered to concentrate in the woods to the north-east of Gross Häuslingen and if 4 RWF was still unable to make headway, to be prepared to advance to attack Altenwahlingen from the north. By the evening the situation began gradually to improve and 1 Oxf Bucks LI's hard work allowed the two rear 4 RWF companies to begin to advance slowly towards the start line to join the remainder of the battalion. At 1847 hours A Company 4 RWF began a slow and contested move forward to join the lead companies who were still trying to clear the crossroads. In an attempt to outflank the opposition on the main axis, the carrier platoon and two sections from C Company moved through the woods on B Company's right to capture the bridge and house at Rethemer Fähre, some half a mile to the south-west of the crossroads. This met with heavy opposition from Kompanie 6./6, commanded by Oberleutnant zur See Fuchs, the first marines to be encountered from Mar.Gren.Rgt.6's second battalion. These marines were eventually forced from this area following an artillery bombardment and the remainder of the company moved up to secure the objective. However, the bridge which carried Route 209 over the narrow, curved lake had been thoroughly demolished.

At 2000 hours C Company 1 Oxf Bucks LI, now commanded by Captain Baxter in place of Major de Warrenne Warren, cleared up the last marines who had resisted A Company during the night from the area of the small pinewood to the east of Gross Häuslingen, and the battalion's positions were finally secured. At 2035 hours the battalion was able to report to 71st Infantry Brigade that 4 RWF was at last advancing through and by 2200 hours the Welsh had three companies digging-in in the area of the crossroads and one, D Company, had managed to enter the western edge of Altenwahlingen, although they were checked here by vigorous small-arms fire. C Company 4 RWF was ordered to despatch a patrol to Kirchwahlingen to check whether the enemy were still holding the village, which was not only in defilade to any future movement up Route 209 but also lay on the only alternate axis if the main road could not be used.

Whilst the fighting at the crossroads had ebbed and flowed, the marines had readied themselves for the next phase of 71st Infantry Brigade's operation, the capture of Altenwahlingen. Kompanie 6./6 which had held the area of the crossroads and Rethemer Fähre, had fallen back in reasonable order to join Oberleutnant zur See Marhenke's Kompanie 7./6 which was already in prepared defensive positions in Altenwahlingen. The marines were supported by the four 10.5cm Flak of Batterie 4./162 which were sited on the fringe of the pineforest in the broken ground of the Timpenberg. The battle for Altenwahlingen began at 2245 hours when D Company 4 RWF pushed on into the village from its foothold on the western edge of the village and systematically began to clear the houses and farms making maximum use of Wasp flamethrowers. The two German companies offered a spirited resistance but they were gradually forced out of the village step by step as the farms burnt down around them. By 2315 hours D Company seemed to have pushed the marines out of the village but, terrier-like, the marines refused to give up their grip and they occupied defensive positions at the eastern end of the village on the higher ground by the cemetery. A last desperate counter-attack launched by Kompanie 7./6 and Oberleutnant zur See Muller's Kompanie 8./6, which had been brought from Böhme, was halted and all the companies withdrew into the woods to the north and east. By the end of the battle, half the village had been burnt down and the marines lost two Leutnants, one Fahnrich, five Maate and 28 marines; a heavy price to pay for one small action.

During the early evening and before the events described above, 1 HLI had been ordered to be prepared to carry out a flanking movement to the north to relieve some of the pressure on 4 RWF whilst the Welsh attempted to move up to the crossroads. This manoeuvre would allow 1 HLI to attack Altenwahlingen from the north if 4 RWF remained unable to attack due to continued disruption in the area of their start line. The first part of this plan was still put into effect even though Altenwahlingen was captured by 4 RWF, as it was felt that flank protection to the north was necessary; and so it later proved to be. At 2230 hours A and B Companies 1 HLI were ordered to advance from the battalion concentration area and secure the high ground astride Route 209 in the area of Timpenberg. Their advance is described by Captain Ramsay who was the second in command of A Company.

'Earlier during the night, as the company had encountered no opposition we established a position in a large farm. One youthful German marine was taken prisoner, giving us an idea whom we were up against and as events showed they were brave and reckless fighters but had not much idea of the tactical situation. On Friday 13th, a day which must have given the superstitious cause to think, A and B Companies were to move across country and establish positions astride the main road leading forward from the area where the bridge was being built, into enemy country. Darkness was just falling as the two companies set off, B Company leading, to make their way by rather indefinite tracks to the area ordered. F echelon transport was taken. The ground was low-lying in parts and intersected by deep drains. Eventually, spurred by a longer halt than usual, A Company commander went forward and found that progress was barred by a deep ditch, crossed only by a plank. Obviously the transport could not go on and so the two jeeps and two carriers were left there and told to await further orders. They eventually made their way back to battalion headquarters through enemy-held ground. The marching personnel then carried on and after a slight brush with an enemy patrol, reached the approximate area of the objective.'

Back in the northern part of the divisional bridgehead 158th Brigade made slow progress on 13 April, expanding the perimeter against pockets of German resistance in the woods and heathland and much of the day was spent mopping-up. At 1600 hours orders were held at Brigade HQ at Otersen and instructions given for the next phase of operations in the brigade area: 7 RWF was ordered to clear the divisional axis, the main road leading north to Verden, and capture Hohenaverbergen; 1 E Lan R was to be relieved by 1/5 Welch in Otersen and then move up to concentrate in Wittlohe prior to advancing to capture Neddenaverbergen; 1/5 Welch would complete the operation with an advance to capture Armsen once the other two battalions had secured their objectives. The 53rd Recce Regiment was tasked to expand the bridgehead in an easterly direction and capture the village of Stemmen. Norman Mitchell takes up the Recce's story.

'...3 Troop, an armoured car troop commanded by Lieutenant Frank Long, proceeded to the village of Wittlohe which had been captured by a company of the East Lancs. They were in the process of digging-in a defensive position around the outskirts, and having exchanged the usual pleasantries with their most forward outpost ("Good luck Recce - rather you than us!"), we proceeded down the road towards Stemmen with the scout car leading the heavy armoured car in the standard first contact procedure. On reaching the farm where we later harboured for the night, Lieutenant Long called up the Support Troop in their carriers to check whether the farm was occupied by the Germans. They reported it clear. In view of the nature of the terrain, hedgerows and heathland scrub, it was decided that the best way to approach and clear Stemmen was for the armoured cars to proceed down the road, with 6 Troop on foot clearing the hedges of any Germans who might be lurking with bazookas. From movement observed from the cars, it was obvious that Stemmen had a well-planned defensive ring of slit trenches, which on our approach were being reinforced by marines. At this point the leading scout car came under small-arms and machine-gun fire and I heard Corporal Lilley shout to his carrier section to take cover. There then developed a heated exchange between his section and the Germans, with my armoured car firing HE into the row of houses which was obviously the local HQ. At this stage dusk was falling and the squadron leader ordered a withdrawal to the farmyard which we had passed earlier. Major Goldsmid then set up an all-round defensive ring around the farm building and within the farmyard.'

With the rest of the division fighting hard to expand the bridgehead, back on the left bank on 13 April 160th Infantry Brigade had another relatively quiet day. The divisional plan in being the night before had intended 2 Mons to cross the Aller in boats at first light, then take over the area between Altenwahlingen and Kirchwahlingen; 6 RWF would then cross the Class 40 bridge at Rethem as soon as it was finished and takeover the area of the Häuslingens. The execution of this plan had however been delayed by the Germans' tenacity on the right bank and as a consequence 160th Brigade had remained in its concentration area in the Westen area. Despite the lack of progress, fighting in the Weser/Aller triangle was finally brought to a conclusion by 4 Welch on this day. The battalion mounted a series of company attacks on the remaining German-held villages and by the evening of 13 April C Company was in Barnstedt, after a hard fight against an enemy who could only be forced out by burning the village down around him with Wasps; A Company was in Ahnebergen; D Company was in Stedebergen and B Company in Rieda. By the next day, German resistance on the left bank had dwindled and B Company 4 Welch was able to establish a post on the bank of the Aller opposite Verden. Virtually all German soldiers had now been killed or driven from the area between the two rivers and organised resistance had ceased.

During the course of 13 April 2 Mons continued to mop up the Rethem area and still found Germans close to the bridging site. At 0140 hours a patrol from A Company was fired at when entering a house near the bridge by a patrol of marines which had managed to reach the house without being noticed. Two Germans were killed and three members of the patrol were injured in the skirmish. At 1300 hours Lieutenant Colonel Brooke was warned that the battalion would not now cross the Aller at Rethem but was to be prepared to move to the Westen area to take over the defence of the bridge site. He visited Headquarters 158th Brigade at Westen later in the afternoon to receive details of the areas he would take over, but a daylight recce by his company commanders was not possible due to failing light. The battalion was warned to take over from the two companies of 1/5 Welch and one company from 1 E Lan R at 0700 hours on 14 April. The 6 RWF meanwhile had received clearer orders on its part in operations that would take place on the right bank once the Rethem bridge was open. The battalion was to come under command of 4th Armoured Brigade and advance from Rethem as an integral part of an armoured manoeuvre. To allow the lorried infantry battalion to operate with armour, the brigade was allocated a squadron of Kangaroo armoured personnel carriers (APC) to carry 6 RWF. At 2000 hours the Kangaroos arrived and married up with the battalion's companies in their concentration area near Stöcken. Despite the lateness in the day, the battalion immediately began rehearsing climbing in and out of their new steeds and learning about their tactical handling. This was a totally new type of warfare for these infantrymen and they spent most of the rest of the night discussing with the officers and men who crewed the vehicles how they would fight together the next day.

Whilst 53rd Division battled to consolidate its bridgehead, 11th Armoured Division was similarly engaged to its south. On the left flank of the armoured division's bridgehead, 13 April brought considerably more success than had the day before. During the night of 12-13 April there was some respite from the counter-attacks allowing bridging operations to get on quickly, with the bridge being completed shortly before dawn. Recce patrols sent out early in the morning reported back that the enemy had pulled back and were preparing new positions in the woods. At 1100 hours 46 (RM) Commando was ordered to advance to capture Hademstorf in order to prevent enemy observation of the bridge, which by now had been completed by the Sappers on the site of the demolished road bridge. The village and the surrounding area was held by Kompanie 1./2 with some 70 SS soldiers from Kompanie 1. and 5./12. Both Elefant tank-destroyers were also in the village but were of no use as they had run out of ammunition. A pincer attack was launched against the Germans with two troops moving across the railway embankment to attack from the south whilst two troops attacked through the woods from the north. The attack was preceded by a short but heavy artillery fire plan. Although the left pincer initially made good progress and was able to establish a small bridgehead over the railway line, the attack ran into trouble in the woods as it swung north towards the village. The commandos were engaged from well-concealed positions by a large number of automatic weapons which quickly caused casualties. All three officers and the troop sergeant major in Y Troop, the leading troop, were either killed or seriously wounded and the attack was in grave danger of being halted. However, the men were rallied by the surviving SNCO, Sergeant Cooper, and under his leadership they slowly fought their way forward through the wood. The second troop following up behind gave added momentum to the attack and the Germans, realising the hopelessness of further resistance, began to flee. The right pincer faced less opposition for here the ground was far more open and the Germans had not had time to establish defensive positions. Furthermore the artillery fire had had a disastrous effect on the morale of the young SS troopers who held this area and most fled up the railway line to the north-east before the attack closed with them. The commandos engaged these targets from the rear causing many casualties. One German officer was so ashamed at the action of his countrymen that he was seen to shoot himself as his troops ran from the battlefield. The final capture of Hademstorf was an easy affair after this collapse and the first troop gained a footing in the village by the railway station, while the second made a wide encircling movement to enter the village from the north-east. The village then fell

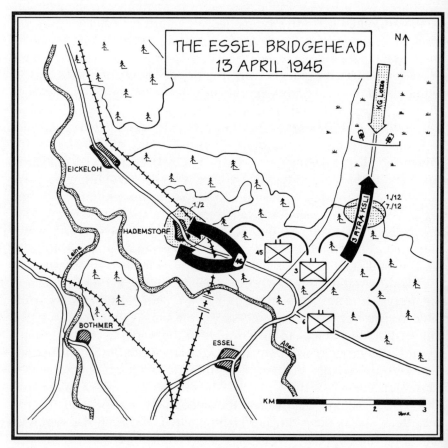

quickly under the impact of 46 (RM) Commando's twin pincers and many prisoners were taken.

Attempts were also made to expand the bridgehead up the divisional axis, the main road leading north-east. Although more armour from 29th Armoured Brigade had crossed the Aller via the new bridge, the close country would only allow at the very most a squadron of tanks at a time to advance. B and C Companies 4 KSLI and A Squadron 3 RTR accordingly resumed their advance up the road and became involved in a series of costly attacks to clear the woods. Facing them initially were the SS troopers from 1./12 and 7./12 and Franzen's Tiger tank. Stiff resistance was experienced throughout the morning despite A Squadron successfully stalking and finally knocking out Franzen's Tiger which had dominated the road for some time.

Unfortunately for the British this sector of the bridgehead had received reinforcement during the night which enabled their advance to be blocked. This reinforcement came primarily from the armoured training school at Bergen which had formed a number of weak battalions by using training personnel, walking wounded and stragglers from all branches of the Wehrmacht. These battalions came under the overall command of Oberst Grosan as part of the Kampfgruppe bearing his name. The Kampfgruppe was of course woefully weak in heavy weapons but it had a Panzer-Panzerjäger Abteilung which consisted of three Tiger tanks, one Panther tank, seven 8.8cm Pak 43 anti-tank guns and two 10.5cm field howitzers; a significant amount of firepower had it been concentrated against a single point. Fortunately for the British only a slice of the Abteilung was allocated to the forces battling to contain the Essel bridgehead. Although Grosan deployed a regiment to the Essel bridgehead battle, only one battalion was to take part in the fighting. This battalion was commanded by Hauptmann Lotze and he and his battalion had marched from Bergen to the front, arriving during the morning of 13 April. Lotze's battalion, with at least two Tigers in support, was immediately deployed forward to help the hard-pressed SS companies in the woods. The crews of two 6pdrs from 4 KSLI's anti-tank platoon spotted these tanks and engaged them. One gun scored seven hits but failed to penetrate the Tiger's massive frontal armour and the tanks returned fire, destroying both guns. The Germans' morale must also have been momentarily lifted by the appearance overhead of a number of Me 262 jet aircraft. The British war diaries make no mention of these aircraft carrying out attacks so it must be presumed that they were unable to acquire targets among the thick pineforests and broke off.

At about 1730 hours 4 KSLI mounted its first attack across open country since crossing the Aller. The attack was supported by A Squadron and initially made good progress despite the enemy fire. However, all but two of the accompanying tanks bogged-in leaving the infantry to advance without the majority of their armoured support. One of the tanks was knocked out by a Tiger which suddenly emerged at very close range and the two reserve companies had to be brought up to help deal with the stiffening German resistance. Although the immediate area was mopped up, it was decided to withdraw the companies to a firm base as the enemy appeared to be too strong and, with the light failing, continuing the battle into the night against unknown but strong forces seemed unwise.

The difficulties being experienced in overcoming the opposition on the intended divisional axis now forced a change of plan, and the decision was taken to abandon further effort in the Essel area. Both 29th Armoured and 159th Infantry Brigades would cross the Bailey bridge at Essel, but then head east following the course of the Aller with the armoured brigade following 159th Brigade as far as Winsen, which lay upstream on the Aller's right bank some four miles to the east. Once Winsen was captured, another bridge would be built there, the one at Essel would be dismantled and the divisional axis swung away to the east. Accordingly, on 14 April, the advance on Winsen began with 1st Commando Brigade being left in place to protect the bridgehead. Unbeknown to the British, the German effort to defeat the bridgehead was now spent and with no further forces available, Lotze's battalion was ordered to remain in place to block any British attempts to break out up the main road, whilst the remnants of Mar.Füs.Btl.2 and SS Kompanie 1./12 and 5./12 were to do likewise in Eickeloh.

The battle for the Essel bridgehead had cost 1st Commando Brigade 29 dead and 91 wounded and 4 KSLI 13 dead and 40 wounded. Some 220 Germans were killed in the area and now lie buried in the cemeteries at Essel, Eickeloh and Schwarmstedt. It had been a ferocious fight.

12

'BELT-FED BAZOOKAS'
13–14 APRIL

Any thoughts the men of 71st and 158th Infantry Brigades may have had that they had finished off the threat from the marines on the right bank was misplaced, for throughout 13 April plans were being made for counter-attacks to be launched during the night of 13-14 April. The attacks would be launched using all available troops and would be designed to destroy the bridgehead opposite Westen, drive a wedge between the 71st and 158th Brigades, before cutting off and destroying 71st Brigade in the south.

As there were insufficient troops to attack the northern part of the bridgehead, additional forces had to be moved to the area. Hauptmann Kessel's ROB-Pi.Btl.Nienburg was moved from its position in reserve at Kirchboitzen to a concentration area in woods in the Stemmen area where it was held pending the launching of the attack. Kessel's battalion, numbering some 600 men, moved on foot over two nights to avoid the threat of air attack and for the forthcoming operation was divided between Mar.Gren.Rgt.5 and 7. Forces also had to be moved to be in a position to attack the bridgehead's left flank. For this task, both battalions of Mar.Gren.Rgt.7 moved south to join Kampfgruppe Tebener. Whilst these deployments were taking place, planning for a general attack on the northern bridgehead was in train. The concept of operations for the attack is known as Hauptmann Kessel's pencilled orders were captured.

BATTALION OPERATION ORDER FOR TONIGHT'S ATTACK.

'Kampfgruppe Neitzel and Kampfgruppe Jordan are eliminating the Otersen bridgehead by a night attack. ROB-Pi.Btl.Nienburg less 3.Kompanie are under command Kampfgruppe Neitzel, 3.Kompanie under command Kampfgruppe Jordan. H Hour 2245 hours. Kampfgruppe Neitzel is attacking Wittlohe and Otersen with two battalions and will capture the two villages. Left battalion in contact with 1.Kompanie Kampfgruppe Tebener and pivoting on the latter will by-pass Wittlohe to the east and capture Otersen. This attack will take place when it is considered that the enemy has been sufficiently weakened by the attacks of Mar.Gren.Rgt.7 but in any event not later than 2200 hours.

(signed) KESSEL Hauptmann'

The counter-attack began at about 2300 hours, opening with fairly heavy artillery concentrations, including airbursts, falling on the British positions. These were followed by infantry attacks on 7 RWF and C Squadron 53rd Recce Regiment. The companies of 7 RWF were in the process of advancing north to capture the village of Hohenaverbergen when the counter-attack hit them. The night was pitch black and the situation rapidly became extremely confused. D Company was overrun and C Company was encircled but not dislodged from holding the objective it had captured earlier during the night. The Germans infiltrated into the woods where 7 RWF had its battalion headquarters and bitter, close-quarter fighting ensued throughout the night. The 1 E Lan R, who had concentrated in Wittlohe as a preliminary to advancing to capture Neddenaverbergen, was attacked by some of the Germans who had bypassed not only the two 7 RWF companies on the high ground north of Wittlohe but also the Recce Regiment squadrons advancing towards Stemmen. Fortunately the attack was weak in numbers and resolve and the only Germans who penetrated the village sought refuge in a barn opposite B Company's position. They were engaged by PIATs and grenades, and two were killed and four taken prisoner. The Recce Regiment did not however escape as lightly. The vigour of the counter-attacks its squadrons faced and the associated confusion is clear from this account from the regimental history.

'C Squadron was to the left, B Squadron, covering RHQ and the Support Group who were established at Otersen, in the centre and A Squadron was to the right. The day (13 April) passed with patrols and a realisation that if the enemy was still lurking in the thick pinewoods frequently interspersed with sandy tracks, he would probably be very difficult to locate and push back completely. At 2300 hours the squadron stood-to for an hour on information given by the night patrols who reported the sound of movement. At 2345 hours the first of four attacks began. This was from the north and was accompanied by a fusillade of small-arms fire and bazooka bombs, one of which penetrated squadron HQ, shook-up the operators and destroyed the wireless link to regiment. Soon the buildings began to burn, and with this back-cloth of crimson and gold the scene began to resemble some medieval impression of hell. Burning buildings, persistent enemy, and vehicles and stores in increasing danger of destruction presented three simultaneous problems; the troops being concerned with the safety of

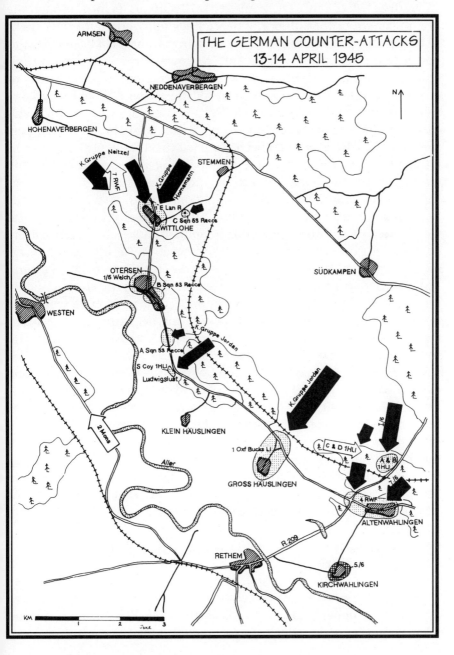

THE GERMAN COUNTER-ATTACKS
13-14 APRIL 1945

themselves and their belongings as well as with the dispatch of the enemy. But the enemy was beaten off and the harbour area had not been entered. There was in fact a short time to breathe.

'At 0145 hours the enemy attacked from the rear in much the same strength as before but were repulsed by 6 Troop on its own, though the bright glare from the still burning buildings silhouetted, for the benefit of the enemy, the remainder of the squadron which had been drawn in nearer to the central courtyard. At 0300 hours on 14 April came a third attack, this time from the west, the most persistent and dangerous of all coming immediately on the heels of the second. These two attacks were believed to have been made by two companies of marines who had been fighting unsuccessfully with 1 E Lan R on our left for the possession of Wittlohe and had been attracted to Stemmen by the hope of a less bloody victory. This time they penetrated the perimeter of the farm defences and fought for a short time in the courtyard, even forming a small ammunition dump there. By now it was a hideous free-for-all struggle; Major Goldsmid, although badly wounded in the face, arms and legs, disregarded his personal troubles and organised the defence with the Humbers firing all they had outwards over the heads of the carrier crews who manned the perimeter slit trenches. Burning vehicles cast an eerie light over the scene, but fortunately the enemy was not able to reinforce his original success, a fact which he seemed to take gradually and reluctantly to heart, for he withdrew at length, urged on his way by a redoubled intensity of fire from every gun the squadron could bring to bear on him.

'The fourth attack at nearly 0400 hours was less bitter and might be likened to a Parthian shot to cover withdrawal. Towards dawn reinforcements from B Squadron arrived, necessarily prevented till then from any active form of assistance by C Squadron's all-round fire. When all was over, Major Goldsmid reported to RHQ to say that everything was in order, that only one man had been killed but a dozen had been wounded, that a good many vehicles and stores could no longer be considered serviceable parts of his squadron G 1098, and finally that he would go to hospital himself to be patched up...'

Corporal Henderson of 5 Troop C Squadron also gives a vivid impression of the fighting.

'We were bedded down nicely when at about 11 o'clock we were awakened by fighting and shouting in the village to our rear. No one knew what was happening until we were informed that a strong party of enemy had attacked the infantry (1 E Lan R) behind us and was holding half the village (Wittlohe). Not so good we thought. Then it was our turn! Whoof, Bang, Crash! They were upon us having crept up to the copse from the village in front of us. Bazookas, stick grenades, a lot of shouting and general confusion, all came at once. They infiltrated into our forward positions and two or three even reached the edge of the farm-yard, but the Besas got to work and we eventually drove them back. I had foolishly not made a trench and in all this I was sweating blue bricks, hacking away roots with my blunt shovel in a foot-deep trench. In the end I gave it up and lay down flat with my nose just sticking over the top. Luckily nothing came my way during this time getting all the ammunition and grenades I could, grenades being my favourite weapon because Jerry does not know which direction they come from and cannot therefore retaliate so accurately. I was between the road and a ditch which had 11 inches of mud in it. I firmly believed that the enemy would come next time up this ditch so I found myself a new position and waited.

'They came in from the right and managed to set the farm-house on fire which had its advantages for both sides, but mainly for us as it lit up the surrounding ground better than any Verey light. There seemed to be hundreds of them by the row they made. The Besas were firing seemingly endless belts and Jerry appeared to be firing belt-fed bazookas back. The blast from those bazookas knocked all the wind out of your body, and as I was 50 yards away on the opposite side of the farm-house I felt very sorry for anyone in that vicinity, and didn't hold out much hope for them. But somehow they stuck to their guns ... A small party then tried to come in from the rear. They must have been absolute fanatics for they came straight for the farm buildings over a completely flat field, shouting in English to us, "Hands up! The war is finished for you.". But you can guess what answer they got. The last attempt came from the left where there was even more shouting and scores of silhouettes, but I think Jerry was a bit shaken by this time as he was definitely not so bold. Nevertheless there was plenty of noise and danger. In the morning we were warmly congratulated by the CO and the Divisional Commander, for during the night chaos had reigned in the bridgehead which had not yet been reinforced with armour owing to the need for bridging, and the division had been attacked by six battalions of marines with the object of blowing the bridge, and they had very nearly succeeded. I was in the only position that was not attacked and did not fire a shot so I can personally take no credit for the squadron's success; but I can always say I was there.'

During the night the Germans also attacked A Squadron and cut the road between them and regimental headquarters, but Lieutenant Ferguson dealt with this successfully with his troop the next morning on his way back to A Echelon for UK leave. Due to the ferocity of the German attacks 2 Mons, defending the bridging operation at Rethem, was given urgent orders at 0300 hours on 14 April to move as soon as possible to take over the defence task at Westen. The battalion was ordered to move at 0430 hours and was in position by 0700 hours, having left one company behind to guard the bridging operation at Rethem. As mentioned in C Squadron 53rd Recce Regiment's account, the Germans also attacked 1 E Lan R in Wittlohe. The attack by three companies of Kampfgruppe Hornemann and marines from Kompanie 13./7 came in with determination, and about one company succeeded in infiltrating right into the village where there was a lively battle in pitch-darkness in which friend and foe alike were indistinguishable. The main brunt of the attack fell around B Company's area on the village crossroads and here 10 Platoon under Lieutenant Kay took a heavy toll of the Germans. The brightest spot of the evening was produced by Sergeant Oram who obviously felt at one stage of the battle that the situation was obscure. He accordingly threw some additional light on proceedings by landing a 77 (phosphorous) grenade in a nearby barn full of hay and B Company's cooks. The barn burnt well and, as described in the regimental history, the cooks provided a shining example of a smart turnout! The German attack on Wittlohe proved abortive and order was soon restored.

The German counter-attack was, however, by no means spent for in the early hours of 14 April attacks were launched by marines on the southern part of the bridgehead in 71st Infantry Brigade's area. In a determined attack to eradicate the Rethem bridgehead, both battalions of Mar.Gren.Rgt.6 and the remnants of Mar.Gren.Rgt.5 were thrown into battle. The ensuing fighting was far more ferocious than that in the north of the bridgehead and the battle raged between Altenwahlingen and Otersen for three hours, with 4 RWF and 1 HLI bearing the brunt of the counter-attack. The 71st Infantry Brigade's deployment immediately prior to the counter-attacks was as follows: 4 RWF had A and D Companies in Altenwahlingen and were holding the area of the crossroads to the west with B and C Companies; 1 HLI had A and B Companies forward on 4 RWF's left flank consolidating in the area of the Timpenberg, whilst C and D Companies 1 HLI were on the move having been ordered to vacate the Gross Häuslingen area to support A and B Companies; and the 1 Oxf Bucks LI companies were still holding the area of Gross Häuslingen and ensuring the brigade axis was kept open whilst 4 RWF and 1 HLI pushed on. Brigadier Elrington had decided to visit battalion headquarters of 1 HLI and had arrived there soon after 0500 hours. Forty-five minutes later the Germans launched their counter-attack which struck all three battalions simultaneously.

Bataillon II./6, notwithstanding its losses from the battle for Altenwahligen the previous day, now threw its entire remaining strength against the tired and vulnerable companies of 4 RWF and 1 HLI. A Company 4 RWF was heavily attacked by Kompanie 7./6 and Kompanie 8./6 near Altenwahlingen and was forced to give ground. Also attacked in strength were C and D Companies 1 HLI who were just passing battalion headquarters in their move forward to support A and B Companies. These latter companies had already had a difficult night and were badly in need of this help. Captain Ramsay, second in command of A Company, takes up the story again.

'Having arrived at the Timpenberg feature Major Hemelryk, who was OC B Company, then went forward to recce his company's position which was to be on the right of the main road. He took a platoon with him to place in position. The platoon having been placed on the ground, Major Hemelryk was making his way back when he was fired on by an enemy patrol and badly wounded. He was carried back to the position where the two company O Groups were waiting at the junction of a track and the main road. It was decided by Major Greenaway, commanding A Company, and Captain Pender who had taken over B Company, to get the platoons in position as soon as possible.

'At this moment a long line of men were seen marching towards us in single file, down the main road. Somehow one never thinks of the enemy approaching in this manner but it has to be remembered that they knew little of the tactical situation. A challenge was replied to by a smart burst of carbine fire and for the next few minutes all hell burst loose. The enemy got down in the ditch and started lobbing over grenades. In reply A Company had three LMGs spraying the road while the remainder of the two companies were sorted out and reorganised in a defensive position in a copse about 300 yards to the rear. Several of our wounded, including Major Hemelryk, had to be left for the moment and Private Blythe, a B Company stretcher bearer, very gallantly stayed with them. For the next half-hour or so our men were trickling back to the defensive position and just as things were quietening down a voice was heard shouting, "HLI here". It was Private Blythe, who had been taken prisoner, accompanied by a German officer. He came with an offer from the German commander to allow us to bring in our wounded. After permission had been obtained from battalion HQ by wireless, Lieutenant Heywood went forward to meet him and after a conversation in broken English and German arranged for the evacuation of 10 wounded personnel including Major Hemelryk. All the stretcher bearers returned safely too with the exception of Private Blythe who was compelled to stay with the enemy to look after their wounded. We heard that he was afterwards released by a subsequent attack and was in due course awarded the MM for his bravery.'

This attack was mounted by Kompanie 6./6 and although its marines were relatively fresh, the complexities of mounting an effective night attack were beyond them and it is clear that they had no idea of the whereabouts of the British. The presence of C and D Companies was most fortunate for battalion headquarters, not to mention the brigade commander, for without them they would certainly have been over-run.

S Company 1 HLI was also attacked in its depth position near Ludwigslust. This was a novel experience for the support company as an unknown company author recounts.

'Excepting of course for the carrier platoon, the company, or only a small part of it, had never come into actual contact with the enemy. The first time this happened was late in the campaign just after we had crossed the River Aller. On the night after the battalion had crossed the river it was again ordered to push on, in this case to assist 4 RWF if necessary. At this time it was quite on the cards that it would not be necessary and everyone was cheerful at the O Group that evening. Especially so was S Company commander because he had been ordered to stay in situ, less the mortar platoon, and if necessary bring the carriers and anti-tanks up to battalion HQ at first light. The "situ" consisted of a largish house, with barn and cowshed attached, lying alongside the axis of advance which ran parallel to the river. One section of the anti-tank platoon occupied the house along with company HQ and the pioneers. The remainder of the anti-tank platoon and one section of carriers occupied a farm cottage about 200 yards away. After the remainder of the battalion had left, everything was quiet and peaceful with the only fly in the ointment being the wooded and unprotected left flank. That night it was definitely a case of "kip down" and in all cases trousers and boots came off. At about 0400 hours the anti-tank platoon commander went forward to battalion HQ and later sent back a dispatch rider to bring up the platoon. Once awake, they started to pack blankets and load the carriers. As suddenly as a flash of lightning, spandaus and other automatics opened up from the blue and grenades from discharge cups smashed against company HQ's house. The two sections of anti-tanks and the carriers were taken completely by surprise. They were herded into a room by very trigger-happy marines, forced to drop their slacks and were searched and stripped of watches, pens etc (poetic justice!).

'Inside the other house confusion would be a very weak word to describe the scene. Half-dressed, everyone was stampeding in a dazed kind of way. By a great deal of shouting order was gained and all possible entrances to the house were covered. At first a lot of indiscriminate firing went on from both sides. In the house we had only two Bren guns and the usual ratio of rifles and Stens, but so great was the volume of fire poured out that the enemy seemed to grow quiet, while we wasted ammunition to such an extent that it was in great danger of running-out altogether. It was half light by now and we could see the shadowy shapes as they worked their way nearer and nearer to the house. As our firing slackened owing to shortage of ammunition, theirs increased from cleverly concealed LMGs. Showing excellent fieldcraft the marines got right into the vicinity of the house and even into some of the out-buildings. They used grenades with great skill and rendered the two rooms on the top floor a shambles and caused several casualties. In return some very fine shooting by cooks, pioneers and others took a heavy toll of the enemy. Even though the road had been cut, vehicles not aware of this were starting to come down and an ambulance managed to make the yard in safety. As well as the ambulance, a company jeep, having missed the RAP[1], made harbour in the yard. The driver, seeing the position, volunteered to go back to contact an armoured car of the recce to help out. Without waiting for an answer he ran to his jeep and managed to run the gauntlet to safety.

'Things were now reaching a climax. Ammo was at a minimum and the marines had closed in and were causing more casualties. Perhaps worst of all they had managed to set fire to the straw loft of the cowshed. This meant that it was only a matter of time before the whole house too caught fire. The result would be a foregone conclusion for, being in the position that they were, the marines could have either have killed or captured us at will. As it was everything was all right. At the critical moment the armoured car, summoned by the jeep driver, arrived and its Besa soon put paid to the marines. We just had time to make a very hurried exit before the fire really took hold. Placed beside others, this was probably a minor incident indeed, but it is certainly one that will live in our memories forever.'

Whilst S Company fought off the marines' attack, A and B Companies spent the rest of the night in a bleak and exposed position. Captain Ramsay describes their situation cut off from the remainder of the brigade.

'Although no further attack was made by the enemy on our defensive position, as soon as first light came up extremely accurate sniping started. About this time I went to see how Major Hemelryk was getting on and found to my sorrow that the gallant commander of B Company had died a few minutes earlier. The cold and damp of the early morning proved very trying for the wounded and it was impossible to evacuate them as no transport had managed to get through and we were still more or less surrounded. We asked battalion HQ if carriers or stretcher bearers could be sent up but the reply came back that they were being attacked themselves and that they could give no assistance in the meantime. A short while later, looking out to our right front we could see bedraggled members of the German marine battalion making their way back towards the enemy's area. They were the remnants of the forces which had counter-attacked other units of 71st Brigade. Though they were too far away for good results to be obtained, we sped them on their way with LMG fire. As soon as it was possible a patrol was sent out to recce forward to our original objective, and as it reported all clear the companies then moved up and occupied positions astride the road. One platoon from A Company was left to watch the left flank and reply to the snipers' fire. It was well on in the afternoon before carriers arrived up the main road and we got the wounded sent back and our breakfast sent up.'

With the HLI fighting a confused battle in the woods, Bataillon I./6 attacked B and C Companies 4 RWF at the Altenwahlingen crossroads and pressing them very hard, managed to cut the main road. A Company was heavily counter-attacked in Altenwahlingen and the recce squadron moved to help prevent the companies from being overwhelmed. The situation was becoming very difficult indeed and it was only the timely intervention of the artillery that enabled the attacks to be beaten off. At 0500 hours all the 81st Field Regiment RA battery commanders with the battalions reported that their areas were surrounded by enemy who had infiltrated in large numbers. Although the three battalion headquarters were in close proximity to each other and the task of coordinating the fire was made easier, the regiment recorded more radio traffic and concentrated firing than at any other time in the campaign. By first light, after confused fighting and severe infiltration to within 300 yards of Headquarters 71st Brigade which cut communications to the battalions, the marines were caught in the open and became what the war diary described as a 'Gunners' Dream'. After heavy artillery concentrations large groups surrendered in turn, but not before they had suffered severe losses. The last attacks were eventually beaten off with the help of B and D Companies 1 Oxf Bucks LI and by 0900 hours the German counter-attack was spent.

During the course of this bitter fighting approximately 130 marines were killed and 79 wounded, whilst 1 HLI suffered 68 casualties. The German dead included the commanding officer of Bataillon I./6, Korvetten Kapitän Melzer[2], and his commanders of Kompanie 1./6 and 2./6, Oberleutnant zur See Peters and Mahler. A further 163, including the commanding officer of Bataillon II./5, were taken prisoner and the four 10.5cm Flak of Batterie 4./162 were captured in the Timpenberg area.

The night battles fought during the early hours of 14 April were not however just confined to repelling German counter-attacks. Shortly after midnight the 4 RWF Carrier Platoon had passed through the cross-roads held by B and C Companies and had moved south to investigate the hamlet of Kirchwahlingen. The hamlet was held by Kompanie 5./6 commanded by Oberleutnant zur See Herbst. This remaining company of Korvettenkapitän Meincke's Bataillon II./6 would appear not to have received the order to withdraw given to the battalion after the fall of Altenwahlingen. It must remain a mystery why Herbst and his soldiers decided not to pull out, having heard resistance come to an end to their north and a night withdrawal eastwards to Böhme would have presented few problems. Herbst was however determined to stay and fight it out come what may and the day before he had ordered the inhabitants to leave. Few did so and the mayor, Winkelmann, had pleaded with him not to defend Kirchwahlingen as it had no value. The Oberleutnant refused this request stating that it was his duty to stay and fight. As the Carrier Platoon reached the hamlet they were met by heavy small-arms fire and the Welsh were forced to dismount rapidly to begin a long and bitter action involving hand-to-hand fighting to clear the houses and farms. The fighting went on throughout the remainder of the night and into the next morning.

Despite the courage of the marines, the failure of the counter-attacks to eliminate the bridgehead led to the German defence of the right bank becoming very fragmented. Elements of Mar.Gren. Rgt.5, Bataillon I./6, Mar.Pi.Btl.2 and ROB-Pi.Btl.Nienburg now withdrew to the area of the villages of Südkampen and Vethem, from where they were to continue to fight stubbornly. Mar.Gren.Rgt.7 pulled back to defend the Verden area against the impending British attack from the south. Only Bataillon II./6 could in any sense be called battleworthy and the marines of this battalion, supported by the batteries 2./604 RAD and 4./117, prepared to defend the villages of Gross Eilstorf and Kirchboitzen to counter the inevitable breakout up the Route 209 axis. As the bridge at Rethem neared completion during the late morning, 71st Brigade redeployed in expectation of 4th Armoured Brigade's advance; 4 RWF swung round so that all four companies in the Altenwahlingen area faced due east and 1 HLI's rear companies were held back in preparation for an advance to the north.

NOTES

1   This is the Regimental Aid Post. The RAP is usually the first point in the casualty evacuation chain and here casualties receive additional first aid prior to movement further back.

2   Melzer lies buried in the small war cemetery at Gross Häuslingen with fifty-eight marines who died with him in the battle for the village.

BREAKING THROUGH THE CRUST
14 APRIL

The capacity for 2.Marine Infanterie Division to prevent the bridgehead from expanding further was now virtually at an end and the violent counter-attacks of 13 and 14 April had exhausted the marines and fragmented their battalions. Those that remained were fully prepared however to fight it out from the villages and hamlets that lay on the British axes of advance.

In the immediate aftermath of the counter-attacks in the southern area of the bridgehead, the marines of Mar.Gren.Rgt.6 had pulled back to recover and regroup in the woods that dominated the routes which led away from the bridgehead to the east. This belt of timber offered further opportunity to exact delay and casualties as the British had no option but to advance through the close country where the routes available to them would be very limited. Here Bataillon II./6 prepared to fight from the close confines of the pine woods, adopting ambush positions from which to attack the British as soon as they started to advance up Route 209 or attempted to make use of the rides through the woods. The marines were grouped into tank-hunting teams equipped with Panzerfausts and automatic weapons, both most effective at the very short ranges in the woods. Road blocks were hurriedly built on Route 209 by felling the oaks that lined either side of the road and positions further in depth were prepared in the next two villages on Route 209 – Gross Eilstorf and Kirchboitzen. Gross Eilstorf was occupied by marines from Mar.Gren.Rgt.5, who had fallen back to the village following the failure of their counter-attack in the Gross Häuslingen area on 13 April, and Kirchboitzen, previously occupied by ROB-Pi.Btl.Nienburg, was now held by marines from Bataillon I./6 who had moved to the village after regrouping. Mar.Art.Rgt.2 had by now at last arrived with its horse-drawn 10.5cm field guns and the batteries had occupied gun positions north of Route 209. Whilst their arrival was to give much needed fire support to the marine battalions, this support was to be short-lived as we shall see.

Commander XII Corps' concept of operations for the next phase of the advance was for 52nd Lowland Division to come up on the left flank to mask Bremen from Ottersberg to Achim. As soon as the Class

40 bridge was completed at Rethem, 4th Armoured Brigade, under command 53rd Welsh Division, would cross, relieve 71st Infantry Brigade and then advance as quickly as possible to Walsrode, where it would then swing north-west in a manoeuvre to outflank Verden from the north. The 7th Armoured Division would then begin its advance on Hamburg whilst 53rd Division expanded the bridgehead to the north and captured Verden. The plan for 53rd Division's northwards advance involved the three infantry brigades advancing up the right bank of the Aller towards Verden clearing the remaining forces of the Aller Line as they did so. The brigades were to leap-frog past each other supported in turn by an armoured regiment and one squadron of Crocodiles.

The 4th Armoured Brigade had played an illustrious part in the war. The brigade had its origins back in 1938 when it was formed as one of two armoured brigades in the Mobile Force, Egypt. This formation, known irreverently at the time as the 'Immobile Farce', later became the famous 7th Armoured Division, also soon to play its part in the events of this account. To mark their service in North Africa, the troops of both brigade and division continued to display badges depicting desert rats on their vehicles and on their uniforms. The 4th Armoured Brigade fought throughout the North African campaign, mostly under command of the armoured division, but left it for the invasion of Sicily where it served as an independent armoured brigade in XIII Corps. The brigade then fought in the Italian campaign on the Adriatic flank from October to December 1943 before returning to England in preparation for Operation 'Overlord'. It landed in Normandy on 9 June and fought as an independent armoured brigade throughout the remainder of the campaign. The brigade was allocated to XII Corps as Corps Troops on 7 March for the Rhine Crossing; thereafter the brigade's operational affiliation changed rapidly, and it fought in turn with 53rd Welsh Division, 52nd Lowland Division and then on 9 April was ordered to rejoin 53rd Division. The brigade was commanded by Brigadier Carver[1] and in April 1945 consisted of three armoured regiments – the Greys, 44 RTR and 3rd/4th County of London Yeomanry (Sharpshooters) (3/4 CLY) – and a motorised infantry battalion, 2nd Battalion the King's Royal Rifle Corps (2 KRRC).

For the breakout phase however this grouping was not ideal for either 4th Armoured or 53rd Welsh. For 4th Armoured the thick woods which would be encountered in the early stages of the breakout required the brigade to have more infantry, whilst the infantry division needed a tank regiment to support its brigades as they advanced north on Verden. General Ross consequently ordered a regrouping. The brigade reconfigured and became in modern military parlance 'square', as it was now to consist of two armoured and two infantry battalions. It lost 3/4 CLY, which was placed under divisional control, but gained 6 RWF, from 160th Infantry Brigade, to be carried in Kangaroo APCs supplied by 49 APC Regiment[2]. The Greys and 3/4 CLY were both equipped with a mix of Sherman V (75mm) and Vc (17pdr) tanks, whilst 44 RTR had the amphibious variant of the Sherman V, the DD[3]. Stuart V light tanks were used by the armoured regiments' reconnaissance troops and for command purposes, whilst 2 KRRC were carried in International half-tracks.

Two regimental sized groups were formed for the brigade's advance, the first was based on 44 RTR and 2 KRRC, the second on the Greys and 6 RWF. As soon as the Rethem bridge was completed the lead

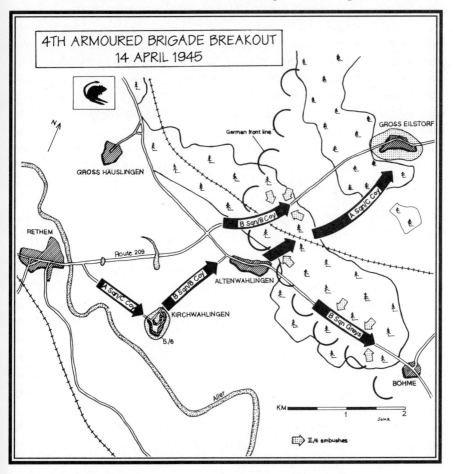

group – 44 RTR/2 KRRC – was to cross, followed by a number of units and sub-units destined to join 158th Infantry Brigade in the north, but which were too heavy to cross the Class 9 bridge at Westen. The 4th Armoured Brigade was to be clear of the Rethem bridge by last light on 14 April when it was hoped that 7th Armoured Division would be able to start crossing. To relieve 4 RWF in the Altenwahlingen area and free them for the northwards advance, the brigade was allocated from 7th Armoured Division an additional infantry battalion, 2 Devons.

On 13 April the Brigade had moved to a concentration area near Hohenholz to await the completion of the Class 40 Bailey pontoon at Rethem, which had continued to be delayed by frequent mortar and shell fire. At 1200 hours on Saturday 14 April the bridge was finally ready and the Carrier Platoon of 2 KRRC, which was to act as a recce screen, rumbled across and advanced east toward Kirchwahlingen, as the craters on Route 209 prevented movement up the main road and the bypass route had to be used. A few minutes after they had crossed, the Germans shelled the site once more. Fortunately no damage was caused but it shook all the high ranking observers, amongst whom was the Corps commander, who had gathered to watch the crossing. Despite this near disaster, the war diarist of 244 Field Company RE was fully justified in proudly recording that the bridge at Rethem had been built under very trying conditions, that it was one of the best they had built and that they had deserved the Corps commander's praise.

Whilst the shells were falling at the bridging site, 2 KRRC's Carrier Platoon was pressing on towards Kirchwahlingen. However, the detour off Route 209 taken by the platoon was far from satisfactory for the brigade advance would be restricted onto a narrow, raised road with the ground on either side boggy and unable to support armour. This would inevitably result in congestion and delay just when speed was needed. For their advance, 44 RTR and 2 KRRC had formed a regimental group of three, combined squadron/company groups. A Squadron and C Company were first group across the bridge and with A Squadron leading slowly advanced up the bypass route. By 1330 hours they had almost reached Kirchwahlingen, but as they drew near the sight and sound of the continuing bitter fighting between Herbst's marines and the men of the Carrier Platoon of 4 RWF became plainly evident. The column caught up with the 2 KRRC Carrier Platoon and the group halted whilst clarification of the situation was sought. Why Herbst never spotted the approaching armour is a mystery. Although the fighting spirit of the marines and their dedication to duty was of an extremely high order, the reason why these men remained to take on such overwhelming odds will never be known. Perhaps they were so involved in their battle with the men of 4 RWF that they simply never noticed the armour approaching.

A Squadron commander eventually managed to get the 4 RWF Carrier Platoon to disengage and advanced with his tanks into the hamlet. Herbst and his marines continued to fight on and they engaged, unsuccessfully, the lead tanks with their few Panzerfausts. When these were exhausted, they shot at the tanks with their rifles in a futile attempt to destroy their optics. However, close-quarter fighting amongst the farms and houses of Kirchwahlingen was not a healthy environment for armour and there were more efficient ways of dealing with the snipers. The 2 KRRC's Wasp flamethrowers were called forward and immediately proceeded to burn down three of the large farm complexes. Fortunately for Kirchwahlingen they ran out of flame fuel thus preventing its complete destruction. Herbst however was killed whilst fighting from the garden of the mayor's house and his deputy, Leutnant zur See Markert, took over to continue the one-sided battle. The marines were now forced out of the back of the hamlet but continued to fight tenaciously from ditches and hedges as they withdrew to the woods to the north. Leutnant zur See Markert was severely wounded during the battle and died of his wounds the next day.

Whilst A Squadron Group was mopping up Kirchwahlingen, B Squadron and B Company, the second squadron/company group, had moved up, managed to bypass the fighting and advanced directly to Altenwahlingen. Here they met up with 4 RWF who they relieved from its task of securing the village. The remainder of the 44 RTR Regimental Group followed on, although Support Company 2 KRRC and a section of carriers had to stay behind in Kirchwahlingen to mop up snipers who were still causing trouble. Once finished with Kirchwahlingen, A Squadron Group followed B Squadron Group and then struck off towards the thick pine woods to the north of the Altenwahlingen. As soon as the woods were entered however, the tanks and half-tracks were engaged and halted by intense machine-gun fire and a hail of Panzerfausts fired by marines from Bataillon II./6 holding positions further back in the trees. Despite the dangerous situation, the tanks were chary of returning fire as they had yet to contact A and B Companies 1 HLI who were supposed to be in the general area. These events are described by Major Gibbs, company commander of C Company 2 KRRC.

'C Company 2nd 60th Rifles were to advance on Gross Eilstorf but on a centre line east of the main Rethem-Gross Eilstorf road. With A

Squadron we debouched from Altenwahlingen in the early afternoon. We had hardly put our noses outside when firing broke out from the edge of the woods just north of the road to Böhme. I led with a motor platoon on its feet supported by a troop of A Squadron with the rest of the company immediately to the rear. The country, being wooded, was an infantry task to clear. The leading platoon got into the edge of the wood, supported by the machine-gun fire of the tanks. I don't think they had many casualties. But the enemy were fighting with no thought of surrender - indeed they were well dug-in and camouflaged, difficult to locate and their positions were in depth back into the wood. The empty half-tracks and company headquarters endured an extraordinary barrage which was difficult to recognise. It was solid shot from anti-tank guns cocked up to clear the trees. They hit one half-track. The tank machine-guns were clearly not having much impact and I was starting to plan a coordinated attack with the rest of the company when to my surprise one of my two Wasps (which were very slow and often broke down because of their excessive weight) hove in sight. So I thought, "We will just try this on them first". The little carrier heaved itself towards the wood, covered by the platoon and tanks. It stopped 25 yards from the edge and let off a squirt of liquid which happily ignited. There were immediate shrieks from the enemy. With a few more squirts the nearest enemy got up and surrendered followed by the rest. I cannot say how many POW we evacuated. Quite a lot. The dead we left for the villagers to bury. Having secured our open flank, we turned north-east to continue our advance. We had broken through the crust...'

At company level there probably were grounds for feeling confident, but the confused situation north of Altenwahlingen could not be quickly resolved and Brigadier Carver was becoming increasingly frustrated as the advance was unable to make headway. The second regiment group, The Greys and 6 RWF, had been delayed by the Crocodiles of C Squadron 7 RTR and the Class 40 vehicles of both 71st and 158th Brigades moving to join their parent units and they could not bypass this congestion due to the boggy ground. The only place between the bridge and Altenwahlingen where vehicles could get off the road was at Kirchwahlingen, but both the hamlet and the road were in full view of the enemy-held woods to the north-east and it was most undesirable to have any more congestion on the single road than was absolutely necessary with the area under sporadic shelling. To relieve the situation it was decided to see whether another route could be opened to the north of Route 209 and an attempt was made to use the track that led direct from the bridge to Gross Häuslingen. The patrol from 3/4 CLY's recce troop which went along it reported very boggy conditions, but nonetheless it was decided to try with armour. Only one squadron from 3/4 CLY managed to go that way before the track collapsed.

At 1715 hours, B Squadron 44 RTR Group which was in the area of the crossroads to the west of Altenwahlingen, was ordered to use Route 209 to try to ease some of the pressure on A Squadron Group in the pinewoods. C Squadron and A Company followed up in reserve. The marines from Bataillon II./6 were not however prepared to let the British have any respite, and they slowed the advance to a crawl on this axis as well. They could not be shifted despite the use of Typhoons from No 184 Squadron, shell-fire, machine-guns and flame-throwers, and by 2100 hours B Squadron Group's attempts to make further progress had come to naught against endless Panzerfaust teams which kept on re-infiltrating behind them through the thick pine woods and the squadron was ordered to concentrate just to the north of the Timpenberg. C Squadron Group was also ordered to move up to concentrate in this area and provide mutual support in the event of any night attacks. Whilst B Squadron Group was inching its way forward, A Squadron Group began to have more success on its axis during the early evening and gradually worked its way forward against the marines in the woods. As night fell, the group managed to get a troop and a platoon established in a school-house some 350 yards from the centre of Gross Eilstorf.

During the latter part of that Saturday afternoon, the other regimental group based on the Greys and 6 RWF eventually crossed the Rethem Class 40 bridge. This was a powerful fighting group with the infantry battalion mounted in Kangaroos provided by F Squadron 49 APC Regiment. This armoured grouping marks a very significant stage in the evolution of British armoured warfare, for the tanks and infantry now had similar mobility and protection and for the first time the two arms could manoeuvre and fight in concert and not as separate entities.[4]

With 44 RTR Regimental Group embroiled in fighting its way through the woods and with progress up Route 209 slow, Brigadier Carver decided to try to regain momentum by passing the Greys Regimental Group straight to Kirchboitzen via the woods north-east of Altenwahlingen. Although this would be a high risk business involving a night advance on a single axis through enemy-held woods, speed was of the essence. To speed things up further, B Squadron Greys was ordered to try and find a route from Kirchwahlingen to the road and track junction midway between Altenwahlingen and Böhme, so as to avoid over-congestion in Altenwahlingen and the blockage in Kirchwahlingen still being caused by vehicles destined for 158th Infantry Brigade. No route was found however due to the ever-present boggy ground and C Squadron Group, the lead group, had to move back to Altenwahlingen, which it eventually reached by 1800 hours. The Group then began to try to clear the road to Böhme. Typhoon support had already been called for on this village, as most of the artillery fire seemed to be coming from this area, with Typhoons from No 175 Squadron of 121 Wing carrying out the attack. Trees felled across the road and parties of marines from Bataillon II./6 armed with machine-guns and Panzerfausts fighting from the thick woods on either side of the road made progress very slow and it was clear that little more would be achieved that day. Sixty-one prisoners from Kompanie 4./6 and 5./6 were captured during the course of Saturday 14 April.

At 2100 hours Brigadier Carver held his orders in Altenwahlingen in which he gave the following tasks, to be carried out during the night of 14-15 April by the two regimental groups:

1. The Greys and 6 RWF were to move to Point 57 east of Gross Eilstorf via Point 21, but were not to make any attempt to clear the woods through which they passed. As soon as possible on 15 April the group was to attack and clear Kirchboitzen.

2. 44 RTR and 2 KRRC were to patrol into Gross Eilstorf during the night. If the village was still held, they were to attack and clear it at first light 15 April; if it was clear, they were to concentrate there and prepare to pass through the Greys on the capture of Kirchboitzen.

The route to Point 57 would take the Greys Regimental Group[5] for the most part through the same thick woods in which so much opposition had already been experienced. To tackle such an obstacle in the normal way with dismounted infantry would have been a slow and costly business, so it was decided to advance in line ahead with alternately a tank then a Kangaroo and so on down the line. Alternate vehicles had their machine-guns trained to right and left and the order was given to shoot their way forward whether or not any enemy showed themselves. The advance would start in the early hours of 15 April and the brigade would receive help for its night advance from artificial moonlight provided by two searchlights belonging to C Troop 344 Search-light Battery.

Whilst the Greys Group prepared for its unconventional night advance, during the early part of the night A and B Companies 2 KRRC mounted patrols to probe the defences of Gross Eilstorf. The patrols met with vigorous reaction and it was clear that no form of night attack could be mounted. An amusing but potentially lethal incident happened during one of the patrols despatched by Major Gibbs.

'I sent out a recce patrol later in the night because the enemy could well have slipped away. Lieutenant Bobby Morrison commanded it. On the outskirts of the village he saw a German sentry. Ambitiously he thought he could capture him. He crept up behind him, put his pistol in his back and said, "Hands up!". The German turned and grabbed Bobby's pistol. Bobby fired all six rounds and missed with the lot! Unarmed, he felt discretion the better part of valour and broke away before the German could use his rifle!'

With 4th Armoured Brigade poised to break out of the southern part of the divisional bridgehead, the remainder of 53rd Welsh Division was directed northwards on Verden. The initial plan for the advance had envisaged an advance by all three brigades. However, due to the threat that still existed to the Westen bridgehead and the confused nature of the continuing fighting in the area of Altenwahlingen, it was not possible to extract 71st Brigade and only one battalion from 160th Brigade could be made available. The main effort had therefore to be provided initially by 158th Brigade, with 160th Brigade, less 6 RWF, joining the advance once 4 Welch had completed its operations on the Aller's left bank and 2 Mons had been relieved from guarding the bridge at Westen. The 158th Brigade's advance would involve it in a series of vil-lage and wood-clearing operations, some of which were to be unop-posed whilst others faced very determined opposition from men still prepared to resist to the last.

NOTES

1   Coincidentally there were three future field marshals all serving within the brigade at this time: Field Marshal The Lord Carver GCB CBE DSO* MC (Commander 4th Armoured Brigade), Field Marshal Sir Roland Gibbs GCB CBE DSO MC DL (Officer Commanding C Company 2 KRRC) and Field Marshal The Lord Bramall GCB OBE MC (Intelligence Officer 2 KRRC). Brigadier Carver was aged twenty-nine, the youngest brigadier in the Army.

2   49 RTR had been converted from the armoured to the APC regiment role in 1945. It reformed on an establishment of two squadrons of fifty-three Kangaroos, each squadron able to lift an infantry battalion of a headquarters and four companies. The regiment came under command of 79th Armoured Division but was reallocated according to need.

3   DD stands for Duplex Drive. Other than its flotation screen and twin propellers, the DD variant had exactly the same characteristics as the standard Sherman V. 44 RTR had converted to the amphibious role for the Rhine crossing and had then retained these tanks.

4   After the War a paper entitled 'Operations East of the River Aller' was written by Brigadier Carver, highlighting the lessons learnt from grouping an armoured regiment and a motor battalion (44 RTR/2 KRRC) and an armoured regiment and an infantry battalion in Kangaroos (Greys/6 RWF). Little has changed in nearly fifty years and many of the principal lessons of 1945 still hold true today.

5   Serving as a troop leader with The Greys was Lieutenant The Viscount Althorp, later to become Earl Spencer and the father of the future Princess of Wales.

THE CAPTURE OF VERDEN
14–17 APRIL

Let us now return to the infantry brigades of 53rd Welsh Division which we had left preparing to advance north up the right bank of the Aller to clear the remaining vestiges of the Aller Line. The majority of the forces which would initially face the advance to Verden were based on Neitzel's depleted Kampfgruppe Verden. The Hungarian battalion had been destroyed and Schaffer's two Kampfgruppe, Hornemann and Tebener, were the only remaining units with any vestige of cohesion. However, both had been badly mauled in the counter-attacks and were in disarray following the failure of their night attacks on the Westen bridgehead. Hungarian stragglers had been swept up into them, along with Kompanie 13./7 and some redundant Luftwaffe personnel who were also incorporated into their ranks. To the left of Schaffer's regiment were the engineer cadets of Hauptmann Kessel's ROB-Pi.Btl.Nienburg, which had also suffered heavy loss during the counter-attacks. Captured orders written by the redoubtable Hauptmann Kessel admit the failure of the counter-attacks but reveal a determination to maintain the defence.

BATTALION ORDERS FOR THE DEFENCE OF THE SECTOR WATERLOO (INCLUSIVE) TO SÜDKAMPEN (EXCLUSIVE).

'The enemy has repelled last night's attack and is now attacking from the Verden road towards Stemmen. 2.Marine Infanterie Division is now holding the general line Armsen-Waterloo-Südkampen-Gross Eilstorf. ROB-Pi.Btl.Nienburg (all three companies) is now under command Mar.Gren.Rgt.7 - right boundary Waterloo (inclusive) left boundary Südkampen (exclusive). Battalion HQ Nordkampen. Outposts and standing patrols are to be pushed out to the south. Kompanie 1 (on right) will maintain contact with Mar.Gren.Rgt.7.'

Signed: Kessel
Hauptmann'

These weakened forces were all that were available to prevent the British advance. Attempts were made to create strongpoints in the villages, and obstacles of felled trees were hastily built on the roads which the enemy were likely to use. Further to the north and in depth of the two Kampfgruppe and ROB-Pi.Btl.Nienburg were the marines of Neitzel's Mar.Gren.Rgt.7. Bataillon I./7 was in the area of the village of Kirchlinteln, but had deployed Kompanie 4./7 forward to the area of Armsen, whilst the remainder of Neitzel's Regiment was in the vicinity of Verden. A few horse-drawn 10.5cm field guns from Mar.Art.Rgt.2 were available for indirect fire support and some 8.8cm Flak had been deployed from the Flak defences in the Verden area to give anti-tank firepower. For the Germans about to face the final phase of the battle for the Aller Line, the prospects must have been grim. Nonetheless, the opposition they were to put up in hopeless circumstances was a credit to their resolve.

The 158th Brigade advance was to take place on three axes: on the left next to the Aller 7 RWF; in the centre 1/5 Welch; and on the right 1 E Lan R. The 7 RWF had the responsibility to clear the divisional axis and the battalion's advance began in the early afternoon from the positions it held on the left flank of the Westen bridgehead. The companies advanced progressively through each other meeting isolated pockets of resistance from troops of Kampfgruppe Hornemann as they did so. As resistance began to stiffen, the commanding officer Lieutenant Colonel Tyler, asked brigade for tank support; this was granted but it was to be some time before the tanks arrived. At 1730 hours B Company reported a well-constructed road-block to the south-east of its objective, the village of Hohenaverbergen. Whilst the pioneer platoon examined the obstacle, Lieutenant Colonel Tyler deployed the other companies forward to be ready in position for the attack, and at 1830 hours the Crocodiles of C Squadron 7 RTR arrived. However, before the orders for the attack could be completed, the Germans launched a counter-attack against B and D Companies in the area of the road-block and both companies were forced to give ground. Lieutenant Colonel Tyler now decided to attack the village using A and C Companies advancing from the south-west. By 1950 hours A Company had crossed the start line and by 2030 hours the company was in the village's outskirts. Defending Hohenaverbergen was Kompanie 13./7, commanded by Oberleutnant Gallhof, reinforced with a platoon of artillery recruits and a number of Luftwaffe personnel. Although the Germans resisted fiercely with rifles, machine-gun fire and Panzerfausts, they were gradually forced out of the village as it burnt around them. Gallhof managed to withdraw north with a number of survivors but 14 marines, three artillerymen and six from the Luftwaffe were killed in the fighting. By 2130 hours resistance had ceased and 7 RWF after a short pause prepared to push on. Throughout the day the battalion had been supported by the Vickers machine-guns and mortars of A and D Company 1 Manchesters which had again caused much destruction among Germans caught in the open on the right bank.

At 1400 hours Major Bowker of 1/5 Welch was ordered by Brigadier Wilsey to advance and capture Armsen some $2^1/2$ miles to the north of the battalion's concentration area and then push on to cut the Verden-Kirchlinteln road. During the counter-attacks of the night 13-14 April, the battalion had been guarding the Westen bridge but had been relieved early in the morning of 14 April by 2 Mons from 160th Infantry Brigade in order to free it for the advance. The battalion subsequently moved to relieve 1 E Lan R in the Wittlohe area where it was due to be joined by a squadron of tanks from 3/4 CLY and half a squadron of Crocodiles from 7 RTR. Major Bowker ordered C Company, supported by the armour, to capture Armsen and then for D Company to pass through them to capture the high ground to the north-west of the village; B Company would then advance to capture the village of Wietzmühlen. Once the position was consolidated, C Company with the armour was to clear the villages of Luttum and Eitze to the west, leaving D Company to advance and cut the road. At 1700 hours the commanding officer was told that he would now have a regiment of tanks, 3/4 CLY, in support, but no Crocodiles. As time was getting on and the light beginning to fade, he ordered his companies to move mounted on the backs of the tanks so as to make best speed. At 1830 hours the advance began and although a Sherman was destroyed and its driver killed when it was hit by an HE 8.8cm shell on the gun mantlet during a halt, Armsen was reached with no difficulty. By 2000 hours it had been captured with little resistance from the artillery recruits of Kampfgruppe Hornemann who had tried to defend it.

D Company now attempted to capture the high ground but ran into trouble and the Welsh were beaten-off by heavy small-arms and mortar fire. This opposition came from the 100-strong Kompanie 4./7, composed of ex U-boat men, who had dug-in on the ridge and in the wood backing it and were prepared to fight it out. This company had been moved forward to hold this piece of key terrain and bolster the very shaky defence. As the Welsh had met determined opposition, the decision was taken to halt the advance until daylight when more information could be gathered on the enemy positions.

1 E Lan R was to face less resolute resistance on the right axis. Having been relieved by 1/5 Welch in the morning, the battalion advanced steadily northwards to its objective, Neddenaverbergen, which was

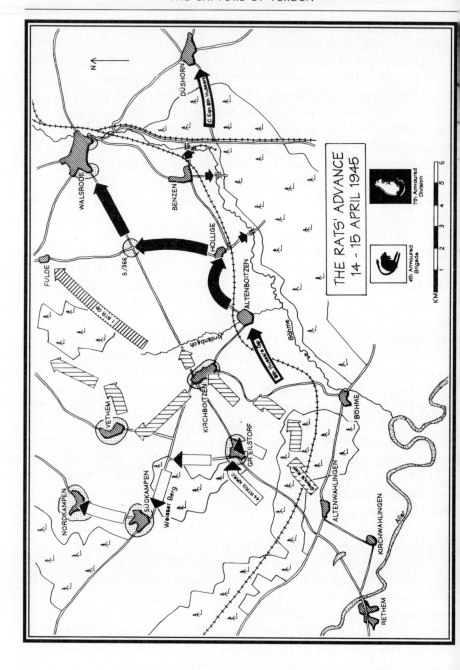

THE RATS' ADVANCE
14 - 15 APRIL 1945

held by artillery recruits from Kampfgruppe Tebener. The advance started quietly enough and Stemmen was cleared with little trouble against only isolated pockets of resistance. Having cleared the village, D Company was fortunate not to be on the receiving end of a concentration fired by their own medium artillery. The company's first objective was the road and rail junction to the north of Stemmen, and just as the first section reached this point the company was warned that they had been mistaken for Germans and that a medium concentration had been called down on them. Fortunately the company radio net was working as they were able to take immediate cover in the cellars of the nearby houses and avoided the storm of steel that descended moments later. Apparently other troops advancing on the right flank had mistaken D Company for a counter-attack force and had ordered up a medium concentration to deal with it. Although some casualties were later caused by enemy shelling during the morning, the enemy fire was not as accurate and the advance continued unhindered. By early afternoon they were close to their objective and H-Hour for the attack on the village was set for 1500 hours. After a short artillery bombardment, B Company entered the village and cleared the western end; A Company then passed through to clear to the eastern. Some machine-gun fire caused three casualties otherwise the village was taken with little opposition and 73 prisoners from Regiment Schaffer were captured in the process. The battalion then consolidated for the remainder of the day in the area of Neddenaverbergen and commanders were briefed on the brigade plan for the attack on Verden. The key to a successful attack was considered to be the control of the Verden-Kirchlinteln road and the wooded area near Kirchlinteln. The plan would start with 1/5 Welch occupying Weitzmühlen, then with 1 E Lan R on the right and 1/5 Welch on the left the brigade would conduct a night advance to secure the main road in order to cut off the Verden garrison from the east before launching the assault on the town.

During the early afternoon of 14 April, a lone Arado Ar 234 Blitz overflew the bridgehead. The aircraft was engaged by H Troop 25th LAA Regiment RA but not surprisingly no hits were scored on the jet-engined aircraft, whose speed was such that it was virtually immune to interception even from Allied fighters. This bomber belonged to the 6.Staffel from III.Gruppe of the bomber unit KG 76[1]. The Staffel had mounted a mid-day attack on the concentrations of British vehicles in the Essel bridgehead area and this aircraft, somewhat off-course for its return journey, had strayed within range of the Bofors gunners. Its parent Kampfgruppe had previously operated from airfields in the Rheine-

Achmer area until forced by 2nd Army's advance to withdraw to an air base at Kaltenkirchen near Hamburg.

Although 14 April had ended with 7 RWF, 1/5 Welch and 1 E Lan R preparing to push on with a night advance having made satisfactory progress during the day, not as much progress was to be made by the brigade during the course of the next day. On the left flank, 7 RWF resumed its advance shortly after midnight and 30 minutes later C Company reported a road-block which the accompanying armour from 3/4 CLY tried unsuccessfully to knock down. Sapper assistance was sought from brigade and by 0100 hours the block was cleared and the company had reached its objective, the road and railway crossing north of Hohenaverbergen. The battalion seems to have then spent the remainder of the day in consolidating its gains rather than advancing, although a patrol was sent to investigate the next village, Luttum.

The 1/5 Welch on the centre axis had a busier time. At 0815 hours D Company with one squadron of tanks mounted another unsuccessful attack against Kompanie 4./7 on the ridge where they had been stopped the night before. At 1300 hours yet another attempt was made which this time was entirely successful; the presence of half a squadron of Crocodiles with the tanks would seem to have made up the marines' minds that resistance was no longer possible. With the ridge clear, D Company and the tanks now swung west and captured the area of the cross-tracks to the north-east of Luttum, and at 1403 hours Major Bowker was visited by Brigadier Wilsey who ordered him to press on and capture Weitzmühlen. The Weitzmühlen area was held by Bataillon II./7 and the village itself weakly held by artillery recruits from Kampfgruppe Hornemann, who had pulled back to it having been forced out of the villages to the south. Major Bowker planned a two-phase attack with C and B Companies attacking alongside each other. Following a short and uneventful advance, the village was attacked and cleared by 1900 hours. Perhaps because of the mauling they had had fighting 4 Welch on the left bank, the marines from Bataillon II./7 failed to resist in the same very robust way as their comrades in the 5th and 6th regiments and gave up quickly.

On the right axis during the early part of the morning, 1 E Lan R had moved to a concentration area. Following a visit to brigade headquarters, Lieutenant Colonel Allen gave orders for an advance northwards to the main road at Kirchlinteln. Once this had been achieved, 160th Brigade were to seize the high ground east of Kirchlinteln before the advance on Verden began. The battalion began the advance at 1600 hours and B Company was soon subjected to shelling from 8.8cm guns whilst it moved down an exposed slope just north of Armsen and took a few casualties. No ground opposition however was met until the advance was some two miles north of the village, where the companies met outposts holding the line of a stream near Specken, providing an obstacle to armoured movement. D Company successfully crossed the only bridge in the area and drove the Germans back to what appeared to be their main defensive position. The armour then attempted to follow. However, when the lead tank from B Squadron 3/4 CLY crossed the bridge the structure collapsed, the tank was tipped upside down and Trooper Green, one of the crew, was drowned. This had been a bad day for the squadron as they had been caught in an artillery barrage that morning which left the squadron leader, Major Phelps, and six other tank commanders wounded. To try to resolve the problem of the stream where they were now stuck, a bulldozer was sent for but it was late on before an alternative route was made and well after midnight before the battalion's vehicles and the tanks advanced again. C Company had in the meantime moved round the right flank to ease the pressure on D Company, the leading company, and the battalion spent the rest of the night consolidating in the area of Specken.

On 15 April 160th Brigade joined the divisional advance. However, as 6 RWF was operating with the Greys and 4 Welch had yet to be replaced on the left bank by 4 RWF from 71st Brigade, the advance was begun by 2 Mons on a single battalion axis. At 1430 hours the battalion began its advance on the right of 1 E Lan R directed on Kukenmoor. Good progress was made and the hamlet was captured by 2100 hours with 52 prisoners taken. The divisional plan was now for 158th Brigade to capture Kirchlinteln and, if fresh enough, then to swing south-west towards Verden. Failing this, 71st Brigade was to pass through 158th Brigade and capture Verden, whilst 4th Armoured Brigade covered this manoeuvre from the right flank.

The 15 April saw the last actions on 2.Marine Infanterie Division's left flank. Here Lotze's battalion and the remnants of Mar.Füs.Btl.2 and the SS companies had remained in place to attempt to block any further British attempts to break out of the Essel bridgehead. It was fortunate for the Germans in their weakened state that the British had decided not to make further effort in the Essel area. Although the Germans had stayed in place for two days, it was clear by 15 April that they would be cut off if they remained on the Aller as there was now virtually nothing to stop the British advancing rapidly to Walsrode and Bergen. Lotze's battalion accordingly withdrew in a north-easterly direction towards Soltau whilst the marines and young SS soldiers headed north for Walsrode. Their withdrawal marked the end of Mar.Füs.Btl.2's gallant and ferocious defence of 2.Marine Infanterie Division's left flank. Also on this day, detailed instructions were issued by OKW in expectation of communications being cut in central Germany when the enemy's east and west fronts met. As the Berlin-incarcerated Hitler would then be prevented from issuing instructions, Dönitz would command all forces in the north, on both east and west fronts, from a headquarters called Führungstab Nordraum; Kesselring would similarly command both fronts in the south. In the event these plans were only partially implemented as the Allies met in central Germany only in the very last days.

During the night of 15-16 April Schaffer's artillery recruits were joined by the remainder of 480.Division which was now deployed to the Aller front from its concentration area to the north of Verden. Verden was the division's home town and it was here that it was formed in November 1944 to replace Division.180 which had been sent to the Netherlands. The division's remaining units were two infantry training regiments, Gren.Ausb.Rgt.22 and 269; an engineer training battalion, Pi.Ausb.Btl.34; a marine reinforcement unit, 22.Mar.Ersatz Abt.; two marine artillery batteries equipped with a total of eight 10.5cm le FH, and various ad hoc mortar, signals and Nebelwerfer units. Gren.Ausb. Rgt.22 took over the area between Kirchlinteln and Kukenmoor, with Gren.Ausb.Btl.16 on the right and Gren.Ausb.Btl.489 on the left, relieving Bataillon I./7 to pull back to an area to the north of Kirchlinteln. Gren.Ausb.Rgt.269 assumed responsibility for the defence of the Bendingbostel area. These regiments received artillery support from Art.Rgt.58 and 5./Volks Artillerie Korps.

To prepare for the final advance to capture Verden, the British also made use of the night of 15-16 April. The 158th Brigade made no further advances and activity was concentrated on preparing for the next day. Work by 555 Field Company RE continued throughout the night on the weak bridge on 1 E Lan R's axis as the intention was for both the battalion and 1/5 Welch's supporting arms to cross it. The patrol sent by 7 RWF to investigate Luttum reported back that the village was held and at 0945 hours on 16 April, Lieutenant Colonel Tyler was ordered to occupy it. As the village was now known to be occupied it was decided to soften up the enemy by attacking with Typhoons prior to the assault. The Typhoons, always a very popular sight for the infantry, attacked at 1230 hours and the battalion was subsequently able to occupy the village without opposition. The companies then took up defensive positions to consolidate their gains and the pattern of the previous day was repeated with a recce patrol being dispatched to investigate the next village, Eitze. The 1/5 Welch, in concert with 1 E Lan R, had meanwhile advanced steadily northwards throughout the day and by evening its companies had established themselves on the high ground to the north-east of Verden and here they dug-in to protect the division's right flank.

1 E Lan R was directed to capture Kirchlinteln on 16 April. During the morning enemy soldiers could be seen through field glasses digging in on the dominating spur to the south of the village and they were heavily engaged by artillery and mortars. These soldiers were from the newly arrived Gren.Ausb.Rgt.22. The advance was led by A and B Companies who had to deal with a great deal of opposition from small groups of machine-gunners who covered all the tracks leading through the woods. As each one had to be separately eliminated, the whole morning was taken up slowly pressing onwards to reach the forward edge of the woods about 800 yards short of Kirchlinteln. Prior to the start of the advance it had been understood that Kirchlinteln formed part of a undefended hospital area and was therefore not to be attacked. With enemy troop activity clearly visible, it was obvious that the Germans had realised Kirchlinteln's tactical importance and were hastily preparing its defence; Brigadier Elrington told the battalion to attack immediately. After a pre H-Hour artillery fire plan, at mid-day A Company began the attack on the town followed by B Company, with both companies supported by tanks from B Squadron 3/4 CLY and Crocodiles.

As the attacking infantry reached the spur the German resistance increased and A Company was heavily engaged on its way up to the village, losing the company commander, Major Whiteside, and two platoon commanders all wounded. During the course of the fighting a Sherman Firefly commanded by Second Lieutenant Rhodes was knocked out and Rhodes killed. He had just fired HE and his machine guns into a trench and thought that it was safe to proceed when he was engaged at a range of four yards by a Panzerfaust. The warhead hit the turret in front of the gunner and the jet instantly killed Rhodes and his gunner, and wounded the operator. The driver escaped unhurt only to be killed by shell-fire a few moments later. Due to the resistance, B Company had to be passed through earlier than intended and with assistance from the Crocodiles was able to capture the spur. Lieutenant Colonel Allen then combined A and B Companies for the assault on the village itself. The battle for the village was over by early evening, both companies having been forced to fight hard to clear the Germans from the houses and farms, particularly around the area of the village cross-roads. The infantry were greatly assisted by the Crocodiles which flamed a very large area. With Kirchlinteln captured, D Company moved up to join the two assault companies whilst C Company provided right flank protection and sent out carrier recce patrols. Sixty-five prisoners from Gren.Ausb.Rgt.22 were captured in the battle for Kirchlinteln and one 8.8cm gun was captured on the southern edge of the village. The regimental history of 1 E Lan R records that the prisoners wore Luftwaffe uniform and those captured by the battalion said that they had been rushed into the breach in the Aller Line so fast that they did not know where they were or in what sort of division they were fighting. The 1 E Lan R's casualties had been four killed and 20 wounded or missing.

During the afternoon of 16 April it was decided that 158th Brigade would not be sufficiently fresh for mounting the attack on Verden. The 71st Brigade was therefore warned to take on this task and the brigade moved up the right bank during the rest of the day to concentrate in the Weitzmühlen area to be poised for an attack on Verden, which would be mounted in the early hours of the morning of 17 April. The axis would be from the east down the main road from Kirchlinteln.

The final destruction of the Aller Line therefore took place on the next day, 17 April, with the capture of the town. Verden had suffered its first major damage on 7 April when German engineers, blowing up the bridges over the Aller as preliminary demolitions, caused extensive blast damage, particularly to the cathedral. Although proposals had been gingerly made by the civic authorities for Verden to be declared an 'open city', these were rejected in Lüneburg and Hamburg. On 14 April wall posters were put up warning that looters would be shot and there was widespread fear among the townsfolk who realised that the town would shortly become a battleground. At 1800 hours on the same day Verden was bombed. The target would seem to have been the Flak battery on the Burgberg on the southern edge of the town, but many bombs fell within the town causing serious damage and killing 31 people. The inhabitants' worst fears for their and the town's futures were not however realised as Kapitän zur See Neitzel had no intention of fighting within the town. His Kampfgruppe had made its stand to the south and east and his troops were now too depleted and exhausted by these battles to take on the town's defence. In the early hours of 17 April Neitzel's exhausted marines withdrew through the town telling the inhabitants that Verden was lost and that the war would soon be over for them.

Whilst these marines were pulling back, 71st Brigade unaware of the German situation were preparing for the battle for the town. The 1 Oxf Bucks LI and 1 HLI left the Weitzmühlen area and moved to the start line which had been secured by A Company 1 Oxf Bucks LI. All indications pointed to a hard fight ahead and there was nothing to suggest that Verden would not be heavily defended. The battalion attacks were to be mounted in two phases: 1 Oxf Bucks LI would attack first, clear the approaches to the town and then break in. The 1 HLI would then pass through to clear the remainder of the town. At 0130 hours C Company 1 Oxf Bucks LI, accompanied by half a squadron of Crocodiles, moved forward down the main road behind a series of artillery concentrations to seize the string of houses on the outskirts of Verden. This was successfully accomplished against minimal opposition, and the many German soldiers dug in among the houses surrendered at the first opportunity. D Company then passed through and occupied a small housing estate. A Company followed and captured the cemetery on the edge of the town against some opposition from two machine-guns; the first gun was silenced by fire from the company, whilst the second was flamed by a Crocodile. During its part in the attack, 1 Oxf Bucks LI captured 112 prisoners and killed one – an indication of the rock-bottom morale which now existed in most of the German forces.

With the approaches to the town secure, at 0530 hours 1 HLI moved through 1 Oxf Bucks LI and began to enter the town. By 0830 hours C and D Companies had reached their objectives and had pushed forward patrols to check the defences within the town. These patrols reported no evidence of opposition so A and B Companies advanced and cleared the remainder of the town and captured an ordnance dump, a field hospital and eight 10.5cm field guns. Despite the Germans' frequent declarations to fight to the last from Verden, the town was essentially handed over as an open city, much to the relief of the townspeople. The daily situation report for 18 April from the OKW however, announced that the town had been lost after many hours of heavy fighting.

NOTES

1   The Arado Ar 234 was the world's first jet engine bomber. KG 76 had formerly been a Ju 88 unit, but from the summer of 1944 had been converted to the new Ar 234 at its bases at Burg bei Magdeburg and Alt-Lönnewitz. First operations with the new aircraft were flown in support of the Ardennes Offensive in December 1944. By 9 April 1945, KG 76 had only four Ar 234 serviceable.

15

'THE RATS ADVANCE'
14–15 APRIL

With Verden captured, we will now step back three days to see how events developed in the southern part of the bridgehead. By mid-April the three corps of 2nd British Army were poised to play their parts in the closing scene of the war. On the right flank VIII Corps was continuing to advance strongly toward the Elbe. Celle had been cleared en route and 15th Scottish Division was closing on Uelzen, the next town, and the corps' left flank was breaking clear of the dead-end of the Essel bridgehead. On the Army's left, XXX Corps was still fighting hard to clear the Germans from the approaches to Bremen, while in the centre, XII Corps readied itself to take up the eastwards advance once again. Speed was still vital, not only for the reasons given in Chapter 1 but also for other strategic reasons that had become apparent. In his report of 14 April to the Combined Chiefs of Staff, Eisenhower identified Norway and the National Redoubt in Bavaria to be the two main areas where prolonged resistance was likely and that operations in both these areas in winter would be well nigh impracticable. Furthermore, as he feared that U-boat warfare could continue to be prosecuted from Norway after Germany had fallen, it was imperative that that country should be promptly liberated. He therefore directed that Denmark be liberated as early as possible so that it could act as a mounting base for an attack on Norway from the east via Sweden, the only viable approach. A thrust to Lübeck and Kiel was an essential preliminary for this manoeuvre and the port of Hamburg would be needed to support the operations in Denmark and Norway; operations on Berlin, however, would continue to take second place. Montgomery was left in no doubt that his advance must press on with maximum speed and this need was impressed on General Dempsey. Dempsey's plan for the advance involved VIII Corps securing a bridgehead over the Elbe to provide XII Corps with a secure right flank from which to mount from an easterly direction the operation to capture Hamburg. With the port in British hands, Denmark would then be cleared.

General Ritchie now completed his plan for his corps' advance from the Aller. The operation would start with 53rd Division and 4th

Armoured Brigade making the initial breakout which would aim to roll up the remainder of the Aller Line and capture Verden, and we have heard how the Welsh fared in this process in the preceding chapter. The 7th Armoured Division, which was concentrated near Nienburg, would then be released to spearhead the eastwards advance on the axis Walsrode-Lüneburg and thereafter the Elbe. The 52nd Lowland Division, which had been continuing to clear the corps' left flank, was warned that it would join XXX Corps for the battle to reduce Bremen and its place in XII Corps' order of battle would be taken by the Guards Armoured Division. The Guards Armoured could be released from XXX Corps, as there was no role for it in the plans being made for the capture of Bremen. The division would be tasked to cross the Aller in the wake of 7th Armoured and then advance in a northerly direction to seize successively the towns of Visselhövede, Rotenburg, Zeven and Bremervörde. In accomplishing this, it would cut the autobahn linking Bremen and Hamburg and dominate the higher ground between the two cities.

We will now take up the story with 4th Armoured Brigade's breakout battle. When last mentioned, the Greys had been poised to start their night advance into the thick pinewoods to the north of Altenwahlingen. The advance was to be led by 2 Troop of C Squadron. The troop set off at 0100 hours on Sunday 15 April with guns blazing to the front and either flank. In a very short time the dry undergrowth had caught fire and the column drove down sandy tracks between walls of flame choked by smoke. On reaching the first bound, the group took up all-round defence and signalled to the following group to pass through it to the next bound. The immediate effect of the forest fire was to force the Germans to withdraw very quickly and the passing of squadron through squadron continued until daybreak when the regimental group, numbering some one 150 tracked vehicles, reached a saucer-shaped dip at the foot of the high ground overlooking Kirchboitzen. At daybreak, hull and turret-down positions were taken up and those present remember having an eerie feeling from not only knowing that they had passed right through the German positions but also because they were able to see the battle that had started to be waged behind them by 44 RTR and 2 KRRC in Gross Eilstorf, only half a mile away.

The village of Gross Eilstorf was defended by marines from the shattered Bataillon II./5, Rethem's defenders, whilst to the south-west Oberleutnant zur See Schrickel's Kompanie 4./6 was dug in on the fringes of the beechwoods covering Route 209. This company had been detached

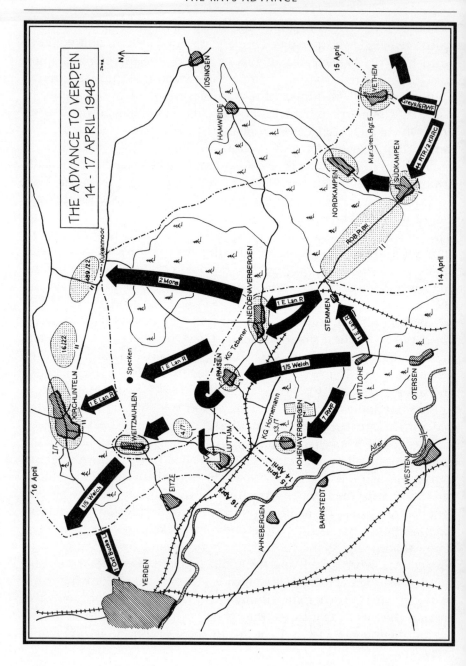

from the remainder of Bataillon I./6 which had fallen back to the villages of Kirchboitzen and Altenboitzen after the failure of the counter-attacks. At 0600 hours on Sunday morning 2 KRRC assaulted Gross Eilstorf with B Company left, A Company right supported respectively by B and A Squadrons 44 RTR. Although the left axis was held up by minor road blocks of felled trees, which took until 0735 hours to be cleared, better progress was made on the right where A Company managed to close up to the village without difficulty. A Company's attack is described by the company commander, Major Gosse.

'The first phase of the attack went quite well and 4 Platoon under Lieutenant Humphreys reached its objective which was a bit of high ground overlooking the first half of the village. One prisoner was taken. The attack then went in with 2 Platoon advancing on the left of the road and 3 Platoon on the right. 2 Platoon soon ran into trouble and Rifleman Downing was killed and Lance Corporals Timson and Hewson and Rifleman Deaves all injured. Lance Corporal Timson later died of his wounds. All these men were very experienced and could be ill-spared. 3 Platoon got on well on the right but were very unlucky as the tanks supporting them thought that they were enemy, opened up and killed one corporal and wounded a rifleman. The Carrier Platoon was meanwhile giving wonderful support and the Germans, though fighting very hard, were obliterated. Rifleman Matthews of 3 Platoon lost his platoon and cleared a large farm single-handed with a German dog as his companion! 4 Platoon then pushed through and cleared the rest of the village which was by then under accurate shell-fire. Altogether 40 enemy were accounted for in a short but bitter struggle.'

While A Company 2 KRRC assaulted from the south, B Squadron moved up from the west and cleared the northern part of Gross Eilstorf. Watching their assault was a young member of Kompanie 4./6, Helmut Krieg.

'Suddenly the artillery fire we had been subjected to lifted and we saw the attackers coming towards us. No infantry were to be seen but just tanks - tanks in long lines. They rolled down the road slowly, shooting into the woods as they came. We waited for the tanks to turn off the road and roll over us but we were to be surprised. The tanks did not turn left in our direction but went to the right. A great weight was lifted from me.'

However, Krieg and his comrades were not to know that the assault had been designed to by-pass their position which was consequently unable to take part in the fighting for the village and was captured complete. When B Squadron broke into the western part of the village, difficulty was experienced with burning houses and sniping and it was not until 1055 hours that brigade headquarters could be informed that Gross Eilstorf was clear and the road passable. One German officer and 94 soldiers were captured in the fight for the village.

On the south-eastern edge of the village an oak tree still bears the scars of the battle. At the base of the tree, a Leutnant and a Fähnrich were buried in a temporary grave having been killed near the neighbouring house. The female occupant of the house tells the following story.

'For some days a battle had been raging to our west in Rethem where the Allies were trying to cross the river Aller. Early in the morning of the 15th of April young German soldiers began coming through the village from the south-east – Kirchwahlingen. They were in a terrible state, one had a very damaged helmet. The shed opposite us was destroyed by fire. The mare, which had had a foal five days before, was killed. Several houses in the village were destroyed, including one which was used as a temporary hospital. I and several of the women buried the young officers next to the oak tree. We covered their faces with a vinegar soaked cloth so that they could be identified at a later date.'

While 44 RTR and 2 KRRC were attacking Gross Eilstorf, the Greys and 6 RWF planned their attack on Kirchboitzen. The plan involved A Squadron with two companies of 6 RWF carried in Kangaroos from 3 and 4 Troops, F Squadron 49 APC Regiment, assaulting from the south. C Squadron would provide fire support from hull-down positions from the south-west whilst B Squadron provided flank protection from the north-west. H-Hour was set for 0800 hours. Kirchboitzen was held by marines from Bataillon I./6 and some marines from Mar.Felders.Btl.2, who had withdrawn north from their position on the Aller near Bierde to avoid being cut off by the expanding Rethem and Essel bridgeheads. The village had been attacked by Typhoons on a number of occasions over the preceding days and destruction of houses and deaths of inhabitants had already occurred.

The attack began at 0815 hours with an artillery fire plan being shot by 4 RHA. Despite the accuracy of the shelling, the attacking troops were met at a short distance from the village by intense small-arms fire and heavy mortar and shellfire. The infantry dismounted too early when still some 300 yards from the village, were quickly pinned down by the Germans' fire and were unable to move for the time being. The leading tank troop, commanded by Lieutenant Andrews, accompanied by the squadron second in command Captain Lewis in his tank, continued to move forward however and reached the village. Various mishaps then overtook the tanks of Lieutenant Andrews' troop with the result that only his and Captain Lewis' tank entered the village. The small-arms fire was still intense and Panzerfaust fire also plentiful. On reaching the church, Lieutenant Andrews was greeted by a salvo of six Panzerfausts fired from 40 yards away. One of the missiles, fired by an inhabitant of the village, struck the ground by the track at the rear of the tank temporarily immobilising it. Apart from that shot no damage was done. The coaxial machine-gun had jammed, so the gunner had the satisfaction of firing high explosive with the certainty of registering a hit. These two leading tanks were quickly followed by the remainder of 1 Troop and the infantry were able to advance again. With the armour dominating enemy movement, the infantry were able to break into the village and then clear it systematically, building by building.

By mid-morning it was all over and at 1000 hours the village was declared clear, with 67 prisoners being taken and two 7.5cm Pak captured. Leutnant zur See Lieberwith and 47 marines were killed in the fight for the village and a 15 year-old Volkssturmmann, Erich Mühle, also died. Those marines who had avoided death or capture in Kirchboitzen, retreated to the woods to the north to take up new positions in the villages of Vethem and Südkampen. As they did so they left behind ambush parties in the woods and hillocks of the Weisser Berg, which straddles the road leading to Südkampen. With the Greys and 6 RWF regrouping after their successful attack, patrols of the Greys' recce troop pressed on up Route 209 from Kirchboitzen to check on the state of the road. They soon reported back that the road was cratered where it crossed the Jordanbach stream north-east of Kirchboitzen and no deviation was possible there[1]. Another patrol was despatched to Altenboitzen, which was situated to the south of Route 209 and had been reported earlier to contain German troops, but the patrol reported back that the village was now clear.

By this time 22nd Armoured Brigade of 7th Armoured Division was across the Rethem bridge and straining at the leash to take over the advance. It was decided therefore that 4th Armoured Brigade should not continue to Walsrode but turn north to clear to Verden and Rotenberg, releasing Route 209 for 7th Armoured Division's use. However, traffic congestion now became a problem again in the restricted area of the bridgehead, delaying this sensible change of plan. Although Brigadier Carver was anxious to get the tail of his brigade clear of Gross Eilstorf as soon as possible to allow 22nd Armoured through, it was not yet safe to move the guns of 4 RHA beyond the village. Against this, he needed to get 1 RTR, one of 22nd Armoured Brigade's regiments, through Gross Eilstorf to Kirchboitzen to relieve the Greys and 6 RWF before his own brigade could take up the new northwards advance. Notwithstanding the desire to press on, there were however some sound administrative reasons for not moving too precipitately; 6 RWF had not had a meal since the previous afternoon, ammunition needed replenishing and the two regimental groups needed to regroup. Despite the pressures from on high, 4th Armoured therefore remained in location for the time being whilst 22nd Armoured moved up as far as it could on Route 209.

With his brigade replenishing, Brigadier Carver completed his planning for the advance on the new axis. He decided to advance north on two regimental axes: right the Greys and 6 RWF with Vethem and Idsingen as their objectives; left 44 RTR and 2 KRRC directed on Südkampen, Nordkampen and Hamweide. Although the right axis with fewer villages and woods offered the best chance for rapid progress, it was essential to clear the left route as the brigade needed it for its resupply route.

The armoured brigade's advance resumed again at 1400 hours. On the right the Greys and 6 RWF soon discovered that Vethem was held and in trying to outflank it, the Stuarts of the Recce troop were engaged by 10.5cm guns firing from the wood line north-east of the village. These guns belonged to a battery of Mar.Art.Rgt.2 which had eventually arrived having acquired its horses. The batteries were to pay dearly over the next two days for their lack of mobility and the contrast between the manoeuvring armour of the British brigade and these antiquated, horse-drawn guns could not be more stark. Operations were hindered by the fact that the area was overlooked by the ridge to the west of Vethem, dominated by a windmill. Attempts to find a route down through the wooded slope south of the road were finally successful, but took time. It was now clear that Vethem was not going to be easy to capture with the bridge over the stream on the southern approach blown and all other approaches difficult and it was apparent that its capture would require at least two of 6 RWF's companies. The area of the stream was boggy and effectively protected the village on all sides but the west, whilst the approaches from the south and east were open and overlooked by both the village and the ridge with its windmill to the north-west. This high ground would have to be taken as it dominated the axes of both regimental groups.

Unfortunately for the German gunners at Vethem, their guns were spotted by the Greys' commanding officer, Major Stewart, as soon as they opened fire and he ordered B Squadron to mount an immediate attack on them; this it did knocking them out at point-blank range. It had now become evident that Vethem was held in some strength so B Squadron was ordered to remain in position in the fringe of the wood where it overlooked the village, whilst C Squadron pushed round further to the north-east to isolate the village. A Squadron was given the task of attacking Vethem with the fire support of the other two squadrons. It duly started to advance but only managed a short distance before it was held up by the stream and the poor going and so B Squadron was ordered to make the attack instead from the east as they were already across the stream. Stubborn resistance was immediately encountered from all forms of small-arms and the ever-present Panzerfausts and although the marines suffered many casualties, Lieutenant Briggs, troop leader of 2 Troop was killed by a sniper firing from an upstairs window and 6 RWF suffered a number of killed and wounded.

With the battle to clear Vethem looking as if it would take time, Brigadier Carver ordered Major Stewart to leave the battle's completion to the commanding officer of 6 RWF. A and B Squadrons and the two companies which were already committed to the attack would be left behind, whilst Major Stewart was to bypass the village with the remainder of the group (one squadron and two companies of 6 RWF) and move to secure the next village, Idsingen; the remainder of the group would join them there once Vethem had fallen. General Ritchie visited the brigade headquarters whilst these decisions were being made and was satisfied that the progress of the battle had opened a gap sufficiently large for the release of 7th Armoured Division.

While the Greys Group was involved at Vethem, 44 RTR and 2 KRRC had been moving north from Gross Eilstorf. As the columns moved through the Weisser Berg they were engaged by machine-guns and Panzerfausts fired by the ambush parties in the woods. These troops were the defenders of Kirchboitzen joined by further marines from the severely depleted companies from Bataillon I./5, who had been retreating in a north-easterly direction following the failure of their counter-attacks on the Gross Häuslingen area. Although they sustained some casualties, 44 RTR and 2 KRRC pressed on and reached the outskirts of Südkampen. The village was held by the headquarters of Bataillon II./5 and the 40 remaining marines from Kompanie 7./5. A Company 2 KRRC was directed to take the village and Major Gosse ordered 3 Platoon to make the initial attack. The platoon found that main bridge over the stream had been blown and a scissors bridge was called up from brigade to span the gap. With 3 Platoon committed on the southern edge, 2 Platoon and the Carrier Platoon made their way round the right flank, entered the village and quickly tidied up the remaining opposition, capturing many prisoners and three Renault light tanks in the process. Where these tanks came from and who crewed them is a mystery[2]. By last light the 44 RTR Group had completed clearing the village. While 44 RTR and 2 KRRC cleared Südkampen, the Greys had managed to reach Idsingen practically unopposed, passing on the way the five 10.5cm guns knocked out earlier by B Squadron. On arrival the troops and platoons were positioned at each of the entrances to the village, which was well in the rear of the fighting in Vethem and Nordkampen, as it was anticipated that withdrawing German troops would almost certainly attempt to enter the village unaware that it had already been occupied. At about 2100 hours this theory was proved correct when numbers of German troops came into the town from the north; 40 were captured, whilst others managed to escape. Worse however was to befall the Germans, for during the early hours of 16 April, soldiers on foot and horse-drawn artillery from Mar.Art.Rgt.2 attempted to enter Idsingen from the west, still unaware that it was held by the squadron of tanks and two companies of infantry. The Germans were engaged by Sergeant Wentzell's troop which opened fire at a range of 100 yards. When the target area was revealed at first light it was discovered that they had killed 20 Germans and destroyed three 10.5cm guns with their horses still in harness.

Despite Major Stewart's success at capturing Idsingen, Vethem had still not been finally cleared due to a stubborn stronghold in the centre of the village held by marines from Jordan's regimental headquarters and from Kompanie 3./5 and 5./5. Even after an area of houses had been cleared, groups of marines kept on reappearing; a typically courageous performance. The whole village was by now ablaze and the two companies engaged in clearing it were somewhat disorganised and very weary. The decision therefore was taken to pull everyone back from the village and flatten it. This was duly done with concentrated 75mm and 17pdr HE and AP gunfire and Vethem was taken with no opposition at 2300 hours. However, it was difficult to reorganise in the village as farm animals, maddened by the fire and shelling, were dashing in all directions, and a few terrified civilians were attempting to rescue their remaining belongings. The ground was hot under foot as there were only three houses which had not burnt to the ground. As the tactic of reducing villages with high explosives saved time and casualties, 44 RTR and 2 KRRC decided to treat Nordkampen in similar fashion. A call was made to the defenders to surrender by a psychological warfare team with a loudspeaker and a small demonstration was laid on in which a house was brewed up; as this brought forth only the Bürger-meister, A Squadron slowly entered the village. As the tanks were greeted with a hail of fire, the whole village was razed to the ground and occupied without further trouble.

On the Greys' axis during the morning the remaining squadrons and companies of the regimental group closed up from Vethem and the advance resumed towards the next objective, the village of Bend-ingbostel. Despite being slowed by boggy ground and a blown bridge, which required a Churchill bridgelayer to be called forward, the advance made good progress and Bendingbostel was captured by 1930 hours. The 44 RTR Group likewise made steady progress from Nord-kampen and despite opposition from an 8.8cm gun in the area of Stel-lichte, which was dealt with by Typhoons, the squadrons and companies pressed on with the northwards advance.

The 4th Armoured's advance had been a most successful manoeu-vre, the brigade had mopped up many groups of withdrawing marines and had cut a swathe through Mar.Art.Rgt.2's gun areas, destroying or capturing 25 10.5cm guns. By 19 April the brigade had taken prisoner nearly 2,000 Germans, mostly marines, and had killed some 150; all for a loss of 15 dead, 62 wounded and four Shermans knocked out. Look-ing back at this time in his memoirs, Field Marshal Carver recorded both his satisfaction and his thoughts on the future organisation of an armoured brigade.

'It had been a most successful battle, a model of its kind, in which we had been able to combine mobility and firepower more effectively than at any time since we had crossed the Somme. It convinced me that the organisation of the brigade into two battle-groups, each of an armoured regiment and a mobile infantry battalion, was the best one for an armoured brigade, certainly for the majority of operations.'[3]

With 4th Armoured to the north of the Corps' axis, the way was now clear for the 7th Armoured Division to breakout. During the long years of the war, 7th Armoured Division had become a household name in

Britain. Formed in 1938 in Egypt it had fought through the North African campaign from the first to the last shot and its members were truly 'Desert Rats'. It had then taken part in the first three months of the Italian campaign before returning to England to prepare for 'Overlord'. The division landed in Normandy on D+1 and thereafter was in the forefront of the fighting throughout the summer of 1944. Following the advance across northern France and into the Low Countries, 7th Armoured became heavily involved in the bitter fighting to clear the west bank of the Rhine. The division crossed that great river four days after the crossing operation and it then played a leading role in the advance to the Weser, as described in Chapter 1. Since 11 April the division had been in a concentration area near Nienburg waiting for the order to move.

In April 1945, 7th Armoured Division consisted of three brigades - 22nd Armoured, 131st Infantry and 155th Infantry, the latter attached from 52nd Lowland Division. The division therefore comprised an armoured brigade of three armoured regiments[4] and an infantry motorised battalion in M5 half-tracks; two lorried infantry brigades each of three battalions; an armoured reconnaissance regiment; and an armoured car regiment. The divisional artillery support consisted of a field regiment (3 RHA) with 24 towed 25pdr guns; a motorised regiment (5 RHA) with 24 self-propelled Sexton 25pdr guns; an anti-tank regiment (65th Anti-Tank Regiment RA) with three batteries of towed 17pdr anti-tank guns and one battery of Achilles M10 self-propelled 17pdr guns; and an anti-aircraft regiment (15th Light AA Regiment RA) with 54 Bofors 40mm guns. It was a powerful organisation fielding some 306 tanks, both light and medium. The division was commanded by Major General 'Lou' Lyne.

General Lyne's plan for the advance by 7th Armoured Division was for 22nd Armoured Brigade to lead with Lüneburg as its objective. The 131st and 155th Infantry Brigades would follow the armour to mop-up bypassed enemy and secure the advance's flanks. Brigadier Wingfield decided to advance on two axes with a regimental group on each: on one would be 1 RTR with a company from 1st Battalion The Rifle Brigade (Motorised) (1 RB) in its half-tracks and a battery of guns from 5 RHA; whilst on the other would be 8th Hussars, the divisional armoured reconnaissance regiment[5], also with a company from 1 RB and a battery from 5 RHA. In reserve would be 5 RTR, 1/5th Battalion the Queen's Regiment (1/5 Queens) mounted in Kangaroos and 1 RB, less the two companies. At 0830 hours on 14 April Brigadier Wingfield held a conference at which he placed the brigade at one hour's notice to cross the Rethem bridge and start the advance. Once across the Aller, the brigade would advance on the two axes with the 8th Hussars Group on the right – Yellow Route – and 1 RTR Group on the left – Red Route.

Let us now look at the German forces which would have to face the tanks of 22nd Armoured. Following the collapse of the Aller Line, the battered battalions of 2.Marine Infanterie Division were pushed back to the north and north-east and had come under command of Korps Ems. The majority of the division was stretched – holding would be too strong a description – on a line between the villages of Jeddingen and Neunkirchen, a front of some 12 miles. In the centre of this frontage lay the town of Visselhövede which now became the focus of the defence. Visselhövede itself was occupied by the remnants of the companies from Mar.Gren.Rgt.5 which had been forced back to the town by 4th Armoured Brigade's advance, and here they drew breath and prepared for its defence; the regiment was still commanded by Kapitän zur See Jordan. Other elements of the division had also managed to reach this area; the five companies of Major Stoschke's Mar.Felders. Btl.2, which had been little involved in the fighting to date, were sited forward of Visselhövede in the villages of Ottingen, Kettenburg and Wehsen, whilst the last remnant of Mar.Füs.Btl.2, a weak company of 80 men, was in the hamlet of Riepholm.

Following the loss of the village of Kirchboitzen, the majority of the marines remaining from Mar.Gren.Rgt.6 had withdrawn in a north-easterly direction to the village of Neunkirchen. Remnants of Bataillon I./6 had however managed to pull back to Walsrode, the next town on Route 209, where the companies hastily occupied positions covering the western and south-western approaches to the town. The bridges over the Böhme river were prepared for demolition. As the marines retreated, an Organisation Todt[6] team blew the demolition charge on the culvert which carried Route 209 over the Jordanbach stream, producing a very large crater which effectively blocked the road. The sole group capable of offering any form of resistance between Kirchboitzen and Walsrode were the gunners from Flak batteries 4./117 and 4./162. These men had prepared hasty defensive positions to the north and east of Route 209 in the area of the hamlet of Schneede. Both batteries had been heavily involved in the fighting and 4./162 had lost all its remaining Flak guns. Although 4./117 had moved on 11 April with its guns to Drei Kronen north of Walsrode, its spare gunners, together with those from 4./162, joined the members of a RAD heavy Flak unit, Schwere Flakabt.366, to form an ad hoc rifle company known as 5./366 under a Hauptmann Tesch. The company deployed around the Route

209 – Hollige-Fulde crossroads; one group located north of Route 209, another on the south on the edge of the pineforest. Further to the east and covering the routes into Walsrode were the remnants of Bataillon I./6 with stragglers from Mar.Gren.Rgt.5 and Mar.Füs.Btl.2. Such artillery support that was still available, was provided by 3.Batterie of Mar.Art.Rgt.2, although one of its three troops was by now without its guns.

The original intention had been for 22nd Armoured Brigade to start its advance on 14 April, with the brigade pushing on as soon as 4th Armoured had broken through the remaining resistance and swung north to clear the centre line. However, with Brigadier Carver's brigade delayed by the stiff opposition, 22nd Armoured was held back on the Aller's left bank for a further night and it was not until the early hours of 15 April that its advance would be able to begin.

With pressure mounting from the Corps commander to get the armoured division's advance underway, it was decided to start 22nd Armoured's advance before 4th Armoured was clear of Route 209. As the 8th Hussars Group was to advance on the southern axis and would therefore avoid the bulk of 4th Armoured Brigade, Brigadier Wingfield ordered the 8th Hussars to start and at 0800 hours the regiment together with A Company 1 RB and K Battery 5 RHA, moved off from its concentration area and an hour later the long column of vehicles had begun to cross the Rethem Class 40 bridge. With fighting still going on in Kirchboitzen, 8th Hussars was ordered to deviate to the south of Route 209, outflanking any enemy opposition and demolitions on the main road, and rejoin it short of Walsrode, the next town on the axis.

The 1 RTR Group, consisting of I Company 1 RB and G Battery 5 RHA, supported by a troop of flail tanks and a detachment from 4 Field Squadron RE, began its advance some three hours after 8th Hussars. During the remainder of the morning, as 4th Armoured began to move off Route 209, the group was able to push its way slowly forward and by mid-day had eventually reached Kirchboitzen. Here 1 RTR dropped off A Squadron to relieve the Greys and then moved on to keep up with 8th Hussars, who were making good progress on the southern axis. By 1500 hours the lead 1 RTR squadron had reached the Jordanbach but were then held up by the engineering effort needed to fill the large crater blown in the road by the Organisation Todt demolition team. This stream's name brought many a wry smile to members of the division. The Class 40 Bailey pontoon bridge built by 7th Armoured Division engineers across the Weser at Nienburg on 13 April had been confidently named the 'Jordan Bridge' as there appeared to be only one more river - the Elbe - to cross. As it happened, the first obstacle encountered by the division on the resumption of its advance was the Jordanbach!

While the 1 RTR Group slowly advanced on Red Route to the north, 8th Hussars Group were making better progress across country via the sandy tracks to the south. By 1130 hours the group had passed through 4th Armoured Brigade and had reached Altenboitzen. Hollige was the next village, where there was a brief encounter with the enemy. A feel for events during this day is provided by the diary entries of Edward Ardizzone, the famous artist, who had been attached to the regiment as a war artist.[7]

'A very cold, grey morning - busy packing-up as we hope to leave. Leave about 9.30 (a long procession, one squadron in front of us and other squadrons behind us) before which we halt in a stretch of open ploughed land. Then across a Bailey bridge and by devious ways with many halts, through wooded country. Sounds of battle in the forest to our left. Column of B Carriers and Kangaroos cross our path. The forest thick pine. In the open places and along the dirt roads many aspen in first leaf ...'[8]

As they passed through the village of Hollige, regimental headquarters was shot at.

'Pass through two half-timbered and brick forest villages. In the second one a man fired a Panzerfaust at our tank from behind the corner of a barn, about twenty paces away. Thank God he missed. Go cautiously forward after this, scanning every nook and corner. Relief when we get out of the village into open country ...'

By early afternoon B Squadron, leading the advance, was able to head north to return to Route 209. As the tanks neared the main road they were engaged by the Flak of 4./117 and the men of 5./366. The war diarist of Batteries 4./117 and 4./162 describes these events:

'15.4.45 ... At mid-day the tanks advanced against these positions. The tanks crossed the main road advancing towards the first group's positions and those of the 2./604 RAD. The company commander located on Schneeheide came under fire from 2 tanks and machine-gun and artillery fire. The second group came under heavy, machine-gun fire and had to vacate their positions. Part of the first group was over-run by tanks. With the exception of one soldier, no news about the fate of those men is known. The remainder of the first group was able to withdraw via Fulde to Drei Kronen.

'Killed: Leutnant Bornhofen from a splinter wound in the head.

'Missing: Wachtmeister[9] Passek, Stabsgefreiter Kruse, Obergefreiter Koch, Gravenits, Strack, Effer and Gefreiter Wieprecht.

'Wachtmeister Passek managed to fire a last Panzerfaust towards an attacking Sherman. Obergefreiter Bartl from the second group fired a Panzerfaust at a tank driving up the main road and destroyed it.

'Missing: Obergefreiter Bartl and Konheiser. Flak-v.Schroers deserted through fear at the start of the attack.

'The soldiers of the second group were reformed on Route 209 by the company commander and repositioned with the 8.8cm guns near the road intersection at the Schneede farm. After a further advance of the tanks these soldiers helped evacuate two 2cm guns and one 8.8cm gun from their positions and thus prevented them from falling into enemy hands. As Walsrode came under fire during the same afternoon all units were withdrawn to Jarlingen.'

Despite their best efforts, the German defence was no match for the British armour and motorised infantry and B Squadron cleared the area quickly, capturing a further three of Batterie 4./117's 2cm Flak. Ardiz-zone describes his impressions of the battle at this time.

'A long halt on a road with silver birch and in open country. Sounds of battle forward and to our left. A big fire ahead too. Some prisoners came back riding on the bonnet of an armoured car. All the time voices on the wireless giving battle positions. Forward onto the main road, past burning cottages and one dead German soldier by the roadside, then up to the high ground overlooking Walsrode. A big fire in the village and one in a farmhouse to the right of us. Dotted about around us are more tanks, half-tracks and a little group of prisoners. Enemy planes overhead and sound of Bren and shellfire ...'

By 1550 hours 8th Hussars Group had established itself astride the cen-tre line on the high ground overlooking Walsrode. While the main body of the regiment had swung north back to Route 209, the Recce Troop had been sent south-east with the dual task of providing a mea-sure of flank protection whilst proving an alternative route in case the regiment was held up on the centre line. This involved them in examining four bridges over the river Böhme. While carrying out their task, small bands of Germans lurking in the woods and farms were successfully dealt with, the farms bursting into flames after a few rounds of 37mm. Civilians questioned by the troop informed them that all the bridges in which they were interested had however been blown.

Sergeant Hearn discovered that the civilians were correct in respect of the first and second bridges. Sergeant Spencer was checking the condition of the third when he got into what might have been a disastrous situation. The road up to the bridge crossed a small stream by a rickety wooden contraption, which collapsed immediately his vehicle reached terra firma on the other side. Sergeant Spencer found himself faced with a blown bridge in front, a collapsed one behind, and on each side of the road that joined them nothing but marshes. To rebuild the wooden bridge with the aid of some telegraph poles, which the section's Stuart pushed down, and some sleepers found alongside a nearby railway line took a couple of hours, during which he was lucky to be left unmolested.

While Sergeant Spencer was practising to be a sapper, Sergeant Hearn discovered that the fourth bridge was a fairly substantial and intact wooden structure, and in the event of it not standing up to the weight of a Cromwell, less than 90 yards away stood a massive stone and concrete railway bridge. Sergeant Hearn's section daintily crossed the wooden one and breasting a small wooded rise on the other side, narrowly missed colliding with a crowded German staff car that flashed past flat out along the broad concrete road making its escape to Walsrode. Some sappers were sent down to pass professional judgement on the wooden bridge and they thought it might take a Cromwell. The troop leader of the leading troop of C Squadron, who had by now reached the scene, was selected as the guinea pig. Recce Troop watched fascinated as the timbers creaked and sagged, but he and his troop all made it. The whole squadron then followed and with the Recce Troop pushed on up the other side.

Back on the centre line B Squadron and A Company 1 RB were located on the high ground to the west of Walsrode waiting for the remainder of 22nd Armoured Brigade to close up before clearing Walsrode. Ardizzone describes the scene.

'7 pm.: Still on the high ground above Walsrode. We seemed to be ringed by fires, some very distant, some nearer. Also distant explosions as bridges are blown by the enemy - some shelling too. The evening sun lighting the scene and the great columns and mushrooms of smoke. Forward again about 7.30 pm. Have the misfortune to misplace a track in a ploughed field near a monolith. Get the tank to the road. Repairs seem almost hopeless. We are visited by an insolent Nazi boy. Getting dark and nervous of being a lone tank crew after dark. Tank mended at last, very late - but we had the company of endless convoys of tanks, Kangaroos and lorries. Find Tac HQ after a devious route through the outskirts of the town. A great fire in a factory lit us part of the way. Arrive at 1 a.m. very tired and dirty. Stumble off my tank and hurt my leg horribly. Go to bed on the floor of a dirty kitchen.'

Although a reasonably sized town, Walsrode was largely undefended and was easily cleared by B Squadron and A Company 1 RB. The south-west entrance to the town had been heavily cratered and was held by a company of marines, probably from Mar.Gren.Rgt.6, armed with Panzerfausts. They were soon disposed of and a road to the south found. Although a bridge on this route was mined and ready for demolition, it was captured intact before the Germans had time to blow it, and those marines able to escape hastily withdrew northwards to the village of Neunkirchen. At 2200 hours Walsrode was occupied by 1/5 Queens[10] who found it crammed with civilians. The town was also being used as casualty evacuation centre and its three hospitals were full of German wounded, among whom were eight Britons. With Walsrode captured, 8th Hussars Group leaguered for the night on the high ground near the town, whilst on the right of the advance the Recce Troop, which had been joined by C Squadron, leaguered to the south of the centre line as they had failed to get through to Düshorn to rejoin the regiment. Their leaguer was in the largest patch of open ground they could find - a field of roots. The vehicles were massed in a tight bunch in the middle and although the troops had not eaten since their very early breakfast that morning, they dared not light any kind of fire and risk revealing their position.

That night the Luftwaffe chose to make one of its rare appearances in strength. In two waves, a mixed force of aircraft attacked the bridge at Rethem as well as the bridgehead area starting at 2030 hours. The first wave consisted of two Me 109s and eight Fw 190s in the fighter-bomber role and the second, about 45 minutes later, a number of Ju 88s and Ju 188s. The Ju 88s would have come from the remnants of the night-fighter units, whilst the Ju 188s probably came from KG 200[11] as records do not show any other unit in Luftflotte Reich in April 1945 being equipped with this type of aircraft. Unfortunately for the pilots, on the night they chose to attack, the Rethem area contained a high density of anti-aircraft weapons. It had been recognised that the crossing would be a priority target, so the light anti-aircraft batteries from 25th LAA Regiment were allocated to provide protection, with H Troop equipped with six 40mm Bofors in point defence of the bridge. Also sited in the area of the bridge was a detachment of searchlights from C Troop 344 Moonlight Battery RA which had been providing artificial light for the manoeuvres of the preceding nights. With 7th Armoured Division also heavily concentrated in the Rethem area as its units moved up, further anti-aircraft assets were available from the three batteries of 15th LAA Regiment. One of these batteries, 41 Battery, had been issued a few days before with four-barrelled .50 calibre machine-guns mounted on M14 half-tracks and its gunners must have been itching to try out their new weapons in earnest.

As the aircraft came into the attack the batteries of 15th and 25th Regiments crashed into action and all guns were able to engage. The wall of fire that met the attackers was such that they were prevented from making low-level runs and the bombing consequently lost accuracy. Nonetheless, a number of bombs landed close enough to the Class 40 bridge to damage the central section sufficiently to force its closure, whilst others landed in the town causing destruction and fatalities among soldiers and civilians. For those subjected to the bombs and bullets this was a very unpleasant experience. Among them was Lance Bombardier John Mercer, a member of the Counter Mortar Officer's[12] staff in 7th Armoured Division, who describes the attack.

'As dusk fell the Luftwaffe came over and bombed and straffed our positions. This was the first time we had met German bombers since the nights at Demouville, though we had seen some German jet fighters in the sky flying incredibly fast... The Luftwaffe attack was both unexpected and extremely unpleasant and I was more scared at Rethem under air attack than I had been at any previous stage of the campaign... Rethem seemed to be the last vicious throw of a defeated enemy as we took cover in a meadow beneath the half-track. The Heinkels (sic) rumbled overhead on their bombing run and we wondered where was the RAF. Maybe I had run out of endurance, maybe the war experience banked in my mind was becoming overdrawn.'[13]

No 257 Battery of 65th Anti-Tank Regiment had the misfortune to be passing through the town at the time of the attack and suffered three killed and four seriously wounded. In addition it lost four trucks including the battery sergeant major's truck and the battery charging plant which it towed. Three townsfolk also died in the raid and more houses in Lange Strasse were burnt down. The Auster aircraft of A Flight No 653 (AOP) Squadron also suffered damage when a bomb landed in the field which served as their landing strip and showered them with earth and stones, tearing their surfaces. The anti-aircraft batteries however had some success, with the .50 calibre machine-guns of 41 Battery shooting down a Ju 88 and damaging a Fw 190, and the Bofors of 42 Battery registering hits on a further Ju 88 and Fw 190. As the aircraft flew away into the night there was feverish activity in Rethem to put out the burning trucks and houses so that they did not serve as beacons for follow-up attacks; fortunately none were forthcoming. Sappers worked on the damaged bridge throughout the night and although by 1000 hours the next day it had been classified Class 24, it did not finally reach Class 40 again until 1800 hours.

While 22nd Armoured pushed slowly forward, 155th Infantry Brigade waited on the Aller's left bank to follow up in its wake. The brigade's task was to mop up any stragglers in the villages of Böhme, Gross Eilstorf and Altenboitzen, and clear the woods between them. The battalions were directed on these tasks as follows: 7/9 R Scots to clear Böhme, 6 HLI Altenboitzen and 4 KOSB Gross Eilstorf. After a very frustrating morning spent at immediate notice to move, at 1430 hours the brigade eventually began to advance with 7/9 R Scots leading. By evening all objectives had been taken and some 28 prisoners from Mar.Gren.Rgt.6 captured. The brigade tactical headquarters was able to move up to the Altenwahlingen crossroads on the right bank leaving the main headquarters stranded on the left due to the closure of the bridge following the air raid.

We had left 1 RTR in the mid-afternoon held up at the Jordanbach demolition. The two squadrons remained in this area awaiting engineer assistance until 1630 hours when the commanding officer, Lieutenant Colonel Hobart, was told to wait no longer and head north-east to the village of Fulde. This more northerly advance now fitted a new divisional axis which had been given to Major General Lyne during the afternoon. The 7th Armoured was now not to take Lüneburg, but was given as its new objective the bridges over the Elbe at the town of Harburg which lay to the immediate south of Hamburg. This would involve a marked swing to the north in the divisional axis and the town of Soltau now became the next major objective. The 1 RTR accordingly struck off across the heathland and meeting only sporadic opposition from groups of marines from Mar.Gren.Rgt.5 and grenadiers of SS-Ausb.u.Ers.Btl.12 HJ, was able to capture Fulde and Hünzingen by

1900 hours. During its advance the following day the regiment swept past the town of Bomlitz. Shortly before the British arrived, an Untersturmführer Frier of the SS battalion had formed up his 40 men in a factory yard, made a short speech then ordered all those under 18 to step forward; 12 moved. These soldiers then had their pay books stamped, 'Dismissed. Bomlitz 16 April 1945' and were ordered to go home which, after some protest, they did. Frier had conducted this ceremony on the site of a large, heavily camouflaged explosives factory concealed in the woods around the town[14]. This factory was never bombed and continued in production right up to its capture. Although 15 April had been a slow and frustrating day for the division, important gains had been made and the way looked clear for the next day's operations.

NOTES

1   A bypass route to the south via the Hellberger Mill does exist but perhaps in 1945 it was a sand track and was not capable of taking armour.

2   The Renault FT 17 first entered service in 1918, had a cross-country top speed of 2mph and was somewhat obsolete by 1945! The Germans recovered large numbers of them after the fall of France and many were put to use maintaining civil order. Latterly some were used as armoured command and observation posts in Normandy in 1944. How these three vehicles came to be in northern Germany is a mystery.

3   Field Marshal Carver, *Out of Step. Memoirs of a Field Marshal*, Hutchinson.

4   The armoured regiments of 7th Armoured differed from the regiments in the other armoured divisions in that their sabre squadrons were equipped with two types of tank – Cromwells and Shermans – on a 3:1 ratio.

5   By 1945 the armoured reconnaissance regiments were organised on the basis of three squadrons of four troops. Each troop consisted of three 75mm Cromwell tanks with a 17-pounder Challenger tank in support.

6   The Organisation Todt (OT), formed in 1938, was a paramilitary construction corps responsible for military construction projects, such as the bunkers of the Atlantic Wall. The OT engineers responsible for this demolition would have come from within Oberbauleitung Unterweser – the local OT formation.

7   Ardizzone had been engaged as a war artist since 1943 and had painted and recorded in his diary his experience of war from Sicily, via Italy and Normandy, to North Germany. His sketches now belong to the Imperial War Museum.

8   E Ardizzone, *Diary of a War Artist*, The Bodley Head. The Bailey bridge referred to here was the Rethem bridge, whilst the noise of fighting was probably from the Greys and 6 RWF as they fought to clear Kirchboitzen. The Kangaroos would have contained 1/5 Queens.

9   These ranks all belong to the Flak arm. The British equivalent ranks would be: Wachtmeister – Staff Sergeant, Obergefreiter – Lance Corporal, Stabsgefreiter – Lance Corporal (administrative) and Gefreiter -Senior Private.

10   Serving in the battalion at this time was one Captain Robert Maxwell. Maxwell was awarded the MC for his part in the January 1945 fighting to clear the Germans from the left bank of the River Roer and he had a respected war service. It is sad that his malodorous record in business did not match his war record.

11   KG 200 had originally been formed as a secret, special transport unit to insert and supply agents. Although the unit operated several captured enemy aircraft for this purpose – such as B-17 Flying

Fortresses -they were used because they had superior range/load carrying abilities rather than to deceive; contrary to some accounts, all captured aircraft flew in Luftwaffe markings. In 1944 KG 200 was reorganised to undertake additional duties, in particular the Mistel attack role which used a Me 109 flying 'piggy-back' to guide an explosive packed Ju 88 onto a target. Ju 88 and 188 were used as the pathfinders and illuminators for these missions. KG 200 held Fw 190 for Mistel guidance and to carry anti-shipping weapons.

12   The task of this organisation was to deploy its half-track based OPs as far forward as possible to get cross-bearings on enemy mortars. The aim was to catch enemy mortars, which had caused so many casualties during the campaign, before they moved.

13   J Mercer, *Mike Target*, The Book Guild.

14   On 19 April No. 4 War Material Reconnaissance Team surveyed the complex which was found to consist of two factories which produced nitro-cellulose powder for artillery and rockets. Fifty, partly underground magazines contained 600,000kg of explosives in stockpile. Many of the factory buildings had been constructed with flat roofs to allow trees to be planted on them for camouflage.

'DIE STUNDE NULL'
16 APRIL – 5 MAY

A t daylight on Monday 16 April, 22nd Armoured Brigade took up the advance once again with 8th Hussars Group on the centre line and further to the north the 1 RTR Group. Intelligence reports suggested that 8th Hussars would be opposed by SS Kompanie 3./12 and 4./12 defending along the line of Route 209 between Walsrode and Fallingbostel, the next town on Route 209. The 13.Kompanie from the same battalion was thought to be in Fallingbostel with its 8cm mortars. Numerous road blocks of felled and booby-trapped trees, mines, blown culverts and bridges were to be expected. Despite these dangers that lay ahead, it was to prove a momentous day for it saw the liberation of two very large prisoner-of-war camps in Fallingbostel – Stalags XIB and 357. The 8th Hussars regimental history describes the opening of that day.

'It was a 5 o'clock in the morning start, in the dark and cold, and a hurried breakfast of a fried egg between two pieces of bread and a mug of tea beside the tanks. Some were parked near a small garden in which were two cherry trees in blossom, and through the branches could be seen the other tanks in the meadow below, their brew fires flickering in the half light. It was an oddly beautiful scene, and a fine dawn which promised an even finer day.'[1]

B Squadron, with one motor platoon of 1 RB in half-tracks under command, was ordered to move east to Fallingbostel. C Squadron likewise was ordered to advance from its night leaguer among the turnips, through Düshorn to Fallingbostel. A Squadron with a section of carriers was to cross the river Böhme and establish itself on the high ground to the north of Fallingbostel. Recce Troop, which had spent the night with C Squadron, was ordered to find the two prison camps that were in the vicinity and which were thought to lie somewhere to the east of the town. The map showed a large expanse of ground covered with regularly grouped blocks of buildings, any of which might have been the camps. It also showed part of an autobahn, which with the mental picture it gave of broad concrete roadways, fly-overs and bridges was likely to prove an unmistakable landmark.

C Squadron reached the railway bridge without incident and the B Squadron Group arrived at the western outskirts of the town where it was held up by infantry. A Squadron reported that the bridge by which they had been ordered to cross had been blown and that it was unable to cross the Böhme anywhere else. By 1100 hours it was clear that the town would need more than one motor company to clear it. Accordingly, at 1250 hours, 1/5 Queens commanded by Lieutenant Colonel Freeland, began to move along Route 209 in their Kangaroos toward Fallingbostel, having been relieved in Walsrode by 2 Devons. As the battalion closed on the town it received a report that the German defenders had with a few exceptions withdrawn, and that a deliberate attack was not now necessary. However, when the lead troops reached the end of the main street, which was by now well alight from the earlier fighting involving A Company 1 RB, they found the vital bridge over the Böhme blown.

A new plan was made which involved A Company 1/5 Queens wading the river to the north-west, supported by B Squadron in an attempt to cut-off any remaining defenders in Fallingbostel. D Company meanwhile would rush across the remains of the demolished bridge and work forward through the town on the right bank to join them. This bridgehead would then allow the sappers to build a bridge and restore the divisional axis. Fire support would be provided by A Squadron from the high ground to the south of the town. All went to plan and by mid-afternoon the town was swiftly captured; the Germans, apart from leaving behind some snipers, having withdrawn. With A Company 1 RB now under command 1/5 Queens held positions in the town and spent the rest of the afternoon mopping up. To save casualties, the guns of 5 RHA were used against the snipers.

Whilst these events were taking place, 8th Hussars recce troop, commanded by Captain Pierson, liberated the two camps. The moving story is told by Captain Pierson.

'Nosing its way cautiously along sandy tracks that skirted or went through the many pinewoods that were the main feature of this country, the leading section of Honeys started off slowly. Though there was no sign of any enemy, similar woods had produced quite a few the day before, and the leading tank occasionally raked the edges of the trees and suspicious hollows or clumps of grass to discourage any Panzerfaust expert that might be waiting hopefully for us to get within range of his very useful weapon. The afternoon before, when he had been missed three times, Lieutenant Anstey, the leading troop commander, confessed to feeling like a goalkeeper in a football match, but this particular sunny morning there was, much to our relief, no sign of them. A wide clearing confronted us, obviously man-made, cut at right angles through the woods, its sandy surface covered with tufts of grass, stretching dead straight to the right as far as the eye could see, and to the left turning out of sight through two small mountains of earth. This must be the autobahn, though scarcely what we had expected, the maps had given no hint of this rudimentary stage in its construction.

'We turned left, came to the large heaps of earth and halted while the leading commander, Corporal Spencer, dismounted to have a look at what lay around them out of sight. No more woods, but a flat open expanse of grass bounded, some thousand yards away, by a long, uneven line of low buildings, out of which, further to our left, rose what looked like half a dozen tall warehouses. Binoculars showed that the main mass of low buildings lay behind a high wire fence and people, at first we saw one, or two moving about, then made out groups of a dozen, and finally realised that the thickening of the bottom half of the fence was in fact a solid mass of them. At this moment the leading tanks of C Squadron, approaching on a different route, came up behind us, and without waiting to see any more we jumped into our tanks and shot out into the open. In high spirits we crossed the grass as quickly as the ground would allow, but as the distance between us grew less we noticed that the predominant colour of the mass that was now streaming out of the gates towards us was grey, dark grey. And at the same moment saw a French flag - or was it Dutch - which in our excitement we had not noticed before, fluttering behind the main gate. Our hopes sank; these were not British prisoners, but another of the camps full of all nationalities of Europe that we had come across so many times before. Perhaps there were some British amongst them, then again perhaps there was no British camp at all, and the Germans had moved XIB as they had moved so many others out of the way of the armies advancing from east to west.

'The leading tank came to a stop as the first of the breathless, shouting stream of humanity surrounded it, and Corporal Spencer, still clinging to a faint hope, bent down and yelled, "English soldaten?". He repeated himself in a moment's hush, and then a hundred hands pointed to his left, and the clamour of the excited crowd broke out with increased intensity. As he looked round for someone out of whom he could get some sense it seemed that every nation was represented, women as well as men, the majority in civilian clothes, with but two things in common, they were all happy and all indescribably dirty. Noticing one persistent man who seemed to have a smattering of English he hauled him up onto the tank and asked which way. The fellow pointed and as the tank moved slowly forward the crowd melted away in front. He glanced over his shoulder and noticed that he was still leading, the Cromwells of C Squadron were as uncertain as he had been as to the route, but were now following hot on his heels. It was going to be a close thing who reached the camp first.

'Parallel to the fence, which we had now reached ran a concrete road, and turning left on this, to the accompaniment of cheers from the waving smiling crowd of prisoners and DPs (displaced persons) that thronged its entire length, he soon passed the tall warehouses that had first been noticed in the distance. The fellow in the turret pointed excitedly forward, but Corporal Spencer could see nothing except a road, tree-lined on both sides, that met ours at right angles. We halted at the junction; to our left the road went under a stone bridge built to carry the autobahn, but with no autobahn to carry looking comically like a piece from a child's set of toy bricks. A quick glance to the right revealed nothing more than an empty road. But the guide was tugging at Spencer's sleeve and jabbering away – and following with our eyes the direction of his pointing arm we saw across the road through a gap between two trees a khaki-clad figure wearing a maroon-coloured beret, clinging to a wire fence beyond and jumping up and down, obviously shouting his head off, though not a word reached us over the noise of the engines and earphones. And then all the way down to the right we could see between the tree trunks more figures racing along the wire. We'd got there, and before the Cromwells, which came up behind just as we moved off down the road giving the glad news over the air. Three or four hundred yards down the road was the main gate to the camp and as we approached the sound of welcome from the crowd that lined the wire and covered the roofs of the camp buildings grew to a roar that penetrated our earphones above the noise of our engines. Inside the main gates was an open space packed with British prisoners, and, beyond another wire fence, what looked like an inner enclosure was black with figures. This was Stalag XIB.

'Quite staggering was the contrast between this scene and that which we had seen at other camps containing prisoners of the Allied nations. Despite the enthusiasm of the men inside you could see at a glance there was order and discipline. The remarkable RSM Lord, Grenadier Guards, of the 1st Airborne Division had already taken charge and was busily engaged in his office giving peace-time orders to his Orderly Warrant Officers. Camp MPs, each with a red armband, policed the gates, and as the crowd came out to meet us there was no ugly rush but a steady controlled stream that surrounded each tank as it stopped, a stream wearing the headgear of what looked like every unit in the Army. The Airborne beret predominated – men of D-Day, Arnhem, even the Rhine Crossing who had only been inside a few weeks – but you could pick out the hats, caps, berets and bonnets of a score of others. And under each one was such a look of happiness and thankfulness that made us as happy to be the cause of it. It was a quiet crowd that thronged around us; they had had their cheer, and now when the moment came for words, few words came. Mostly they were too moved to speak, men who could only grin broadly and clasp your hand as the tears ran down their cheeks. You couldn't speak yourself, only shake as many as possible of the hands that stretched towards you, and grin back, trying to take it all in, and marvel. For these men didn't look like prisoners; their battle-dresses were pressed and clean, here and there web belts and gaiters were scrubbed white and the brasses gleaming, they might have been off duty in a town at home instead of just walking out of prison wire behind which they had been for anything from five weeks to five years.

'Memories of that scene leaves a picture of a healthy and, if not overfed, certainly not starving crowd; of apologetic requests for cigarettes and one man turning green with his first puff, having given up the habit for his three years inside; of the creases in the tartan trews and the shining buttons on the jacket of a CSM in the 51st Highland Division, who admitted having marched 3 or 4 hundred miles from East Prussia, and who didn't look as if he had been more than 3 or 4 hundred yards from his own front door; of the Camp MO indignantly denying any cases of typhus; of the German Commandant and a few of the camp guards standing apart in a small group watching unmoved the reversal of his role, and handing over his automatic with an offer to show us over the nearby storehouses; scraps of conversation, "I've been waiting five years for this day" – "three days ago we expected you," and in contrast, "You've come too soon, my jacket's still wet," this from one who had washed his battledress specially for the occasion; and from one as impressed by our appearance (we hadn't washed or shaved for nearly 48 hours) as we were by theirs, "You look like real soldiers". There were several requests to see a Jeep, which we could not unfortunately produce at that moment; much signing of autographs on both sides and nearly always the first question "What's your mob?" and finding several members of the Regiment in the camp, taken at Sidi Rezegh in 1941; and finally, on asking news of their erstwhile captors, being told that they were not long gone and were carrying Panzerfausts. This was more serious, with all these fellows about, and on asking the police to clear the road we got the most startling proof of the state of camp discipline. For at a word from a tall figure wearing the Airborne beret, RSM Lord, the Camp MPs went round, and in a very few moments and without a murmur these scores of men, some of whom were tasting freedom for the first time in more than five years, made their way back behind that same barbed wire and netting that to them must have been the symbol of all that was hateful and depressing in this life.

'We left as the vanguard of visitors, the VIPs and not so VIPs, the Press and the frankly-curious, all wishing to get a first-hand glimpse of the first large, predominantly British camp to find itself in the path of the British Army of Liberation. And we left taking with us an impression that will never fade of men whose courage and hope had been kept alive through long years of boredom and privation by their faith in their comrades and their country; and whose behaviour in their moment of triumph when faith had been rewarded was an example of the highest traditions of the Army to which they belonged. And that might have been the end of our part in the proceedings of what was for all of us a great occasion. But later on that day we happened to pass that way again when things were more normal; erstwhile prisoners were strolling about in groups, or sitting in the sun enjoying a smoke and waving contentedly at the passing traffic. But all was not quite normal, for as we came up to the main gates where we had received such a reception a few hours earlier, we saw a troop of armoured cars obliging some movie cameramen by driving slowly past a group of wildly waving and shouting ex-prisoners; and, for a brief moment, as we beheld the scene as spectators and not actors, we felt again all the emotions of that most memorable day.'

But at the other camp, Stalag 357, it was a different state of affairs. Edward Ardizzone, visiting the camp soon after its liberation, recalled his impressions.

'Here we were the first troops to arrive and when we halted in the wire approach to the camp we were surrounded by a great crowd of men almost hysterical with joy. They nearly overwhelmed us, climbing over our cars, patting us on the back, shaking our hands, bombarding us with questions, shouting, laughing, some even crying.

'Here, unlike the other camp, was none of that air of discipline and smartness. The clothes most of the men wore were nondescript. Many wore gym-shoes and few had either hats or caps.

'I am not for a moment suggesting that morale and discipline had gone, far from it. But these men, unlike the others, had been prisoners for a long time, some for as much as four or five years, and even their faces showed it. It was a very moving and wonderful experience. As I have said some men were crying and I do not think we ourselves were far from tears; but perhaps the saddest and most moving sight of all was when, after disentangling ourselves from the crowd and having been given a parting cheer as we drove away, we looked back and saw so many hundreds still clinging to the wire as if by habit, a habit caused by long imprisonment. They could not realise that they were free.'

The total freed from Stalags XIB and 357 was some 10,000 British and American prisoners, and 12,000 Allied nationals. After liberation, as was often the case, there were ugly incidents in which freed Soviet prisoners and forced labourers began to pillage the surrounding countryside. A number of barrack blocks were burnt down and a luxurious officers' mess destroyed. RSM Lord contained these incidents by deploying patrols and providing guards for the farms and many local people owe their lives to his action. Nine days after liberation, the last group of ex-prisoners, with RSM Lord among them, left Stalag XIB forever.

Whilst elements of the 8th Hussars Group were involved in Fallingbostel, by the evening of 16 April 1 RTR Group had made solid progress and advanced to within two miles of the west of Soltau, which it reported strongly held by infantry and 8.8cm guns. The 8th Hussars Group was in the area of Dorfmark, four miles to the south-west of Soltau whilst 131st Infantry Brigade, which had been in reserve throughout the advance, was in Walsrode. The 155th Infantry Brigade had spent the day mopping up isolated pockets of resistance and had concentrated in the Walsrode area for the night. The next day would be busy, for the brigade had been given written orders to clear the divisional axis between Fallingbostel and Soltau and then capture Soltau whilst 22nd Armoured by-passed it to the west. On 16 April 2.Marine Infanterie Division received its first and only mention in an OKW situation report when it was announced that the division had prevented an enemy breakthrough on the lower Aller; for the marines the opportunity for a success such as this was long since past.

The battle for Soltau started in the early afternoon of 17 April, although the town had already suffered grievously from the effects of war when 200 American bombers dumped their bomb loads on the town on 11 April, killing 65 inhabitants and destroying 60 houses. The battalion from 155th Infantry Brigade tasked with its capture was 7/9 R Scots, with 5 Innis DG placed under its command for the operation. The plan for battle was to mount an advance to contact up the Dorfmark to Soltau road starting at 1200 hours from Dorfmark. The advance would be led by the Recce Troop of 5 Innis DG and the Carrier Platoon from 7/9 R Scots, followed by a squadron/company group as an advance guard. The main body would be the remainder of the infantry battalion with half the available Crocodiles; the other Crocodiles and the remaining tank squadrons would be held in reserve. The German defenders, led by Oberstleutnant Körner who commanded the cavalry riding school in the town, amounted to approximately a battalion and consisted of Volkssturm, some SS from the Hitlerjugend battalion and the staff of the riding school. Körner established company strongpoints on the approach roads and planned to fall back into the town as the pressure mounted, before fighting to the last within the town itself.

The advance duly began at mid-day with the infantry being carried on the tank decks. The strongpoints held up the advance for a while and it took time to overcome them or find by-pass routes and it was not until early evening that A and C Companies began to break into the town. Liberal use was made of the supporting Crocodiles to destroy pockets of resistance and snipers and by 2330 hours the town had fallen allowing the infantry companies to consolidate in the town centre. Two hundred and twenty prisoners were taken for a loss of three dead and two wounded. Whilst the infantry brigade cleared Soltau, 22nd Armoured made good progress and by nightfall on 17 April it had outflanked Soltau, with the two regimental groups securing villages some 15 miles to its north.

Also moving up on 17 April, was the Guards Armoured Division which had begun its long move to join XII Corps' advance. The Guards Armoured Division had been formed in 1941 from Household Division infantry battalions, and in 1945 consisted of an armoured brigade – 5th Guards Armoured, and an infantry brigade – 32nd Guards Brigade. The division had first come into action in late June 1944 when it arrived in Normandy and had then fought with distinction throughout the campaign in North West Europe. Although it might be thought that a formation with its background would be tactically conservative, the Guards Armoured went further than either of the other two armoured

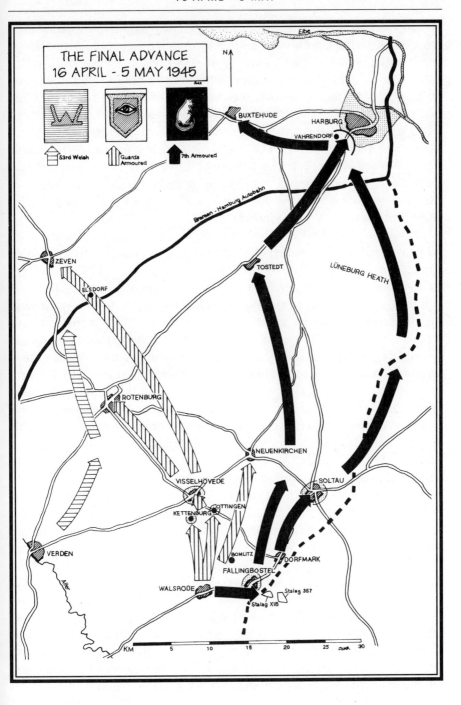

THE FINAL ADVANCE
16 APRIL - 5 MAY 1945

53rd Welsh

Guards Armoured

7th Armoured

divisions in integrating its armour and infantry into permanent mixed groups. This was largely due to the innovative flair of the divisional commander, Major General Alan Adair. The division's orbat and equipment was similar to 7th Armoured being based on armoured regiments with Sherman tanks, a motorised battalion with M5 half-tracks and lorried infantry battalions; 2 Welsh Guards was equipped with Cromwell tanks having been the armoured recce regiment. By dusk on 17 April, 32nd Guards Brigade had reached Walsrode, whilst 5th Guards Armoured Brigade waited in a concentration area to move forward and cross the Aller. The last act of defiance by 2.Marine Infanterie Division was now to take place over the course of the next two days against the Guards in the area of Visselhövede.

The armoured division formed two groups to lead its advance: the Scots-Welsh Group (2 Welsh Guards and 2 Scots Guards) and the Coldstream Group (1 and 5 Coldstream Guards). The Scots-Welsh Group pushed north from Walsrode during the morning of 18 April and made good progress until it met Major Stoschke's companies in Kettenburg. An attempt was made to bypass Kettenburg to the east but this ran into further of Stoschke's companies in Ottingen. F Company 2 Scots Guards fought an extremely bitter action to clear the marines from Kettenburg, with the regimental history describing the fight as being one of resistance to the death and it took until 1930 hours before Kettenburg was cleared. As heavy fire was coming from the woods which dominated any approach on Visselhövede from the south and with darkness falling, preparations for the main attack were postponed to the next day.

Whilst the Scots-Welsh Group was involved in the Visselhövede area, the Coldstream Group bypassed to the east and advanced on Neunkirchen, which was held by Kapitän zur See Hartmann and the remnants of his Mar.Gren.Rgt.6. The depleted force of marines attempted to block the advance but were soon overcome and the village fell without difficulty. The Guards Armoured Division history describes the division's impression of the enemy.

'They were nearly all ex-sailors, many of them until lately members of submarine crews. They had had little time for military training and therefore lacked the fighting skill of the paratroops, but their discipline and bravery were exemplary. They were all equipped with bazookas, which they used in particularly daring fashion; their tactics often involved them necessarily in annihilation but their aggressive spirit certainly delayed our progress most effectively.'[2]

Soon after dawn on 19 April under the cover of a heavy artillery bombardment the Scots-Welsh Group launched its attack on Visselhövede. Right Flank Company carried on the backs of the Cromwells came under heavy fire from the woods but managed to by-pass this opposition and press on towards the town. So that there would be no more interference from this direction, F Company was ordered to clear these troublesome enemy, which they proceeded to do during the rest of the morning. Supported by the Welsh Guards' Cromwells, G and Right Flank companies broke through the perimeter defence on the railway embankment on the town's southern edge and fought their way into the town against determined opposition from the marines. Whilst the Scots-Welsh Group attacked from the south, the Coldstream Group attacked from the north to capture the northern sector of the town. After a fierce fight the town was captured, and the two groups consolidated their sectors with the Scots-Welsh Group establishing their HQ in a hotel in the main street. Two Cromwells were positioned outside the hotel and peace reigned.

Whilst the British rested after the fight, without warning Bataillon I./7 fell upon the town from the north. Although the marines had been pushed out of the town they had not withdrawn, but had occupied a thick wood to regroup before mounting a counter-attack. They had then worked their way undetected back into the town using the cover of the thick garden hedgerows. Both tanks were knocked out by Panzerfausts and two mortar carriers were destroyed in the main street. The centre of the town was soon engulfed in hand-to-hand fighting, a G Company platoon was surrounded in a house in the main street and the members of the HQ in the hotel had to fight-off the enemy attack with their pistols. Confusion reigned for two hours with radio communications lost and movement impossible between houses due to the torrent of small-arms fire. Help eventually came from a tank commanded by Captain the Hon. Mildmay from 3 Squadron which managed to make its way back into the town blazing away with its Besa. This tank and its commander both had lucky escapes with a Panzerfaust exploding against a wall beside it and Captain Mildmay having an earpiece of his radio headset shot-off. It was only due to the presence of this tank, and a troop from 1 Squadron which also later joined the fray, that the Guards gradually began to repulse the attackers, though most of the tanks ran out of Besa ammunition and had to resort to firing at individual Germans with their main armament. By the evening the town was firmly in British hands and nearly 400 prisoners taken. It had been a very hard day and the regimental history of

2 Scots Guards records that the fighting in and around Visselhövede being about the toughest the battalion had experienced. Among the prisoners were Kapitän zur See Jordan and five of his regimental staff who had been captured in a house only two away from the HQ in the hotel. The gallant Kapitän did not however survive the war for he was shot dead by a sentry the next day when he tried to escape from the brigade prisoner-of-war cage wearing plain clothing. A tragic but perhaps predictable end for a man who had fought unceasingly since the opening shots were fired at Rethem 10 days before. The fall of Visselhövede and the death of Kapitän Jordan was the finale to 2.Marine Infanterie Division's short but bloody part in the war. The marines' spirited defence of the town was a fitting climax to their determination and courage; 52 lie buried in Kettenburg and 47 in Visselhövede.

The story is now nearly over. Having captured Soltau, 7th Armoured Division continued to advance strongly towards its next objective, the bridges over the Elbe at Harburg. The division cut the autobahn between Bremen and Hamburg on 19 April and on the next day began to close with the defences of Harburg. On 18 and 19 April, Rethem suffered for the last time when a handful of Ar 234 bombers from KG 76 flew in at 2,000 feet to mount low-level attacks on the Bailey bridge and concentrations of vehicles. Little damage was caused, although in one of the attacks the post office was hit by a bomb and the wife of the postmaster, Müller, and her sister both died in the rubble; there were no British casualties. On 21 April the high wooded ground above Harburg was reached, but as the country was unsuitable for armour, the division was ordered to adopt defensive positions until VIII Corps crossed the Elbe and secured the bridgehead. The enemy maintained an aggressive defence against the armoured division, which reached its climax on 26 April in the area of Vahrendorf, a village just to the west of the main road leading into Hamburg through Harburg. Here a composite force of SS, Kompanie 7./SS-Ausb.u.Ers.Btl.12 HJ, marines and soldiers accompanied by two self-propelled assault guns mounted a last, fanatical but useless counter-attack against 1/5 Queens and 2 Devon. The attack was repulsed, 60 of the youths were killed and 70 captured and thereafter the divisional front remained quiet until the end.

Having captured Visselhövede, the Guards Armoured Division then advanced north-west towards the towns of Rotenburg and Zeven[3] which were captured on 22 and 25 April respectively. In so doing, the remnants of the marine division were pushed away to the north where they played no further part of significance. The remnants of the division, some 3,000 marines, ended the war in the Cuxhaven area although some made it back to Schleswig-Holstein where they were to surrender with the other thousands of German soldiers bottled up in the area. A German situation map for 20 April records the locations of only Bataillon II./7 and the Felders.Btl. The Korps Ems' strength return for 21 April shows starkly the losses that the division had sustained in 12 days of fighting.

Unit	Officers	Men
Mar.Inf.Div.Stab (HQ)	12	65
Mar.Gren.Rgt.5	1	100
Mar.Gren.Rgt.6	18	365
Mar.Gren.Rgt.7	20	410
Mar.Füs.Btl.2	3	80
Mar.Art.Rgt.2	9	270
Mar.Pz.Jäg.Abt.2	4	80
Mar.Pi.Btl.2	3	65
Mar.Felders.Btl.2	10	300

The marines had done all that was expected of them and they had fought courageously with immense spirit to the last. There was never the slightest chance that they would prevent the British advance but they had held it up for a number of days and one can only admire them for their tenacity, given their state of training, the woeful lack of armour and heavy weapons, and the general air of defeat and collapse. It was not without a grudging sense of admiration that they were given the nickname 'Blue SS' by their British opponents.

Having cleared the Zeven area, Guards Armoured returned to XXX Corps' command on 29 April. Whilst the two armoured divisions were pushing ahead, 53rd Welsh continued in its task of clearing the area to the east of Verden and then the area between Zeven and Rotenburg. The division 'loaned' 160th Brigade to 7th Armoured Division to help clear the troublesome pocket of Kampfgruppe Grosan, which was bottled up in the woods north-east of Soltau and posing a threat to the tactical headquarters of both 2nd Army and 21st Army Group which had moved up to the Soltau area. On 22 April 53rd Welsh and Guards Armoured were given orders to take part in a drive to the north-west to cut the Hamburg autobahn near Elsdorf; 71st Brigade and 53rd Recce Regiment would lead the advance. The advance began on 23 April and progress was slow but steady against large groups of Germans supported by artillery. It was whilst Brigadier Elrington was directing his brigade in this operation that tragedy overtook him. He was blown up in his jeep when it ran over a mine on a road verge and he died shortly afterwards; one of many senior divisional officers who met their deaths this way. By 25 April his brigade had reached its objective and the next day orders were given for a final drive to the west on Bremen, in concert with 52nd Lowland and the Guards Armoured. The division was not however to take part in the assault as resistance collapsed and the brigades were ordered to hold their ground.

Events now moved swiftly. VIII Corps, having fought a fierce action against Panzer Division 'Clausewitz', resulting in the annihilation of the German formation, had captured Uelzen on 18 April and by 22 April had reached the Elbe. One week later Operation 'Enterprise' successfully put the Corps over the Elbe at Lauenburg; Lübeck was captured on 2 May and the Baltic finally reached at Travemünde the next day. Bremen finally fell to XXX Corps on 28 April and the remnants of 1.Fallschirm Armee and Korps Ems were pushed away to the north-east to be bottled up in the marshlands that lie between the Weser and Elbe estuaries. Holland was over-run by the Canadians and the Soviet armies had begun the battle for Berlin. The fronts opposing the Americans were collapsing and the end was very near. Hitler committed suicide on 30 April and on 2 May opposition collapsed on the whole north-western front. On 3 May the city of Hamburg was formally surrendered to General Dempsey and occupied by 7th Armoured Division that same day; 53rd Welsh followed up in the armoured division's wake to take over responsibility for the great but shattered city. Throughout north-west Germany columns of thousands of dejected German soldiers blocked the roads as they came on foot, in horse-drawn carts, weaponless and leaderless to give themselves up to the British. The defeat of the nation and the Wehrmacht was absolute and for the Germans this period became known as 'Die Stunde Null', the Hour Zero.

Dönitz, whom Hitler had appointed as his successor, attempted to keep the fight going to the last and the summary hanging of deserters by the naval police continued apace in these final days. But even Dönitz, a most fanatical member of the Nazi hierarchy, realised that the end had come and began to make preparations for suing for peace. At 1830 hours on 4 May the Instrument of Surrender was signed at Montgomery's tactical headquarters on Lüneburg Heath. The German delegation, led by Generaladmiral von Friedeburg, who had been Commander-in-Chief of the Kriegsmarine for a week, and General Kinzel, Dönitz's Chief-of-Staff at Führungsstab Nordraum, agreed to surrender to Montgomery all forces in Holland, North West Germany (including the offshore islands), Schleswig-Holstein and in Denmark. The surrender took effect at 0800 hours on 5 May; three days later the unconditional surrender was signed at Reims by Jodl. For the British the procession was now ended, and for the combatants in North West Germany who had fought to the bitter end, peace had come at last.

NOTES

1   O. Fitzroy, *Men of Valour, History of the 8th King's Royal Irish Hussars,* Tinling & Co.

2   Capt the Earl of Ross,*The Story of the Guards Armoured Division,* Geoffrey Bles.

3   The last VC of the European war was posthumously won on 21 April during the advance to Zeven, when Guardsman Eddie Charlton of 2 (Armoured) Battalion Irish Guards single-handedly held up a German counter-attack near the village of Wistedt.

EPILOGUE

Although the battle for Rethem and the Aller bridgehead have left few historical ripples, its ferocity was stamped on the memories of all those who fought there. For the British participants in particular, it will long be remembered as a gruelling battle and a most unpleasant shock. The old comrades of both sides still talk of the battle on the Aller when they hold their reunions. The 'Alten Kameraden' of 2.Marine Infanterie Division meet annually in April in the Gasthaus at Rethemer Fähre and reminisce about the war and their parts in the battles fought by the division. Their reunion usually ends with a visit to one or more of the local cemeteries where their comrades lie. The British old comrades likewise meet in their regimental associations and the events of these times are similarly remembered.

Few of the British formations and units of 1945 exist today. The British were quick to remove the wartime Territorial divisions from their order of battle once peace came and they soon passed into the pages of history. In July 1946, following occupation duties in Hamburg and the Ruhr, 53rd Welsh Division ceased to exist. The 7th Armoured Division was disbanded in 1948, although it was later reprieved for a few years before final disbandment in 1958. Both divisions, however, live on in three brigades of today's Army: 160th (Wales) Infantry Brigade is a TA brigade with its headquarters in Brecon, 7th Armoured Brigade is based in Germany and carries on many of the traditions of the division that bore the same number, whilst the 4th Armoured Brigade, also in Germany, enjoys an unbroken link with its famous forebear. Both these armoured brigades performed with distinction in the Gulf War of 1991, when their members proudly wore their respective 'rat' formation badges. Of the regiments and battalions there are few traces as the numerous and continuing reductions in the size of the Army have removed most of them from the order of battle.

It has taken many years for the Germans to make good the human loss of war. Due to the appalling casualty toll they exacted on other nations and peoples, the Germans' own terrible losses are perhaps sometimes overlooked, and these losses were felt particularly keenly by rural Germany. The casualties suffered by the Wehrmacht were far in excess of those of the First World War, usually considered as holding grim pride of place. Rethem lost 76 men in the First World War and 120 in the Second, and Hülsen 35 in the First and 61 in the Second. The fighting also claimed the lives of many local civilians.

From the physical viewpoint the area today is not markedly changed from 1945. Although the villages have expanded and have their quota of modern houses, the large red-brick farm complexes continue to predominate and despite the wartime damage there are still many fine buildings to be seen. Agriculture dominates the local economy, with the sandy soils being particularly favoured for asparagus. The low land is now well drained, fewer of the bogs exist and the rivers have had levees built to prevent flooding. The extensive post-war buildings in Rethem show clearly the wholesale destruction caused to the town. Most of the buildings in the Old Town have been restored or rebuilt in their original style allowing it to retain something of its original village atmosphere, despite the roar of traffic passing by on Route 209. Haus Wehland where Jordan had his headquarters still stands, although in a state of some disrepair. After the war a wooden bridge was built over the Aller by British engineers but this was replaced in the mid-1950s by the concrete one which now carries Route 209. Rethem is still connected to the railway system and has not suffered a Beeching-style cut, although the station is now a private house and the sidings on which the railway Flak were located have been reduced. Little imagination is needed to picture the scene in 1945 and the approach used by 2 Mons is just as it was, with Edward Wilson's description holding true to the letter.

Although some buildings still display the evidence of April 1945, war damage is not easily seen and the Germans have been skilful in repairing the marks caused by bullet and splinter. Weapons are still occasionally found and a recent ploughing of the field in front of the railway embankment produced a MG 42 and Stg.44 in remarkably good condition. The area around Elfriede abounds with splinters, cartridge cases and live rounds and shells are sometimes unearthed in the gardens and fields. In the woods, hollows mark the spot where men dug in and shells landed and on Timpenberg parts of A Company 1 HLI's position covering Route 209 can be clearly seen.

The sites of Stalag XIB and 357 can still be visited. Much of the site of Stalag XIB now plays host to a neat housing estate, but concrete foundations and short, ghostly flights of steps leading to doors and buildings long-since gone are visible in the woods. Little remains to be seen of Stalag 357, its site now a melancholy heathland. A small factory producing concrete pipes occupies a wartime building – the only structure still existing from either camp – and within a birch wood lies a cemetery for uncounted thousands of Soviet prisoners who died of typhus and neglect at the camp in 1941 and 1942.

Most of the villages and towns in the area contain cemeteries for the German soldiers who died in the local battles; all also include a memorial stone to their dead who disappeared on the Eastern Front. At Rethem, a well-tended cemetery near the railway embankment, occupying the same site as the one chosen by the British when they cleared Rethem after the battle, is the final resting place for the 77 who died in the town's defence. The British dead lie in the beautiful cemetery of the Commonwealth War Graves' Commission at Becklingen, south of Soltau, where they lie with thousands of other Allied soldiers, sailors and airmen who were killed in this area of northern Germany. Here may be seen the graves of Jake Wardrop, Eddie Charlton VC, and all the others named in the book. They rest peacefully in a cemetery maintained in the style of an English country garden, contrasting starkly with the surrounding sombre pine woods.

APPENDIXES

Appendix A
ORDER OF BATTLE OF BRITISH FOR-MATIONS, MID-APRIL 1945

Abbreviations:

Air Cdre	Air Commodore
Bn	Battalion
Brig	Brigadier
FM	Field Marshal
Lt Gen	Lieutenant General
Maj Gen	Major General

21ST ARMY GROUP (FM Montgomery)
2nd British Army
1st Canadian Army (Lt Gen Crerar

2nd British Army (Lt Gen Dempsey)
VIII Corps
11th Armoured Division
6th Airborne Division
15th(Scottish) Infantry Division
6th Guards Armoured Brigade
1st Commando Brigade
XII Corps
Guards Armoured Division (from 16 April)
7th Armoured Division
52nd (Lowland) Infantry Division (to 19 April)
53rd (Welsh) Infantry Division
4th Armoured Brigade
XXX Corps
Guards Armoured Division (to 16 April)
3rd Infantry Division
43rd (Wessex) Infantry Division
51st (Highland) Infantry Division
52nd (Lowland) Infantry Division (from 19 April)
8th Armoured Brigade
Army Troops
79th Armoured Division
Independent Armoured (4) and Infantry (7) Brigades
Army Groups RA
AA Regts RA
Army Groups RE

VIII Corps (Lt Gen Barker)
11th Armoured Division
29th Armoured Brigade

159th Infantry Brigade
1st Commando Brigade
6th Airborne Division
3rd Para Brigade
5th Para Brigade
6th Airldg Brigade
15th Scottish Division
44th Infantry Brigade
46th Infantry Brigade
227th Infantry Brigade
Corps Troops
6th Guards Armoured Brigade
The Royal Dragoons (Armd Car)
63rd Anti-Tank Regt RA
121st LAA Regt RA
Corps Troops RE
Corps Troops R Signals

11th Armoured Division (Maj Gen Roberts)
29th Armoured Brigade (Brig Harvey)
23rd Hussars
3 RTR
2 FF Yeo
8 (Motorised) RB
159th Infantry Brigade (Brig Churcher
1 Cheshire
4 KSLI
1 Hereford
1st Commando Brigade (Brig Mills-Roberts
45 (RM) Commando
46 (RM) Commando
3 Commando
6 Commando
Divisional Troops
Inns of Court Regt (Armd Car)
15/19th Hussars
13th RHA
1st Mountain Regt RA
151st Field Regt RA
75th Anti-Tank Regt RA
58th LAA Regt RA
11th Armoured Divisional Engineers
11th Armoured Divisional Signals

6th Airborne Division (Maj Gen Bols)
3rd Parachute Brigade (Brig Hill)
8 Para

9 Para
Canadian Para Bn
5th Parachute Brigade (Brig Poett)
7 Para
12 Para
13 Para
6th Airlanding Brigade (Brig Bellamy)
1 Royal Ulster Rifles
12 Devon
52 LI (Ox & Bucks)
Divisional Troops
6th Airborne Recce Regt
6th Airldg Lt Regt RA
6th Airldg Anti-Tank Regt RA
3rd Para Sqn RE
591st Para Sqn RE

15th Scottish Division (Maj Gen Barber)
44th (Lowland) Brigade (Brig Cumming-
   Bruce)
8 R Scots
6 R Scots Fus
6 KOSB
46th (Highland) Brigade (Brig Villiers)
9 Cameronians
7 Seaforth
2 Glasgow Hldrs
227th (Highland) Brigade (Brig Colville
10 HLI
2 Gordon Hldrs
2 A and SH
Divisional Troops
15th (Scottish) Recce Regt
131st,181st and 190th Field Regts RA
102nd Anti-Tank Regt RA
119th LAA Regt RA
15th Divisional Engineers
15th Divisional Signals
1 Middlesex (MG)

6th Guards Armoured Brigade (Brig
   Greenacre)
4 (Armoured) Gren Gds
4 (Armoured) Coldm Gds
3 (Armoured) Scots Gds

XII Corps (Lt Gen Ritchie)
Guards Armoured Division (from 16
   April)
5th Guards Armoured Brigade
32nd Guards Brigade
7th Armoured Division
22nd Armoured Brigade
131st Infantry Brigade
155th Infantry Brigade (from 5 April)
52nd Lowland Division (to 19 April)
155th Infantry Brigade (to 5 April)
156th Infantry Brigade
157th Infantry Brigade

53rd Welsh Division
71st Infantry Brigade
158th Infantry Brigade
160th Infantry Brigade
Corps Troops
4th Armoured Brigade (from 27 March)
86th Anti-Tank Regt RA
112th LAA Regt RA
Corps Troops Engineers
Corps Troops Signals

Guards Armoured Division (Maj Gen
   Adair)
5th Guards Armoured Brigade (Brig
   Gwatkin)
2 (Armoured) Gren Gds
1 (Armoured) Coldm Gds
2 (Armoured) Irish Gds
1 (Motorised) Gren Gds
32nd Guards Brigade (Brig Johnson)
5 Coldm Gds
2 Scots Gds
3 Irish Gds
2 (Armoured) Welsh Gds
Divisional Troops
2nd Household Cavalry Regt (Armd Car)
55th and 153rd Field Regts RA
21st Anti-Tank Regt RA
94th LAA Regt RA
Guards Armoured Divisional Engineers
Guards Armoured Divisional Signals

7th Armoured Division (Maj Gen Lyne)
22nd Armoured Brigade (Brig Wingfield)
5 Innis DG
1 RTR
5 RTR
1 (Motorised) RB
131st Infantry Brigade (Brig Spurling)
1/5 Queens
2 Devon
9 DLI
155th Infantry Brigade (from 5 April)
   (Brig McLaren)
7/9 R Scots
4 KOSB
5 KOSB
Divisional Troops
8th Hussars (Armd Recce)
11th Hussars (Armd Car)
3rd and 5th RHA
15th LAA Regt RA
65th Anti-Tank Regt RA
7th Armoured Divisional Engineers
7th Armoured Divisional Signals

52nd Lowland Division (Maj Gen
   Hakewill Smith)
155th Infantry Brigade (to 5 April) (Brig

McLaren)
7/9 R Scots
4 KOSB
5 KOSB
156th Infantry Brigade (Brig Barclay)
4/5 R Scots Fus
6 Cameronians
7 Cameronians
157th Infantry Brigade (Brig Grant)
5 HLI
6 HLI
1 Glasgow Hldrs
Divisional Troops
52nd Recce Regt
79th,80th and 186th Field Regts RA
54th Anti-Tank Regt RA
108th LAA Regt RA
52nd Divisional Engineers
52nd Divisional Signals
7 Manchester (MG)

53rd Welsh Division (Maj Gen Ross)
71st Infantry Brigade (Brig Elrington)
4 RWF
1 Oxf Bucks LI
1 HLI
158th Infantry Brigade (Brig Wilsey)
7 RWF
1 E Lan R
1/5 Welch
160th Infantry Brigade (Brig Coleman)
6 RWF (to 14 April)
4 Welch
2 Mons
Divisional Troops
3/4th CLY (from 14 April)
81st,83rd and 133rd Field Regts RA
25th LAA Regt RA
71st Anti-Tank Regt RA
53rd Divisional Engineers
53rd Divisional Signals
53rd Recce Regt
1 Manchester (MG)
A Flt 653 (AOP) Sqn
4th Armoured Brigade (Brig Carver)
Greys
44 RTR
3/4th CLY (to 14 April)
2 (Motorised) KRRC
6 RWF (from 14 April)
4th RHA
A Sqn 49 APC Regt (from 14 April)

2nd Tactical Air Force (AVM Coningham)
(HQ – 34 (PR) Wing:16,69,140 Sqns)
2 Group
(AVM Embry)
136 Wing: 418, 605 Sqns

137 Wing: 88, 342, 226 Sqns
138 Wing: 107, 305, 613 Sqns
139 Wing: 21, 464, 487 Sqns
83 Group (AVM Broadhurst)
39 (Recce) Wing:400,
414,430 Sqns
121 Wing: 174,175,184, 245 Sqns
122 Wing: 3, 56, 80, 274, 486 Sqns
125 Wing: 130, 350, 610 Sqns
126 Wing: 401, 411, 412, 442 Sqns
127 Wing: 403, 416, 421, 443 Sqns
143 Wing: 168, 438, 439, 440 Sqns
Air OP: 653, 658, 659, 662 Sqns
84 Group (AVM Hudleston)
35 (Recce) Wing:2,4,268 Sqns
123 Wing: 164, 183, 198, 609 Sqns
131 Wing: 302, 308, 317 Sqns
132 Wing: 66, 127, 322, 331, 332 Sqns
135 Wing: 33, 222 Sqns
145 Wing: 74, 329, 340, 345 Sqns
146 Wing: 193, 197, 257, 263, 266 Sqns
Air OP: 652, 660, 661 Sqns
85 Group (AVM Steele)
147 Wing:219,410,488 Sqns
148 Wing:264,409,604 Sqns
38 Group (AVM Scarlett-Streatfield)
Airborne Forces Sqns
46 Group (Air Cdre Darvall)
Transport Sqns
Royal Air Force Regiment
Armoured Sqns
LAA Sqns
Rifle Sqns

Notes:
1 2 Group comprised medium (Boston and
  Mitchell) bomber squadrons and Mosquito squadrons.
2 83 and 84 Groups comprised Spitfire,
  Typhoon, Tempest and Mustang
  squadrons. 84 Group primarily supported 1st Canadian Army.
3 85 Group comprised Mosquito
  squadrons.

Appendix B.
**ORDER OF BATTLE OF GERMAN FOR-
MATIONS, MID-APRIL 1945**

Abbreviations:
Gen.Feldm.	Generalfeldmarschall
Gen.Obst.	Generaloberst
Gen.Lt.	Generalleutnant
Gen.d.Inf.	General der Infanterie
Gen.d.Fs.Tr.	General der Fallschirm truppen
Obst	Oberst
Kapt.z.S.	Kapitän-zur-See

KKapt.z.S.   Korvettenkapitän-zur-
              See

Oberbefehlshaber Nordwest
(Gen.Feldm. Busch)
25.Armee (Gen.Obst. Blaskowitz)
XXX.Armeekorps
LXXXVIII.Armeekorps
1.Fallschirm Armee
II.Fallschirmkorps
LXXXVI.Armeekorps
Armeegruppe Student/Blumentritt
XXXI.Armeekorps z.b.V.
2.Marine Infanterie Division
Stellv.XI.Armeekorps
Panzer-Division 'Clausewitz'

1.Fallschirm Armee (Gen.d.Inf. Blumen-
tritt) to 10 April then Gen.Obst. Student)
II.Fallschirmkorps (Gen.d.Fs.Tr.Meindl)
7.Fallschirmjäger Division
8.Fallschirmjäger Division
Division Nr.346
Reste 245.Division
LXXXVI.Armeekorps (Gen.d.Inf. Straube)
Panzer Ausb. Verband 'Grossdeutschland'
15.Panzergrenadier Division
Division Nr.471
Division Nr.490
Schatten 325.Division

Armeegruppe Student/Blumentritt
(Gen.Obst. Student to 10 April then
Gen.d.Inf. Blumentritt)
XXXI.Armeekorps z.b.V.(Korps Ems)
Division z.b.V.172
Division Nr.480
Kampfkommandant Bremen
8.Flakdivision
2.Marine Infanterie Division
2.Marine Infanterie Division
Kampfgruppe Grosan
Regiment Totzeck
Stellv.XI.Armeekorps (Korps Hannover)
(Gen.d.Inf. Lichel)
Art.Ausb.Abt.19
Pz.Pi.Ausb.Btl.19
Lehrstab XI Bergen
Nebeltruppen-Schule (Celle)
Fhj.Lehrg.d.Inf.(Hannover)

XXXI Armeekorps z.b.V. (Korps Ems)
(Gen.d.Inf. Rasp)
Division z.b.V. 172 (Gen.Lt. Schwerin)
2./Mar.Alarm Btl. Wesermünde
Polizei Btl. Ottersberg
Rgt.Stab. z.b.V. Maislinger
Flak Ausb.Btl.52
Werfer Ausb.Rgt.2

Festungs Art.Rgt.1350
Division Nr.480 (Gen.Lt. Gilbert)
Gren.Ausb.Rgt.22
Gren.Ausb.Rgt.269
Art.Ausb.u.Ers.Rgt.22
Pi.Ausb.Btl.34
Schwere Art.Ausb.Abt.58
Kampfkommandant Bremen (Gen.
Becker)
SS-Ausb.u.Ers.Btl.18 (Horst Wessel)
Gren.Ausb.Btl.376
4./Mar.Alarm Btl.Wesermünde
Polizei-Btl.Oberneuland

2.Marine Infanterie Division (Vizead-
miral Scheurlen to 8 April then Kapt.z.S.
Hartmann / Obst. Bassewitz-Levetzow)
Infantry
Mar.Gren.Rgt.5 (Kapt.z.S. Jordan)
Mar.Gren.Rgt.6 (Kapt.z.S. Hartmann)
Mar.Gren.Rgt.7 (Kapt.z.S. Neitzel)
Mar.Füs.Btl.2 (KKapt.z.S. Gördes)
Divisional Troops
Mar.Art.Rgt.2
Mar.Felders.Btl.2
Mar.Pi.Btl.2
Mar.Pz.Jäg.Abt.2
Nachrichten-Abt.2
Versorgungs-Rgt.200
Attachments
SS-Ausb.u.Ers.Btl.12(HJ)
ROB-Pi.Btl.Nienburg
Pz.Jäg.Abt.101
Flakregiment 122(E)
11./101 Festungs-Pak-Abt.
Ungarisch Art.Ausb.Btl.7
Ungarisch Btl.Kolotay
Mar.Kfz.Abt.

Kampfgruppe Grosan (Obst Grosan)
Pz.-Pz.Jäg.Abt. (Maj Hache)
Rgt. (Maj Kahle)
Rgt. (Maj Köhler)
Ungarisch Rgt. (Obst Alturiay)

Regiment Totzeck (Obst Totzeck)
Werfer Ausb.Btl.Böhme
Inf.Btl.Gürtler
Inf.Btl.Thomsen
ROB.Btl.Altschwager

Luftflotte Reich (Gen.Obst. Stumpff)
Day Fighter Units
JG2, JG4, JG7, JG26, JG27, KG(J)54, JG400
Night Fighter Units
NJG1, NJG2, NJG3, NJG4, NJG5, NJG6,
    NJG11, NJG100
Night Ground-Attack Units
NSGr.1, NSGr.2, NSGr.20

Tactical Recce
NAGr.1, NAGr.6, NAGr.14
Bomber Unit
KG76
Special Unit
KG200

Notes:
1 JG stands for Jagdgruppe (fighter group); NJG for Nachtjagdgruppe (night fighter group); NSGr. for Nachtschlachtgruppe (night ground-attack); KG for Kampf-gruppe (bomber group); and NAGr for Nahaufklärung (short-range recce).
2 The JG were generally equipped with Me 109 and Fw 190 (although JG7 had Me 262 and JG400 Me 163); the NJG with Ju 88, Me 110 and Me 109; the NSGr. with Ju 87 (Stuka); the NAGr. with Me 109, Me 262 or Fw 189; KG 76 with Ar 234; and KG 200 with Ju 88, Ju 188, Fw 190, Misteln and transport aircraft various.

Appendix C
BRITISH AND GERMAN WEAPONS, VEHICLES AND AIRCRAFT

BRITISH INFANTRY WEAPONS
Lee-Enfield Rifle. The Lee-Enfield No 4 .303in rifle was the standard magazine-fed, bolt-action rifle. It had an effective range of 400 yards.
Bren Light Machine-Gun. The Bren .303in machine-gun was the section level weapon. It was air-cooled, gas-operated and fed from 30-round magazines. The Bren was very accurate and robust and could be used with a bipod or tripod. Its effective range, bipod-mounted, was 1,000 yards.
Besa Machine-Gun. The Besa was a 7.29mm machine-gun of very similar design to the Bren, developed for use in tanks. The name Besa was derived from the towns or firms which featured in its design: *B*rno (in Czechoslavakia), *E*nfield and *B*irmingham *S*mall *A*rms.
Sten Sub Machine-Gun. The Sten was a very light, cheaply made, mass produced 9mm sub machine-gun. It had an effective range of 30 yards and was notoriously unreliable.
Vickers Medium Machine-Gun. The Vickers was a water-cooled, recoil-operated .303in machine-gun. The gun was mounted on a tripod and was belt-fed. Extremely accurate and reliable, the Vickers had a maximum effective range of 1,800 yards and was usually fired at the rate of 120 rounds per minute.
PIAT (*P*rojector *I*nfantry *A*nti-*T*ank). The PIAT was the infantryman's hand-held anti-armour weapon. Although its spring-loaded firing mechanism could project the 2_lb bomb 100 yards, it was notoriously inaccurate and required strong nerves on the part of firers who had to fire it at compensatingly very close ranges.
2in Mortar. The 2in mortar had a maximum range of 500 yards. The weapon was held at platoon headquarters.
3in Mortar. The 3in mortar equipped the mortar platoons of infantry battalions and could fire a 10lb bomb 2,800 yards.
4.2in Mortar. The 4.2in mortar equipped the mortar companies of the divisional support regiment. It fired a 20lb bomb to a range of 4,000 yards. (All British mortars could fire HE or smoke rounds)

BRITISH TANKS
Cromwell. The Cromwell belonged to the 'cruiser' family of tanks being lightly armoured but fast. The tank weighed 27_ tons and had a 75mm gun as main armament and two Besa machine-guns. The Cromwell was out-matched in firepower by its German opponents but was superior to them in speed, reliability and fire control. The 75mm gun could penetrate 60mm of armour at 1,000 yards and the tank had a top speed of 40mph.
Sherman Firefly. The British adapted the standard US tank by fitting to it the 17pdr gun; thus modified it was called the Firefly. This very effective gun had an extremely high muzzle velocity and could destroy the heavy German tanks, such as Tiger and Panther. The Firefly weighed 31 tons and the 17pdr could penetrate 190mm of armour at 1,000 yards. The Sherman was the most widely used Allied tank; it suffered however from a high silhouette and a tendency to burn quickly when hit.
Comet. Issued in December 1944, the Comet was the last in the line of cruiser tanks and equipped the armoured regiments of 11th Armoured Division. It was essentially an up-armoured and up-gunned Cromwell and had similar performance. It weighed 32 tons and was armed with the 17pdr gun. See Sherman Firefly.
Crocodile. The Crocodile equipment consisted of an armoured two-wheeled trailer containing 400 gallons of flame fuel plus five pressure bottles of nitrogen, sufficient for 80, one-second bursts with the flame being projected to a maximum of 110

yards. The flame projector in the Churchill VII tank took the place of the hull machine-gun and was operated by the hull gunner. The trailer could be jettisoned and the tank was then able to operate as normal. Although vulnerable due to the flame's short range and requiring protection by other tanks, they were extremely effective.

Stuart. The Stuart Mk V light tank, nicknamed the Honey, was used by the reconnaissance troops of armoured regiments and was also found in the armoured reconnaissance regiments. To reduce the silhouette, some had their turrets removed and a .50 calibre machine-gun replaced the 37mm gun of the turret.

BRITISH ARTILLERY

25pdr Field Gun. The 25pdr was the standard field artillery gun. The gun was very robust and battle-proven and had a maximum range of 13,400 yards. It was towed by the Morris C8 tractor which carried its crew, ammo and stores.

5.5in Medium Gun. The 5.5in gun equipped the medium batteries. The gun was reliable, accurate and could fire a 100lb shell 16,000 yards.

Sexton. The Sexton was a tracked, self-propelled 25pdr field gun married to the Ram chassis. See Kangaroo below.

17pdr Anti-Tank Gun. The 17pdr towed anti-tank gun was not as satisfactory as the self-propelled versions for the quick actions required in an advance. For this reason, many of the towed batteries were converted to much-needed infantry. See Sherman Firefly.

Archer. The Archer was a self-propelled version of the 17pdr gun. The limited traverse gun was mounted in a rearward-facing, open-topped superstructure over the fighting compartment of a Valentine tank. See Sherman Firefly.

BRITISH ANTI-AIRCRAFT ARTILLERY

.50 Calibre Machine-Gun. The .50 calibre machine-gun was an American weapon. It was an air-cooled, recoil-operated machine-gun firing ammunition from a disintegrating link. In the anti-aircraft role it had an effective ceiling of 5,500 feet.

40mm Bofors Gun. The 40mm Bofors gun fired a HE tracer shell with a percussion and self-destruct fuse. The automatic rate of fire was 120 rounds a minute and the gun had a maximum effective ceiling of 23,000 feet.

BRITISH ARMOURED VEHICLES

Kangaroo. The Kangaroo APC was based on the Ram, the Canadian version of the M4 Sherman. These tanks had been selected for use as the APC for 21st Army Group as they could not be upgunned due to the small size of the turret ring. The Kangaroo had the same mobility and armour as the Sherman, less over-head cover for the mounted section, but was too heavy for its role.

Carriers. The tracked carrier was ubiquitous in infantry battalions and was used for a multitude of roles. By 1945 the Windsor carrier was the main variant. This vehicle had a top speed of some 30mph on roads and had good cross-country capability.

Wasp. The Wasp was a flame-throwing equipment mounted on a Universal carrier. The flame gun, which had a range of 35-45 yards, was fed by two large fuel tanks carried on the vehicle's rear deck. The Wasp had a two-man crew.

Armoured Cars. The Humber Mk 4 and the Daimler Mk 2 were the two armoured cars in general use. Both were four-wheeled, weighed over 7 tons and had a top speed of 45mph. Both had turret-mounted guns, the Humber a 37mm and the Daimler a 2pdr. The Humber would have predominated in 53rd Reconnaissance Regiment and the Daimler in 11th Hussars.

Scout Cars. Two types of four-wheeled scout cars were in general use and both were popular and essential vehicles for recce and liaison work. The Daimler weighed nearly 3 tons and was capable of 55mph; whilst the Humber was slightly heavier and faster, and could carry three men. Both were open-topped, and armed with a .303in Bren.

M5 Half-Track. M5 half-tracks, made by the US firm International, were among the most widely used Allied vehicles during the war. The vehicle weighed 10 tons and was armed with either a .30 or .50 calibre machine-gun. The motorised battalions and the assault troops of the reconnaissance regiments were equipped with the M5 which could seat up to 13, including the driver. Other M5 variants were modified for load carrying, ambulances, command posts and for use by REME fitters. The M14 variant had a mounting for four .50 calibre machine-guns.

Buffalo. The Buffalo was an American, tracked amphibious carrier. The vehicle was capable of carrying 30 troops or 4 tons of cargo. The variant with the rear ramp could carry a Jeep, carrier, 6/17pdr anti-tank gun or a 25pdr field gun. The Buffalo was a very noisy vehicle and its tracks, which propelled the vehicle through water, required continual maintenance. It was armed with two .30in machine-guns on the hull sides and for forward-firing either a Polsten 20mm cannon or a .50 machine-gun.

BRITISH AIRCRAFT
Typhoon. The Hawker Typhoon was a single-seat fighter-bomber. It was a rugged, reliable aircraft particularly suited to the ground-attack role. The aircraft was armed with four 20mm cannon in the wings and could carry either two 1,000lb bombs or eight 60lb rockets - four under each wing.
Tempest. The Hawker Tempest was an uprated variant of the Typhoon and was faster and more manoeuvrable. It carried the same weapon loads. It achieved its greatest success as a destroyer of V-1 flying bombs.

GERMAN INFANTRY WEAPONS
Gewehr 98/40. The Mauser 7.92mm Gewehr 98/40 was the infantryman's standard rifle. It was a magazine-fed, bolt-action weapon with an effective range of 550 yards. By 1945, the Karabiner 43 self-loading rifle was also commonplace.
7.92 MG 42. MG 42 was a belt-fed 7.92mm general purpose machine-gun capable of use in the light, medium or anti-aircraft role. It had a very high cyclic rate of fire (900-1,200rpm) and it gained fame and respect on the battlefield where it will be remembered for the chilling rattle of its bursts of fire.
Sturmgewehr (Stg) 44. The Stg.44 was a 7.92mm automatic carbine which fired the short 7.92mm round. The weapon carried a 30-round magazine and had an effective range of 330 yards. It was extremely simple and cheap to manufacture being made largely of steel pressings.
Panzerfaust. The Panzerfaust was a propelled, hollow-charge grenade fired from a tube and is the forebear of all 'disposable' anti-armour weapons. The shoulder-fired warhead had a range of some 80 yards and could penetrate about 160mm of armour.
Panzerschreck. The Panzerschreck was a shoulder-fired rocket launcher and was a direct copy of the American bazooka. The 5-foot weapon had a 3.5in calibre and weighed 20lb. The hollow-charge projectile could penetrate 84mm of armour at a range

of 110 yards. Like all bazookas, the firer's position was disclosed by a long, flaming back-blast.
8cm GrW 34 Mortar. The GrW 34 mortar was the standard medium mortar. It could fire a 6lb bomb some 2,600 yards.

GERMAN ARTILLERY
10.5cm le FH. The 10.5cm light field howitzer was the maid-of-all-work of the German field artillery. Although it fired a heavier shell than the British 25pdr, it only had a maximum range of 11,600 yards - well short of the British gun.
15cm s IG 33. The 15cm heavy infantry gun was used as a conventional artillery weapon and has the distinction of being the largest calibre classed by any nation as an infantry gun. Its maximum range was 5,500 yards - astonishingly short, and well below the range of today's medium mortars.
Nebelwerfer. The Nebelwerfer was a projector for firing rocket-propelled warheads. The rockets were developed in three calibres: 15cm with a 22lb warhead and a range of 7,300 yards; 21cm with a 100lb warhead and a range of 8,600 yards; and 30cm with a 145lb warhead and a range of 5,000 yards. The title Nebelwerfer or 'smoke projector' was a cover name to conceal its true purpose. The rocket artillery was a formidable weapon and was greatly feared by the Allies.

GERMAN TANKS AND ARMOURED VEHICLES
Panzerkampfwagen V Panther. The Panther tank was developed and rushed into production in late 1942 as a direct consequence of the appearance of the revolutionary Soviet T34 tank. The Panther was plagued by teething problems in its early variants but by the war's end had developed into an excellent fighting vehicle. It weighed 44 tons and was armed with the effective 7.5cm KwK 42 (L/70) gun which could penetrate 118mm of armour at 1,000 yards.
Panzerkampfwagen VI Tiger. The Tiger tank was a formidable vehicle, at its most potent in defence. Weighing 56 tons, armed with a 8.8cm KwK 36 gun and with 4 inches of sloped frontal armour it was impervious to many of the Allied tanks and anti-tank guns. Its low speed and very slow turret traverse, due to the sheer weight of armour, made it vulnerable to being stalked and attacked from the flanks or rear

and it was at its most potent in defence. The Tiger's gun could penetrate 168mm of armour at 1,000 yards.

Panzerjäger Tiger (P) Elefant. The Elefant was a heavy tank destroyer with a limited traverse gun in a fixed superstructure. Weighing over 71 tons, it was technically complicated and unreliable and by 1945 was obsolete. The vehicle was vulnerable to infantry close-attack as it had many blind spots and was generally used in a static role. It was armed with the 8.8cm Pak 43/2 (L/71) gun - a devastating weapon that could destroy any Allied armoured vehicle.

Sonderkraftfahrzeug (SdKfz) 251. The SdKfz 251 was a 9-ton half-tracked APC capable of lifting 11 riflemen. It had a top road speed of 33mph. This vehicle was the workhorse of the Panzergrenadier units and served in all theatres in many different variants. The standard infantry vehicle was armed with two 7.92mm machine-guns.

GERMAN ANTI-TANK GUNS (Panzerabwehrkanone (Pak))

Pak 40. The Pak 40 was a powerful and effective 7.5cm anti-tank gun, although heavy. It could penetrate 84mm of armour at 1,000 yards.

8.8cm Pak 43. The 8.8cm Pak 43 was an outstanding design. The gun's carriage was a cruciform platform carried on two, two-wheeled trailers. The gun had a very low silhouette and could penetrate 170mm of armour at 1,000 yards.

GERMAN ANTI-AIRCRAFT ARTILLERY (Fliegerabwehrkanone (Flak))

2cm Flak 38. The 2cm Flak was a very successful design and could be found in single or quadruple-barrelled versions. It could be used in either the anti-aircraft or ground role, having an effective ceiling/range of about 1,750 feet. In the four barrel version (Flakvierling) it could fire 750rpm.

3.7cm Flak 43. The Flak 43 came in either single or two-barrelled versions. A robust design, it fired a HE shell to an effective ceiling of 13,780 feet and had a ground range of 7,100 yards. It could fire 180rpm.

8.8cm Flak 37. The 8.8cm Flak was the best known German weapon of the war. Its prowess was built on its anti-tank capabilities, although it was not a 'super weapon'

and was no better than its British and American equivalents (3.7in Mk 3 and 90mm M1). In the anti-aircraft role it had an effective ceiling of 26,000 feet and in the anti-tank role fired a round capable of penetrating 4 inches of armour at 1,100 yards.

10.5cm Flak 39. The 10.5cm was developed from the Flak 37 to engage higher and faster aircraft. Due to its weight (13.8 tons on the move) the Flak 39 was usually found in static sites or mounted on railway flats. It could however be carried between two, two-wheeled trailers. The gun had an effective ceiling of 31,000 feet and a maximum ground range of 19,250 yards.

GERMAN AIRCRAFT

Focke-Wulf (Fw) 190. The Fw 190 was generally regarded as Germany's best piston-engined fighter. It had a top speed of 426mph and was armed with two 7.92mm machine-guns and two 20mm cannons. It could carry a wide range of under-fuselage and under-wing bombs, guns and rockets.

Messerschmitt (Me) Bf109. The Me 109 was a single-seat, piston-engined fighter. It was armed with two nose-mounted 7.92mm machine-guns, one 30mm cannon firing through the propeller hub and two 20mm cannons mounted under the wings. It had a maximum speed of 387mph.

Junkers (Ju) 87 (Stuka). The Ju 87 Stuka was used as a dive-bomber and ground-attack aircraft. The D variant was most commonly used in the latter role and could carry two 1,100lb bombs under each wing.

Ju 88. The Ju 88 was a highly versatile aircraft and was used as a low, medium and high level bomber, night-fighter and intruder, torpedo-bomber, anti-tank fighter and even pilotless missile. It had a crew of four and was able to carry a bombload of 6,600lb.

Ju 188. The Ju 188 was a twin-engined bomber and long-range reconnaissance aircraft. It could cruise at 250mph and carry a bomb load of 2,200lb.

Arado (Ar) 234B. The Ar 234B Blitz was the world's first jet bomber. The single-seat aircraft had twin Jumo turbojets providing a top speed of 461mph and could carry a bombload of 11,000lb. The Arado was produced in two variants: the B1 reconnaissance aircraft and the B2 bomber.

SOURCES AND BIBLIOGRAPHY

PUBLISHED SOURCES

Alford, Richard, *To Revel in God's Sunshine* (Westmoreland Gazette, Kendal, 1981)

Allen, Peter, *One More River* (J. M. Dent and Sons Ltd, London, 1980)

Ardizzone, Edward, *Diary of a War Artist* (The Bodley Head Ltd, 1974)

A History of 44 RTR in the War of 1939–1945 (44 RTR Association, Brighton, 1966)

Barclay, C. N., *History of the 53rd (Welsh) Division* (William Clowes & Sons Ltd, London, 1956)

Barker, A. J., *German Infantry Weapons of World War 2* (Arms and Armour Press, 1969)

Barnett, C. (Ed), *Hitler's Generals* (Weidenfeld and Nicolson, London, 1989)

Bender, R. J. & Taylor, H. P., *Uniforms, Organization and History of the Waffen-SS, Volume 3* (R. James Bender Publishing, San Jose, California, 1986)

Brett, Lt Col, G. A., *History of the South Wales Borderers and the Monmouthshire Regiment, Part III, The Second Battalion the Monmouthshire Regiment, 1933–1952* (Hughes and Sons Ltd, Pontypool, 1953–54)

Burden, Brig, G. W. P. N., (Ed), *History of the East Lancashire Regiment in the War, 1939–1945* (H. Rawson & Co Ltd, Manchester, 1953)

Carver, FM, Lord, *Second to None. The Royal Scots Greys 1918–1945* (Messrs McCorquodale and Co Ltd, Glasgow, 1954)

— *Out of Step. Memoirs of a Field Marshal* (Hutchinson, London, 1989)

— *The History of The 4th Armoured Brigade*, (J. J. Augustin, Glückstadt, Germany, July 1945)

Courage, Maj, G., *The History of 15/19 The King's Royal Hussars, 1939–1945* (Gale and Polden Ltd, Aldershot, 1949)

Cowburn, P. M., *Welsh Spearhead, A History of the 53rd Reconnaissance Regiment 1940–1946* (Wilhelm Müller jr, Solingen-Ohligs, 1946)

Crew, F. A. E., *Medical History of the Second World War, Army Medical Services, Campaigns, Vol IV, North-West Europe* (HMSO, 1962)

Crookenden, A., *History of the Cheshire Regiment in the Second World War* (W. H. Evans Sons & Coy Ltd, Chester, 1949)

Crow, Duncan, *Armoured Fighting Vehicles of the World, Volume 3, British & Commonwealth AFVs 1940–1946* (Profile Publications Ltd, 1971)

D'Arcy-Dawson, John, *European Victory* (Macdonald & Co, London, 1945)

Dierich, W., *Die Verbände der Luftwaffe 1935–1945* (Motor Buch Verlag, Stuttgart, 1976)

Dönitz, K., *Memoirs* (Greenhill Books Ltd, 1990)

Durnford Slater, Brig, J., *Commando* (Greenhill Books Ltd, 1991)

Edwards, R., *German Airborne Troops* (Macdonald and Janes, 1974)

Ellis, Maj, L. F., *Victory in the West* (HMSO, 1968)

— *Welsh Guards at War* (Gale and Polden, 1946)

Erskine, D., *The Scots Guards, 1919–1955* (William Clowes & Sons Ltd, London, 1956)

Essame, H., *The Battle for Germany* (B. T. Batsford Ltd, 1969)

— & Belfield, E. M. G., *The North-West Europe Campaign 1944–1945* (Gale and Polden Ltd, Aldershot, 1962)

Farrar-Hockley, A. H., *Student* (Ballantine Books Inc, New York, 1973)

Fitzroy, Olivia, *Men of Valour, History of the 8th King's Royal Irish Hussars, 1927–1958* (Tinling & Co, Liverpool, 1961)

Forty, G., (Ed), *Tanks Across the Desert* (William Kimber, 1981)

Foster, Maj, R. C. G., *History of the Queen's Royal Regiment, Volume 8, 1924–1948*, (Gale and Polden Ltd, Aldershot, 1961)

Fraser, Gen Sir, D., *And We Shall Shock Them* (Hodder and Stoughton, 1983)

Führer Conferences on Naval Affairs 1939–1945 (Brasseys Naval Annual, London)

Graham, Col A., *Sharpshooters at War; the 3rd, the 4th and the 3rd/4th County of London Yeomanry 1939 to 1945* (Sharpshooters Regimental Association, London, 1964)

Gunston, Bill, *British Fighters of World War II* (Aerospace Publishing Ltd, London, 1982)

Hamilton, Nigel, *Monty, The Field Marshal 1944–1976* (Hamish Hamilton, London, 1976)

Hastings, Maj, R. H. W. S., *The Rifle Brigade in the Second World War, 1939–1945*, (Gale and Polden Ltd, Aldershot, 1950)

Hinsley, F. H., *British Intelligence in the Second World War, Volume 3, Part 2* (HMSO 1988)

Hogg, Ian, *German Artillery of World War Two* (Arms and Armour Press, 1975)

Jewell, Brian, *Over the Rhine* (Spellmount Ltd, 1975)

Keilig, W., *Das Deutsche Heer 1939–45* (Podzun, Bad Nauheim)

Kemp, Lt Cdr P. K., *4th Battalion King's Shropshire Light Infantry (TA) 1745-1945* (Wilding & Son Ltd, Shrewsbury, 1953)

— & Graves, J., *The Red Dragon – The History of the Royal Welch Fusiliers 1919–1945* (Gale and Polden, Aldershot, 1960)

Kesselring, Feldmarschall, *Memoirs of Field Marshal Kesselring* (William Kimber, 1953)

Klapproth, Willy, *Kriegschronik 1945 der Stadt Soltau und Umbegung* (Stadtverwaltung Soltau)

Lohmann, W. & Hildebrand, H., *Die Deutsche Kriegsmarine 1939–1945, Volume 2* (Bad Nauheim, 1956)

Lomax, Maj Gen, C. E. N., *The History of The Welch Regiment, 1919–1951* (Western Mail and Echo Ltd, Cardiff, 1952)

Lucas, James, *Last Days of the Reich* (Arms and Armour Press, London, 1986)

Madej, W. Victor, *German Army Order of Battle, The Replacement Army, 1939–1945* (Game Publishing, Allentown, Pennsylvania, 1984)

Mason, Francis K., *German Warplanes of World War II* (Aerospace Publishing Ltd, London, 1983)

Macdonald, Charles B., *US Army in World War II, European Theatre of Operations, The Last Offensive* (US Government Printing Office, Washington DC, 1973)

Mehner, Kurt, *Die Deutsche Wehrmacht 1939–1945,Führung und Truppe* (Rinteln, 1990, private publication)

Mercer, John, *Mike Target* (The Book Guild Ltd, Lewes, 1990)

Meyer, Heinz, *Von der Invasion bis zur Kapitulation* (Verlag K. W. Schütz, Preußisch Oldendorf, 1987)

Mills, Maj Gen, G. H., *The Annals of The King's Royal Rifle Corps, Volume VII, 1943–1965* (Celer et Audax Club, Winchester)

Mills-Robert, Brig, D., *Clash by Night – A Commando Chronicle* (William Kimber, 1956)

Montgomery of Alamein, *Normandy to the Baltic* (Hutchinson)

Muir, A., *The First of Foot, The History of The Royal Scots* (Blackwood and Sons Ltd, London, 1961)

Myatt, Maj, F., *The British Infantry 1660–1945* (Blandford Press, Poole, 1983)

Neillands, Robin, *The Raiders. The Army Commandos 1940–46* (Weidenfeld and Nicholson, London, 1989)

Neville, Lt Col Sir J. E. H., Bt, (Ed), *The Record of the 43rd in the Second German War, Volume 4, June 1944–December 1945* (Various)

North, John, *North-West Europe 1944–1945* (HMSO, 1953)

Oatts, Lt Col, L. B., *Proud Heritage. The Story of the Highland Light Infantry, Volume 4, 1919–1959* (Thomas Nelson and Sons Ltd, Glasgow, 1963)

Padfield, Peter, *Dönitz – The Last Führer* (Victor Gollanz Ltd, 1984)

Price, Alfred, *Luftwaffe Handbook 1939–1945* (Ian Allan Ltd, 1986)

— *The Last Year of the Luftwaffe, May 1944 to May 1945* (Arms and Armour Press, 1991)

Quarrie, Bruce, *German Airborne Troops, 1939–45* (Osprey Publishing Ltd, 1983)

Randel, Maj, P. B., *A Short History of 30 Corps in the European Campaign* (BAOR, 1945)

Rosse, Capt the Earl of & Hill, Col, *The Story of the Guards Armoured Division*, (Geoffrey Bles, London, 1956)

Saft, Oberst Ulrich, *Krieg In Der Heimat* (Druckerei J.Gronemann, Walsrode, 1988)

Samain, B., *Commando Men. The Story of a Royal Marine Commando (45) in North-West Europe* (Stevens and Sons Ltd, London, 1948)

Sandars, John, *British 7th Armoured Division 1940–45* (Osprey Publishing Ltd, 1977)

Saunders, Hilary St George, *The Green Beret* (Michael Joseph Ltd, London, 1949)

Schramm, Percy, *Aus dem Kriegstagebuch des Oberkommandos der Wehrmacht* (Deutscher Taschenbuch Verlag, München, 1962)

Scott, Packer and Groves, *Record of a Reconnaissance Regiment, History of the 43rd Reconnaissance Regiment 1939–1945* (The White Swan Press, Bristol, 1949)

Seaton, Albert, *The Fall of Fortress Europe 1943–1945* (B. T. Batsford Ltd, 1981)

Seaton, Albert, *The German Army 1933–45* (Weidenfeld and Nicholson Ltd, London, 1982)

Sellars, R. J. B., *The Fife and Forfar Yeomanry 1919–1956* (William Blackwood and Sons Ltd, London)

Shulman, Milton, *Defeat in the West* (Secker & Warburg, 1947)

'Taurus Pursuant': A History of the 11th Armoured Division (BAOR, 1945)

'Team Spirit'. Administration of 53rd Welsh Division During 'Operation Overlord'. June 44–May 45, Germany, 1945

Tessin, Georg, *Verbände und Truppen der Deutsche Wehrmacht und Waffen-SS 1939–1945*, (Frankfurt, 1966)

Trevor-Roper, H. R., *Hitler's War Directives 1939–1945* (Sidgwick and Jackson, London, 1964)

US War Department, *Handbook on German Military Forces* (Louisiana State University Press, London, 1990)

Various, *A Short History of the 6th Battalion the Royal Welch Fusiliers,*

North West Europe, June 1944–May 1945 (Gwenlyn Evans and Son, Caernarfon, 1946)

Verney, Maj Gen, G. L., *The Desert Rats* (Hutchinson, 1954)

Wake, Maj Gen Sir H. Bt & Deedes, Maj, W. D., *Swift and Bold. The Story of the King's Royal Rifle Corps in the Second World War, 1939–1945* (Gale and Polden, Aldershot, 1949)

Warlimont, Walter, *Inside Hitler's Headquarters 1939–45* (Weidenfeld and Nicholson, London, 1964)

Wegmann, Günther, *Das Kriegsende zwischen Ems und Weser 1945* (Kommissionsverlag H. Th. Wenner, Osnabrück, 1982)

Young, David, *Four-Five, 45 Commando 1943–71* (Leo Cooper Ltd, London, 1972)

UNPUBLISHED SOURCES
German
Gefechtsbericht des Flakregiments 122(E).

Gefechtsbericht 4.Komp.Mar.Füs.Btl.2

Gedenkblatt des A.und E.Btl.12 SS-Division 'Hitlerjugend'.

Oberkommando des Heeres Tagesmeldung West 2–18 April 1945.

Gen.Kdo.Ems A.K. Korps-Befehl 3 to 12.

Admiral z.b.v. beim Ob.d.M. Teilnahme des Ob.d.M. Führerlage 2, 5, 21 and 30 March, and 6 April 1945.

Blumentritt Paper 'Armee Blumentritt 8.4.45 – Kapitulation.' 29 Sep 46.

British
Operations East of the River Aller – 4th Armoured Brigade.

Lieutenant Colonel Crozier Papers – Imperial War Museum.

No 2 Operational Research Section/2nd Tactical Air Force Joint Report No 3 'Rocket Firing Typhoons in Close Support of Military Operations'.

An Account of the Operations of Second Army in Europe 1944–1945, Volume II – HQ 2nd Army.

Lt Col Harris, G. W., Narrative of the Historical Branch of the Cabinet Office, Chapter VII, Books I and II, 1956.

Capts Wright, H. B., and Harkness, R. D., A Survey of Casualties Amongst Armoured Units in North-West Europe, 1946, (PRO 205/1165).

British Army of the Rhine Battlefield Tour, Operation 'Plunder', Operations of 12 Corps, 23–25 Mar 45, 1947.

The River Rhine to the Baltic Sea, 8 Corps, March–May 1945.

INDEX